NOT TO BE
MISSED

ALSO BY KENNETH TURAN

Call Me Anna: The Autobiography of Patty Duke
Free for All: Joe Papp, the Public, and the Greatest
Theatre Story Ever Told
Never Coming to a Theater Near You
Now in Theaters Everywhere
Sundance to Sarajevo: Film Festivals and the World They Made

NOT TO BE MISSED

FIFTY-FOUR FAVORITES
FROM A LIFETIME OF FILM

KENNETH TURAN

PublicAffairs
New York

PublicAffairs books are available at special discounts for bulk pur-
chases in the U.S. by corporations, institutions, and other organizations. For more information, please contact the Special Markets
Department at the Perseus Books Group, 2300 Chestnut Street, Suite
200, Philadelphia, PA 19103, call (800) 810-4145, ext. 5000, or e-mail
special.markets@perseusbooks.com.

Book Design by Jack Lenzo

Library of Congress Cataloging-in-Publication Data
Turan, Kenneth.
Not to be missed : 54 favorites from a lifetime of film / Kenneth
Turan.
pages cm. Includes bibliographical references and index.
ISBN 978-1-58648-396-8 (hardback)—ISBN 978-1-61039-376-6
(ebook) 1. Motion pictures. I. Title.
PN1994.T855 2014
791.43'75—dc23
2014007773

First Edition
10 9 8 7 6 5 4 3 2 1

To those who watch and dream,
and to B, always

No form of art goes beyond ordinary consciousness as film does, straight to our emotions, deep into the twilight room of the soul.

—INGMAR BERGMAN

CONTENTS

Introduction · *xiii*

IN THE BEGINNING

Introduction · 3

Fantômas, 1913–1914 · 5

SILENT COMEDY DOUBLE FEATURE

Sherlock Jr., 1924 *and* *Pass the Gravy,* 1928 · 9

THE THIRTIES

Introduction · 21

I Am a Fugitive from a Chain Gang, 1932 · 23

Bombshell, 1933 · 28

The Dybbuk, 1937 · 33

LEO MCCAREY DOUBLE FEATURE

Make Way for Tomorrow, 1937 *and* *Love Affair,* 1939 · 39

THE FORTIES

Introduction · 51

Pride and Prejudice, 1940 · 53

ERNST LUBITSCH DOUBLE FEATURE

The Shop Around the Corner, 1940 *and*

    To Be or Not to Be, 1942 · 59

The Lady Eve, 1941 · 69

Strawberry Blonde, 1941 · 75

Casablanca, 1942 · 79

Random Harvest, 1942 · 85

Children of Paradise, 1945 · 90

Great Expectations, 1946 · 95

Bicycle Thieves, 1948 · 100

The Third Man, 1949 · 105

THE FIFTIES

Introduction · 113

All About Eve, 1950 · 115

The Asphalt Jungle, 1950 · 120

Sunset Boulevard, 1950 · 125

Casque d'Or, 1952 · 132

The Importance of Being Earnest, 1952 · 137

Singin' in the Rain, 1952 · 141

The Earrings of Madame De . . . , 1953 · 147

Seven Samurai, 1954 · 151

Kiss Me Deadly, 1955 · 156

Seven Men from Now, 1956 · 160

Sweet Smell of Success, 1957 · 165

Vertigo, 1958 · 170

THE SIXTIES

Introduction · 181

The Man Who Shot Liberty Valence, 1962 · 183

The Gospel According to St. Matthew, 1964 · 188

Point Blank, 1967 · 192

Le Samouraï, 1967 · 198

Kes, 1969 · 202

THE SEVENTIES

Introduction · 209

The Godfather, 1972 · 211

Chinatown, 1974 · 217

THE EIGHTIES

Introduction · 225

The Day After Trinity, 1981 · 227

First Contact, 1983 · 232

Distant Voices, Still Lives, 1988 · 236

THE NINETIES

Introduction · 243

Howards End, 1992 · 245

Leolo, 1992 · 250

Unforgiven, 1992 · 256

THE NEW CENTURY

Introduction · 265

Spirited Away, 2001 · 267

The Best of Youth, 2003 · 272

The Five Obstructions, 2003 · 278

DOCUMENTARY DOUBLE FEATURE

Stranded, 2007 *and Senna,* 2010 · 282

A Prophet, 2009 · 291

Of Gods and Men, 2010 · 296

Footnote, 2011 · 301

ORSON WELLES DOUBLE FEATURE

Introduction · 309

Touch of Evil, 1958 *and Chimes at Midnight,* 1965 · 311

The Fifty-Fifth Film · 321

A Second Fifty-Four · 325

Acknowledgments · 329

Index · 331

INTRODUCTION

The writing of prefaces is, for the most part, work thrown away.

—ANTHONY TROLLOPE

Anthony Trollope hated wasting time. He wrote forty-seven novels, including the Palliser and Barsetshire series, plus assorted nonfiction and even a play or two. Trollope was so disciplined that if he finished one novel with a few minutes to spare in his writing schedule, he started another one. Really. So why was he taking valuable minutes writing a preface to *The Vicar of Bullhampton*, which he feared nobody would read.

Trollope wrote it, I feel sure, for the same reason I'm writing this introduction: he felt the need to explain his intentions and motivations, to put what he had written into a context that would allow readers to more fully understand what he had done.

The book before you now may seem straightforward enough. It's a collection of essays on my fifty-four favorite films. But to me it raises all kinds of questions. Why this book? Why fifty-four films and what criteria were used to select them? And why, for that matter, become a film critic in the first place?

The answer to the last question, at least, should be obvious. I became a critic out of a deep passion for films and their ability to simultaneously do something I love: take me out of this world and return me to it not only entertained but, if I am fortunate, with my emotions and my understanding enlarged.

So when one of my editors at the *Los Angeles Times* accuses me of personalizing the films I write about, I plead guilty as charged. I look on the best of the movies I've seen—the films discussed in this book—as friends who've enriched my life. As director Werner Herzog said, a memorable film "sticks to you forever. It never leaves you. It becomes part of your existence."

Underlying all the questions this book raises, however, is the most basic one: How did I happen to become a critic in the first place—a query that leads to my Brooklyn childhood.

The Brownsville area of Brooklyn where I grew up in the 1950s and early 1960s had more in common with the immigrant Jewish neighborhood of the 1920s and 1930s Alfred Kazin describes in *A Walker in the City* than with the epicenter of hipness the borough has become. I not only had no thought of being a film critic as a child, I had no idea the profession even existed. I was just a kid who enjoyed movies and saw them every chance I could, which was not as often as I would have liked.

Because my old-country father was uncompromisingly observant, the traditional Saturday matinees at my two local movie houses, the ornate pleasure dome that was the Loew's Pitkin and the more proletarian Brandt's Sutter, were open to me only if I was willing to risk his wrath, which I rarely did. That said, I do have a vivid memory of sneaking out to see a vibrant, cleft-chinned Kirk Douglas so bringing to life the title role of *Ulysses* in 1957 that I still have trouble visualizing the Homeric epic without him in it.

Since my theatrical attendance was limited, I was fortunate to come across *Million Dollar Movie*, a local television program with wonderful theme music that showcased older Hollywood features nightly on WOR-TV Channel 9. (Decades later, when I saw *Gone with the Wind* for the first time, I blurted out, "Oh my god, they stole the theme music from *Million Dollar Movie*" before I realized the reverse was true.)

With my sister grown up and out of the house and my parents too exhausted by work to be interested, I curled up by myself and experienced all manner of movies from *King Kong* to *I Was a Fugitive from a Chain Gang*. I did my watching alone, I formed my opinions alone, I talked to no one about what I had seen. I was in effect becoming a critic though I didn't know it.

Also a likely factor in my critical development, though it took me years to realize it, was the exposure I had as a child growing up in the Orthodox Jewish world to the tradition of Talmudic exegesis, the thorough examination of a biblical text. Taking the next step and analyzing a film, trying to figure out how and why it was doing what it was doing, was second nature to me, an exercise I engaged in well before I had any kind of official critical job.

Once I abandoned Brooklyn to go to college at Swarthmore, just down the road in Pennsylvania but a universe away in other respects, the pace of my movie viewing increased. Screenings of both Hollywood and foreign classics every Friday and Saturday night exposed me for the first time to films that could be as profound and moving as any novel. I further educated myself by poring over 16-millimeter rental catalogs and helping to select those all-college films.

The next step was choosing journalism over the academy as a graduate school path. At Columbia's journalism program I took a seminar in film reviewing offered by Judith Crist, one of New York's top critics. She was the first to make me believe I could do this work professionally, and, as anyone who ever met her knows, when Judith Crist spoke, you listened. And so the journey began.

When you love something you do it a lot, and over the decades since I started to take film seriously I've seen more thousands than I can count. (My friend and colleague David Ansen, *Newsweek* critic for more than thirty years and now artistic director of the Los Angeles Film Festival, has kept track; he was at 9,536 and counting the last time I checked.) Sometimes I feel a kinship with the seventy-something horseplayer quoted in handicapper Andrew Beyer's classic *Picking Winners* who told Beyer, "Son, if I'd spent the time studying law books that I've put into the Racing Form, I'd probably be on the Supreme Court now."

Compiling a book like this seems to be the logical culmination of all the watching and reviewing I've done since my first pieces appeared in the *Washington Post* (where I was a staff writer) and the *Progressive* magazine in the mid-1970s. As I look back on it, writing about film has been a voyage of discovery with two interlocking purposes: I write to be a guide for the perplexed (to borrow Maimonides' wonderful title), to help viewers find films they will love. But writing reviews soon became more than that. Through focusing intently on what I liked and disliked, it gradually became a process of finding out what was important to me on a broader scale. A way to find out, in short, who I am.

Being useful as a reviewer always came first, however, and has always been the central element in how I view what I do. This relates to something I learned as an undergraduate. My Orthodox Jewish background had left me with minimal knowledge of other religions, so I signed up for a course in the New Testament. There I was told that the word "gospel" meant good news and referred specifically to the notion of spreading the good news about Jesus. It struck me that spreading the good news about films that were worth a viewer's time was a goal worth having for a critic.

Similarly, it was the drive to write a useful book that convinced me not to go the maximalist "one thousand films to see before you die" route. Like antitax zealot Grover Nordquist, eager to make government small enough to be easily drowned in a bathtub, I wanted to keep my list short enough so that even a busy person like Mr. Nordquist could reasonably choose to see them all. Something in the fifties felt right, in addition to alliterating nicely with film.

With thousands of films to choose from, getting the list down to just fifty-four (the reason for that specific number will be revealed a bit later) was challenging. These are the films that mean the most to me, that touch me most deeply, that I can see over and over again without fear of getting bored. But I'd fallen in love so often at the movies, embraced so many different films that appealed to a variety of diverse moods, that I felt like a cinematic Casanova forced to decide between multiple passions. I experienced this so strongly that I've appended an essay describing both how that process worked and what my fifty-fifth film would have been, as well as a list of another fifty-four favorites for readers who have the strength and desire to go on. And, just for fun, I've added a "what to watch next" choice at the end of each essay as well as suggestions for further reading.

Choosing the specific films became a trickier proposition than I'd anticipated. While I didn't want to disappoint or even anger those who did not find their favorites (believe me, it has already started to happen, even in my own house), this selection of films I can't live without couldn't be helpful to others if I wasn't true to myself. The best part of the dissent is that it's proof of how much people care about films, how terribly deeply, as the Ingmar Bergman epigraph indicates, they affect people. If your favorite isn't here, it's not because I loved it less but because I loved others more.

I also resisted the impulse to present myself as the most ecumenical of critics, someone whose favorites casually extend to the farthest reaches of the globe. If more of the films I love came from the studio system than elsewhere, if I had a pronounced passion for French cinema and film noir, if I found room for a trio of inside Hollywood films (*Bombshell*, *Singin' in the Rain*, and *Sunset Boulevard*) but somehow left off justifiably popular items like *Star Wars* that I truly enjoyed, it would just have to be that way.

As I began to write I took the opportunity to link films in double feature essays when they seemed to go together, but reserved the privilege not to do so when they didn't. So films by

Ernst Lubitsch, Leo McCarey, and Orson Welles got the double feature treatment but the two works by Mervyn LeRoy (*I Am a Fugitive from a Chain Gang* and *Random Harvest*) felt so different I kept them separate.

Once the list was complete, it was fascinating to be struck by unseen parallels—I'd never thought to connect *The Dybbuk* and *Vertigo* in terms of obsessive love lasting beyond the grave—and to see who besides directors showed up more than once.

Protean costume designer Edith Head surprised me by being credited in four very different films (*The Lady Eve, Sunset Boulevard, Vertigo, The Man Who Shot Liberty Valence*), while Lee Marvin (*Seven Men from Now, Liberty Valence, Point Blank*) showed up more than any other actor. I was shocked to see one of my favorites, James Cagney, in only *Strawberry Blonde*, while an actor I rarely think about, Charles Boyer, made it in twice with *Love Affair* and *The Earrings of Madame De . . .*

All that said, I took it as a good sign that my list ended up striking something of a balance between films like *Casablanca* and *The Godfather* that everyone has seen and those like *First Contact* and *Leolo* that have a more limited following. I rewatched each one before writing my essay, and made sure each fit a specification Roger Ebert once laid down. "Every great film," he wrote, "should seem new every time you see it."

If writing reviews has been a gradual process of finding out who I am and what is important to me, putting this book together was akin to undertaking a spiritual autobiography, a way to make explicit what has been implicit for all these years. As a glance at the list will attest, I am a romantic (if pressed for my top film, I invariably pick *Children of Paradise*). I believe moral choices can be as exciting as the ones in thrillers. But more than that I am, for better or worse, a classicist. I trust in the traditional values of character development and story and I still have faith in the notion of film as a popular art, emphasis on both words, a conviction that the greatest films ever made can be accessible to the widest of audiences.

Putting this book together reaffirmed that despite the culture's renewed infatuation with the blandishments of television, I am an unreconstructed, unapologetic partisan of the cinematic experience. Yes, TV makes it easy by coming into your home. And though it can be superb, at the end of the day it's a vest pocket experience that doesn't have the capacity to envelope you the way film does. In fact, there's very little TV does that film couldn't do if it put its mind to it, that film wouldn't be doing right now if it hadn't shamelessly abdicated its adult entertainment responsibilities.

Backing me up on this is author George R.R. Martin, whose novels are the basis for the hugely popular TV series *Game of Thrones*. Martin recently purchased an entire New Mexico movie theater, the jewel box Jean Cocteau in Santa Fe. "If you're watching something in your living room," he told National Public Radio, "it just doesn't have the same impact." I rest my case.

Why fifty-four films? Once I decided on a number in the fifties, fifty-four came into my mind for what seemed like no particular reason. But as soon as I mentioned the number to UCLA History Department chairman David Myers, the former director of the university's Center for Jewish Studies, he immediately said, "three times *chai*," and I knew at once that that was exactly the reason I'd gravitated toward fifty-four.

Chai is the Hebrew word for the number 18, as well as the word for life (as in the traditional toast *L'chaim*, to life), so any multiple of eighteen is considered a lucky number. I believe I've been fortunate to be in a line of work that allows me to experience more movies than any sane person would attempt, and this book is my way of sharing the best of that good fortune with the wider world. With any kind of luck, the films that have rewarded me enormously will bring you the same measure of pleasure and pure joy.

IN THE BEGINNING

"It would have been more logical," star Mary Pickford once said, "if silent pictures had grown out of the talking instead of the other way around." I share her enthusiasm for this particular cinema, once wildly popular, then derided, now restored to respectability and more.

There are but three silent films on this list, only one of them feature length. Two more features—*7th Heaven* and *Show People*—appear among my second fifty-four but I could have chosen a lot more: *Napoleon, Dr. Mabuse The Gambler, Lucky Star, Cabiria*. The possibilities are almost endless but in terms of favorites my passion for *Fantômas* plus the opportunity to pair Buster Keaton, one of silent comedy's most accomplished practitioners, with Max Davidson, a man little known today, was not to be resisted.

Though Americans tend to think of cinema as *cosa nostra*, our thing, the French have an equal if not greater claim. It was in Paris on December 28, 1895, that moviegoers had the first opportunity to buy tickets to a screening, and films like *Fantômas* showed a precocious visual awareness that is still striking today. In his series *Cinema Europe: The Other Hollywood*, historian Kevin Brownlow claims that had World War I not intervened, Europe's cinematic preeminence might never have gone away.

FANTÔMAS

1913–1914

Directed by Louis Feuillade. Starring Rene Navarre, Edmund Breon.

His very name made all Paris quake, his epithets extended the fear: Lord of Terror, Emperor of Crime, Genius of Evil. He was Fantômas, and he lived to wreak havoc in the world.

Even if you're unfamiliar with this French criminal wizard, you may have seen the classic image from the cover of the first Fantômas pulp novel, published in February 1911. It showed an enormous individual in full evening dress and elegant mask, a bloody dagger in his right hand, looming over the Eiffel Tower and striding across Paris like he owned the place. Described on the comprehensive Fantômas website as "a figure of unmotivated evil, moral transgression and diabolical perversity," this was a character who knew how to make an entrance.

That book was the first of thirty-two wildly popular novels by Pierre Souvestre and Marcel Allain, who over three years exhausted teams of stenographers and turned out a 380-page novel per month, more than 12,000 pages all told. All featured the master criminal Fantômas, his implacable nemesis Inspector Juve of the Sûreté, and Juve's right-hand man, the elegant journalist Jerome Fandor.

Graced with vivid cover illustrations by Gino Starace that continue to command high prices among Parisian antiquarian book dealers, the Fantômas novels sold upward of 5 million copies for publisher Fayard. Who liked them? Who didn't?

Poetically described by John Ashbery, who wrote an introduction to an English language reissue of that first novel, the book's "popularity cut across all social and cultural strata. Countesses and concierges; poets and proletarians; cubists, nascent Dadists, soon-to-be-surrealists. Everyone who could read, and even those who could not, shivered at posters of a masked man . . . contemplating hideous misdeeds from which no citizen was safe."

Ashbery was not exaggerating the artistic appeal of the series. Magritte, Cocteau, Dali, and Picasso were fans, as were writers like Apollinaire, Colette, and even James Joyce, who, ever the wordsmith, coined the adjective "enfantomastic." The original man in black, Fantômas is something like the secret sauce of modern popular culture, adding piquancy and taste to a variety of disciplines. Especially film.

Not surprisingly, the stories caught the attention of León Gaumont, one of the titans of the emerging French film industry, and between 1913 and 1914 the studio's head of production, director Louis Feuillade, turned five of the Fantômas novels into silent features ranging in length from fifty-five to ninety minutes: *Fantômas in the Shadow of the Guillotine, Juve vs. Fantômas, The Murderous Corpse, Fantômas vs. Fantômas,* and *The False Magistrate.*

Feuillade, who later directed the similarly mysterious *Les Vampires* and *Judex,* stuck close to the original books, likely for commercial reasons. Though each of the five films is broken out into chapters, they were not consumed like a serial, one segment at a time, but were meant to be taken in whole for maximum effect.

Critic Roy Armes, an authority on French cinema, insists that these films' popularity among the avant-garde "should not lead us to see Feuillade as any sort of frustrated artist or poet of cinema, suffocating in a world dominated by business decisions."

In his day, "a filmmaker's only viable ambition was to reach the widest possible audience."

Still, Feuillade directed these uncannily compelling films with so much energy and flair that future directors never forgot the viewing experience. Louis Malle noted simply, "Fantômas has scared me and thrilled me since childhood," while Alain Resnais shrewdly observed that "Feuillade's cinema is very close to dreams, therefore it is perhaps the most realistic."

Realism is not the first thing viewers necessarily think of when considering the Fantômas films, which are, after all, a century old and need certain allowances made. Don't look for elaborate camera moves or dazzling cutting: they're not there. Scenes cloaked in darkness look identical to ones made during full sunlight (day-for-night shooting had not yet been invented), and a train wreck known as "the catastrophe of the Simplon Express" is shot with an obvious model train. And, yes, some of the actors' gestures and expressions are florid and exaggerated, but there's not as much of this as you might expect. We should all look so good when we hit the century mark.

The films starred Edmund Breon as Juve, Georges Melchior as the dapper Jerome Fandor, and Renée Carl as Lady Beltham, mind bendingly described in an intertitle as "mistress, accomplice, and victim of Fantômas." René Navarre plays the man himself, the criminal mastermind who looked best dressed in sinister head-to-toe black with the merest slits for eyes but is introduced to the camera morphing from one disguise to another. The message is inescapable: if Fantômas can become anyone, then no one is safe.

The Souvestre and Allain plots are brisk and ultra-complicated. Though they involve genre staples like train wrecks and stolen necklaces, they also specialized in the kind of outré situations that must have delighted surrealists: bodies crushed, corpses disfigured, a man murdered so Fantômas can make nefarious use of the skin of his hands. (Don't ask.) Awful things done in an age of innocence.

It's not just the crimes Fantômas and his minions commit that create the frisson of pure evil that surrounds the man; it's the daring way he makes his appearances, often simply materializing out of thick black curtains as if he's been part of the background all along. The audacity, the flair, the sheer nerve, and the pure evil combine in a way that was cinematic almost before that was a word.

What makes all this fantastical criminal activity so potent is the nature of the film's exteriors. They weren't shot in some Never-Never Land but on the crowded streets of contemporary Paris, so much so that glimpses of civilians staring at the camera are not uncommon.

Those sequences do more than create a wondrous documentary portrait of Paris at the time. The inescapable sense of reality this ordinariness provides is essential to the film's theme that Fantômas's terrible crimes are happening right under our oblivious noses while we, like the narcoleptic citizens of *The Matrix*, have no idea what's going on.

Finally, there is something in the simplicity of Feuillade's style that gives these films their force, a way that his archetypal visuals are as unnerving as being in someone else's dream. Stunning images like the one that closes *The Murderous Corpse*—Fantômas dressed head to toe in black, his arms raised in pure exultation against the white ruins of a building he's just reduced to rubble—dazzle us with the purity of their vision, and their evil. To paraphrase the Virginian, when you call these films primitive, smile.

What to Watch Next:
Dr Mabuse, The Gambler (1922), directed by Fritz Lang.

Further Reading:
Pulp Surrealism: Insolent Popular Culture in Early Twentieth Century Paris, by Robin Walz.

SHERLOCK JR.

1924

Directed by Buster Keaton.
Starring Buster Keaton, Kathryn McGuire.

PASS THE GRAVY

1928

Directed by Fred R. Guiol.
Starring Max Davidson, Spec O'Donnell.

They worked tirelessly for decades in the same corner of the same industry in what was then a very small town, but, twenty years apart in age, there is no record of their being friends or even having met. One is revered today, the other next door to forgotten. But Buster Keaton and Max Davidson are united by their ability to use the essence of who they were to make people laugh and laugh again.

How widely the posthumous reputations of these two men have diverged becomes apparent if you attempt to find their films on DVD today. While there are numerous choices where Keaton is concerned—his work is on offer on a film-by-film basis as well as on massive multidisc compilations like *The Art of Buster Keaton* and *The Ultimate Buster Keaton Collection*—Davidson's efforts did not become available for home viewing in any form until 2011 and then only in a European-format edition produced by the Munich Film Museum.

But back in the day the levels of public recognition these two comedians enjoyed were not as different as we might imagine. Keaton was always one of the reigning monarchs of silent comedy, even before he moved on to features, but Davidson, who stayed in shorts, was quite well-known also.

The advertising for Davidson's comedies for the Hal Roach Studios, for instance, mentioned him in the same breath as Laurel and Hardy and Our Gang. And a full-page 1927 trade ad in *Motion Picture News* celebrates his success with audiences by proclaiming, "Exhibitors know that in these dialect comedies are rich opportunities for side-splitting comic situations together with touches of pathos. Great audience entertainment! And no one is better suited to interpret these comedies than Max Davidson."

Davidson was born in Berlin in 1875, came to the United States as a teenager, and had a career that started on stage and stretched from silent films well into the sound era. The goatee and wild hair that made him look like a slapstick Leon Trotsky are unmistakable even as late as his stint as a jury member in *Reap the Wild Wind* (1942), starring John Wayne.

As a journeyman comedian, Davidson worked with everyone from Mabel Norman and Jackie Coogan to the Three Stooges. He also had a small role in the modern section of D.W. Griffith's *Intolerance*, and some film historians believe that it was Davidson who first suggested to his stage acting friend Griffith that this new film medium might be worth looking into.

Davidson's best work came in a series of two-reel shorts, twenty minutes of superb comedy construction and timing, that he did for Hal Roach Studios in the late 1920s. These included *Should Second Husbands Come First*, *Why Girls Say No*, and the aptly named *Jewish Prudence*, films where he played a character, whether named Cohen or Ginsberg, Gimplewart or Weinberg, who was unmistakably Jewish.

The essence of Davidson's appeal was his skill as a maestro of reaction shots. No one was better at registering shock and dismay, often with the kind of wordless delicacy that close to disappeared in the sound era. Davidson had a remarkable variety of gestures and grimaces—he was the complete opposite of Keaton's celebrated stone face—with an unmistakable impish quality thrown into the mix.

Davidson also conveyed a quality of sympathetic, believable humanity that transcended stereotype. If the heart of the audience for these "ethnic comedies" was Jewish—it's been estimated that America's Jewish population rose from 229,000 in 1877 to 4,228,000 in 1927—Davidson's appeal was universal and his career was very much a mainstream affair.

Ten of Davidson's Hal Roach Studios comedies survive. The most celebrated—and the funniest—is *Pass the Gravy* (1928), considered "culturally significant" enough to merit inclusion in the Library of Congress National Film Registry in 1998.

The film's renaissance began a few years earlier, in 1994, at the world's preeminent silent film festival, Le Giornate de Cinema Muto in Pordenone, Italy, where it appeared without fanfare but was selected as the funniest silent short of a rich program called Unknown American Comics.

The genius of *Pass the Gravy* is that it takes a single uncomplicated setup and gradually rings every possible comic iteration out of it. Events go from real to unreal in an instant and, as the situation builds and builds, everything slowly spirals out of control.

At first the characters are so generic they don't all have names, but one who does is Schultz (Bert Sprotte), a fierce-looking man who is inordinately proud of his prize-winning rooster, Brigham. Living next door is Davidson, who raises flowers and has an irascible son named Ignatz (freckle-faced Spec O'Donnell), who, the subtitle pointedly informs us, "raises what is not polite to mention."

Two other, older children are also involved in the plot, Schultz's son (Gene Morgan) and Davidson's daughter (Martha Sleeper), who, as movie chance would have it, have just become engaged. Though the two fathers don't get along—Brigham is forever eating the flower grower's seeds—the engagement seems like a fine time to "bury the hatchet."

A dinner is planned to mark the celebration, and Ignatz is given two dollars to purchase a chicken. But the shameless young man, thinking to save the money for himself, pounces on Brigham instead and before you know it the bird is basting in the oven and the families have gathered to devour it. After some ethnic humor—Davidson advises Schultz to "take the white meat, it's more expensive"—the bird turns, so to speak. Ignatz suddenly realizes that he's left Brigham's name tag on the now cooked leg, revealing his perfidy for the world to see.

This knowledge gradually spreads from person to person around the table until the only people who don't know are Davidson's character and Schultz. Some of the funniest parts of *Pass the Gravy* involve attempts by the engaged couple to pantomime to Davidson what has happened, unsuccessful efforts that only increase his look of Talmudic befuddlement. It cannot end well for him, and it doesn't.

Slight though *Pass the Gravy* was, it had major talent behind the camera. Supervising the film for the Roach studio and often credited as codirector was Leo McCarey, whose future included two personal favorites, *Make Way for Tomorrow* and *Love*

Affair, plus an Oscar for directing *Going My Way*. Future film-maker George Stevens was the editor. Many decades later, Stevens reached back and hired *Pass the Gravy* director Fred Guilol to cowrite the script for *Giant*.

Summing up Davidson's appeal, Robert Farr wrote in the silent film journal *Griffithiana* that he was "a skilled comic actor who effortlessly projected vulnerability, resignation over life's little tragedies, and genuine warmth. The little man who can never quite assimilate into 20th century urban culture speaks to us all. Max is one of us."

So, what happened to Max Davidson? One of the theories advanced was that Nicholas Schenck and Louis B. Mayer, the Jewish executives who ran MGM, the distributors of Hal Roach Studio films, came to be embarrassed by what they considered ethnic stereotyping. Roach himself told film historian Richard W. Bann that Schenck "was increasingly uncomfortable with the Jewish family angle in the Davidson comedies." For whatever reason, in 1928, the same year *Pass the Gravy* appeared in theaters, Hal Roach Studios ended Davidson's contract, and his road to oblivion began.

If *Pass the Gravy*, successful in its day, is now largely forgotten by the general public, the opposite is true of Keaton's *Sherlock Jr.* Made in 1924, four years before *Gravy*, and running the not quite feature length of forty-five minutes, it was in its time one of Keaton's least successful films both financially and critically.

The $448,337 earned by *Sherlock Jr.* (they kept careful records in those days) made it one of Keaton's lowest-grossing films, and the reviews were by and large equally dismal. *Picture Play* lamented the film's lack of "ingenuity and originality," while *Variety* famously complained that the film was as funny as "a hospital operating room."

Opinions have changed today, however, with *Sherlock Jr.* now considered one of Keaton's most adventurous films, called "a piece of native American surrealism" by Pauline Kael and significant enough to merit an entire volume of its own in the Cambridge Film Handbooks series. It both illustrates why Keaton, a master of both movement and stillness, was so brilliant and why that brilliance so connects with contemporary audiences.

With Keaton it always comes back to the face, the Great Stone Face, a face, someone said, "that asks to be left alone." It inspired Luis Bunuel, Federico Garcia Lorca, and Samuel Beckett, who had it in mind when he wrote *Waiting for Godot.* James Agee believed it "ranked almost with Lincoln's as an early American archetype, it was haunting, handsome, almost beautiful." The most expressive blank face in film history, it continues to astonish, even today.

The awareness behind that face brought an engineer's mind and a poet's sensibility to silent screen comedy, ending up, in critic Peter Hogue's words, with "some magical and unlikely wedding of surrealism and Yankee pragmatism." Keaton and his peers had come out of vaudeville, and they used the enormity of their experience—Keaton had given an estimated 10,000 performances with his parents by the time he was twenty-one—to help create effects that built beautifully on what they had done on stage.

The spareness of Keaton's work is one of the qualities that give it an exquisitely modern feeling. No matter what happened to Buster's character, and extreme scenarios were his specialty, he never got overly emotional or pleaded for an audience's sympathy. Rather, like a comic philosopher of despair, he accepted the world and his lot in it and tried to make the best of an increasingly preposterous situation.

Keaton himself often wondered what the modern fuss over his films was all about. If he could see how much he is now revered, his late wife Eleanor told me in a 1995 interview, "He would be in total shock. He wouldn't believe it—in fact he didn't believe it when his films started coming back."

To understand that point of view, Eleanor Keaton emphasized, you had to understand the prevailing attitude when Keaton was in his prime. Movies were a new form, considered as ephemeral and disposable as paper napkins. Keaton's films were created, Eleanor Keaton emphasized, strictly to make money for the short period until the next one would be ready, "and that would be the end of them. This kind of interest, Buster couldn't visualize it."

That matter-of-factness, however, didn't preclude enormous pride in being able to handle the often grueling physical nature of his pictures. Keaton's vaudeville training had given him a spectacular physicality; not only did he not use a double in his prime, he often doubled other actors. Keaton's balance and agility were wonders to behold. He displayed a cheetah's fluid grace when he ran, and no one took a pratfall or stepped off a cliff, came through a window or went out a door, with so much sangfroid.

No Keaton film is more impressive than *Sherlock Jr.*, where the actor breaks the theatrical fourth wall and any other walls that get in his way. It's hard to name another movie that more casually plays with the notions of film, dream, and reality than this story of a projectionist who moonlights as a private detective and imagines himself into the on-screen action. Keaton himself called it "the trickiest of all pictures I ever made," and the sheer joy of that unalloyed inventiveness is as tonic as ever.

Sherlock Jr. begins with a simple title card offering a pedestrian proverb as a premise: "Don't try to do two things at once and expect to do justice to both." Keaton's character may work in a small town movie theater, but he has hopes of greater things, which is why the film opens with him reading "How to Be a Detective" while his boss expects him to be sweeping up the place.

For all the originality that is to come, *Sherlock Jr.* starts in an ordinary way, with a small skit in front of the theater involving not one or two but three different people searching for a dollar in the trash Keaton is sweeping up. As with Max Davidson, repetition was counted on to add to the laughter.

Even the plot proper begins slowly with Keaton paying a call on "the girl in the case" (Kathryn McGuire) and presenting her with a box of chocolates. No one did shyness quite like Keaton, who gave the impression it might actually unhinge him if even the hint of visible emotion were required.

Showing up soon after is Keaton's romantic rival, "the local sheik" (Ward Crane). This practiced seducer immediately steals a pocket watch owned by the girl's father (the star's own father, Joe) and manages to transfer the blame to Keaton.

Our hero is barred from the house but, nothing daunted, decides to follow the advice in his how-to book and shadow the sheik around town. This does little to advance the plot but leads to one of Keaton's most unnerving stunts. The actor gets drenched by a powerful burst of a water from the spout of a huge water tank; the force of the water was so strong that it crashed his head on nearby railroad tracks and broke the actor's neck, though that fact wasn't discovered until a routine physical exam years later.

"As a detective, he was all wet," the intertitle reads, so Keaton goes back to his other job, movie projectionist, which is where *Sherlock Jr.* really takes off. The movie he projects ("Hearts and Pearls or The Lounge Lizard's Lost Love") is credited to Veronal Films, a reference to a sleep-inducing barbiturate of the day and the first hint we have that something out of the ordinary is about to take place.

No doubt exhausted by his exertions, Keaton falls asleep in the booth. In this dream state he leaves his body and, noticing that the actors in the film have been replaced by his girl, the sheik, and other people in his life, he walks down the aisle and understandably attempts to join them. This does not turn out to be easy.

For the movie universe is intent on keeping Keaton out. On his first attempt, it simply tosses him back into the audience, but when, nothing daunted, he manages to sneak into the frame the movie tries other ways to keep him off balance. In a brilliant series of sight gags that come out of nowhere, Keaton keeps exactly the same position in the frame but gets transferred to a completely different reality from shot to shot to shot, finding himself alternately at the edge of a cliff, stranded in the desert, or facing a group of lions. He may dive off a rock in the middle of the ocean but where he ends up is head-first in a snowbank.

This run of images is one of the most remarkable visual sequences of the entire silent film period because of its quintessential cinematic nature. Difficult to achieve (Keaton used surveying equipment to get his position exactly right) and almost impossible to describe with words ("he becomes the victim of film language" is one of the better attempts), it is completely and immediately understandable the minute you see it unfold on the screen. Plot is abandoned and pure visual pleasure takes its place.

When the story picks up again, an upscale Keaton, immaculate in evening clothes and now known as Sherlock Jr., "the world's greatest detective," is called on to solve the case of a missing necklace that is suspiciously like the case of the missing watch that began the film.

The search for the bad guys ends, as many of Keaton's films do, with a magnificent chase sequence, with the star ending up steering a motorbike through chaotic Los Angeles traffic (according to Keaton authority John Bengston, the architectural landmark Schindler House is visible in the distance), even though he is sitting on the handlebars as he does it. "It wasn't easy to keep a balance," the director told Christopher Bishop in a 1958 interview. "I got some nice spills, though, from that thing."

That kind of down-to-earth nonchalance, a stubborn refusal to take yourself too seriously, was a hallmark of Keaton's style both on and off camera. "He didn't have a big ego, he was never impressed with himself, he'd performed from the time he was four years old and this was all in a day's work for him," Eleanor Keaton told me. "Geniuses were great thinkers to him; he thought calling him that was unreliable information."

When Keaton died in 1966, he was buried with a rosary in one pocket and, at his wife's suggestion, a deck of cards in the other. "He had to have a deck, he was never without one," Eleanor Keaton said. "That way, wherever he was going, he was ready." It's not hard to imagine Max Davidson, who'd had an equally tumultuous show business life, joining him in a hand.

What to Watch Next:
Seven Chances (1925), directed by Buster Keaton.
Jewish Prudence (1927), directed by Leo McCarey.

Further Reading:
My Wonderful World of Slapstick, by Buster Keaton and Charles Samuels.
Buster Keaton: Interviews, edited by Kevin W. Sweeney.

THE THIRTIES

T his was the time when movies began to speak. Not just Greta Garbo in *Anna Christie*, who famously demanded, "Gimme a whiskey, with a ginger ale on the side—and don't be stingy, baby" ("Garbo Talks!" roared the ads), but everybody.

It was a decade, as even the titles of films like *Bombshell* and *I Am a Fugitive from a Chain Gang* indicated, that started with a ferocious burst of uncensored energy. The ability to speak filled the movies with a kind of dynamism that never went away.

By the end of the decade, the enforcement of the Production Code brought a kind of decorum to Hollywood filmmaking, but that in no way affected an emotional sophistication so potent that both *Make Way for Tomorrow* and *Love Affair* inspired films decades later. *Make Way* led Japanese master Yasujiro Ozu to make *Tokyo Story*, and Leo McCarey himself remade *Love Affair* as *An Affair to Remember*.

As to *The Dybbuk*, though in one sense it's part and parcel of the thriving world of Yiddish language film that the Holocaust snuffed out, it's in another way a world unto itself, a film that seems to have emerged fully formed from its premodern setting with all its strangeness and majesty untouched.

I AM A FUGITIVE FROM A CHAIN GANG

1932

Directed by Mervyn LeRoy. Starring Paul Muni, Glenda Farrell.

A man retreats from the camera, disheveled, unshaven, a look of awful fear on his face. The night is dark and the woman he loves, horrified, distraught, calls after him, "How do you live?" He answers with a savage, exultant "I steal . . . " and the screen goes pitch black.

That chilling, almost terrifying ending, one of the most famous in Hollywood history, brings to a close *I Am a Fugitive from a Chain Gang* as bleak and fatalistic a film as the studio system ever produced, yet one that is thrilling to watch because of the relentless energy of the filmmaking and the intensity of Paul Muni's performance in the title role.

It's been more than fifty years since I first experienced that ending on a small television set in my family's Brooklyn apartment, but I still remember how much it disturbed me. I had never seen anything that hopeless, even nihilistic, had never seen a film that so mocked the notions of institutional justice and honor. Having a Hollywood movie end in such a cold, amoral way, with its decent, striving hero turned irrevocably from good to bad, was completely outside my experience. Was it even legal to end films that way?

It wasn't until decades later that I found out that *Chain Gang* was part of a classification critics call pre-Code films, features made in the brief window after sound fully arrived in 1930 but before the enforcement of the moralistic Production Code in 1934, a window when Hollywood pushed boundaries of all sorts and made films that featured strong violence and stronger sexual content, not to mention candor about nudity, drug use, and homosexuality.

"Pre-Code Hollywood did not adhere to the strict regulations on matters of sex, vice, violence, and moral meaning forced upon the balance of Hollywood cinema," writes Thomas Doherty in his thoughtful history, *Pre-Code Hollywood*. "More unbridled, salacious, subversive, and just plain bizarre than what came afterwards, they look like Hollywood cinema but the moral terrain is so off-kilter they seem imported from a parallel universe."

While the sexual nature of pre-Code movies is much celebrated—and features in a key *Chain Gang* scene—it's less well-known that another aspect of the genre was the determination to be socially conscious before the existence of the phrase.

To see, for instance, William Wellman's pair of 1933 films, *Wild Boys of the Road*, about homeless children, and *Heroes for Sale*, where a World War I veteran gets a morphine addiction instead of the honor he deserves and then experiences the horrors of the Great Depression, is to see a kind of Hollywood engagement with the problems of the day that took decades to reappear.

In *Chain Gang* narrative was almost literally ripped from the headlines of the day. Stories of the travails of Robert E. Burns had first appeared in newspapers, then were serialized in *True Detective Mysteries* magazine and finally published as a 1932 book, *I Am a Fugitive from the Georgia Chain Gang!*

Though Burns was still in hiding when the film was made, he was apparently smuggled into Hollywood to consult on the script and enhance verisimilitude. As directed by Mervyn LeRoy and written by Howard J. Green and Brown Holmes under the strong supervision of Warner Bros. head of production Darryl Zanuck, *Chain Gang* stuck reasonably close to the book's story, though, under pressure from the state, it dropped any references to Georgia from the title and the script.

Not one to hide a movie under a bushel, Warner Bros. pushed this film as hard as it could. "Every Anguished Bloodstained Word Is True," read one frenzied ad. "Thousands suffered the torments of the damned that it might be made." The studio's reward, in addition to robust box office results, was three Oscar nominations (including best picture and actor), a Vitaphone musical parody called *20,000 Cheers for the Chain Gang*, and the encomiums of powerful folk like newspaper tycoon William Randolph Hearst.

"I wish everybody in this nation of ours could see 'I Am a Fugitive from a Chain Gang,'" the great man wrote. "It is a most revealing and horrifying picture: a most amazing presentation of frightful conditions actually prevailing in certain parts of the country." Given everything, the reform of the chain gang system and a pardon for Burns were simply a matter of time.

A great deal of *Chain Gang*'s effectiveness is due to the casting of Muni in the title role, here named James Allen. An actor who married naturalness, intensity, and a deeply soulful face, Muni (who'd last played an Al Capone knockoff in *Scarface*) imbues Allen with both poetic and heroic characteristics which ensure that we care about what happens to him. Which is a lot.

The film introduces Allen as a returning World War I veteran comparing future plans with buddies on the troop carrier taking them home. "We'll be reading about you in the newspaper," says an impressed shipmate, little dreaming what the context of that prophecy will be.

Once back home in bucolic Lynndale, where the girl next door says she liked him better in uniform and his sanctimonious minister brother says, "Now tell us all about the war," Allen finds himself too ambitious, too newly inspired to do something worth-while to be satisfied with his old job in the shipping department of "The Home of Komfort Shoes."

An engineer in the war and determined to be part of build-ing something in peacetime as well, Allen leaves town. Despite his best intentions, however, he soon finds himself unemployed and penniless, a classic "forgotten man" reduced to sleeping in fifteen-cents-a-night flop houses and trying unsuccessfully (in a scene reminiscent of *Heroes for Sale*) to pawn his Belgian Croix de Guerre.

Involved unintentionally in a robbery in an unnamed state, Allen gets apprehended, tried, and sentenced to ten years hard labor in the blink of an eye. Before he can comprehend what's happening to him, he finds himself on the Merritt County chain gang, shackles and chains on his legs day and night and all the horrors of this savage system displayed before him.

These chain gang scenes are inherently dramatic. This is a pitiless, dehumanizing place where you can be beaten for almost anything, from wiping the sweat off your face without asking permission to instinctively expressing compassion for a fellow hu-man being.

Underlining the hopelessness of Allen's situation is the un-blinking, neo-noir cinematography of veteran cameraman Sol Polito, whose classic compositions of men in stripes swinging sledge hammers look unremittingly bleak, and Mervyn LeRoy's unblinking directorial style.

LeRoy, who'd directed Edward G. Robinson in *Little Caesar* the year before, brings the immediacy of engaged journalism to his approach. Though the situations are melodramatic, the direc-tor's relentless, matter-of-fact style drives home the message that this is a place it's worth risking death to escape.

Escape Allen does, stopping only for a brief interlude with the been-around Linda (Noel Francis). It's a racy pre-Code scene where the era's sexual candor pays off in unexpected dramatic impact.

Allen ends up in Chicago and attempts with seeming success to build a new life, but he finds to his horror that his past won't let him be. Always there is the fatalistic sense that he can't escape, a feeling that emerges as subtext when he talks about his work as an engineer: "I build bridges and roads for people to use when they want to get away from things. But they can't get away. Nobody can."

For James Allen, the chain gang is a nightmare he can never awaken from, a past that dogs him like a hellhound on his trail. *I Am a Fugitive* teases us with the possibility of a Hollywood ending, but to expect one here is to wait in vain.

What to Watch Next:
Heroes for Sale (1933), directed by William Wellman.

Further Reading:
I Am a Fugitive from the Georgia Chain Gang! by Robert E. Burns.

BOMBSHELL

1933

Directed by Victor Fleming. Starring Jean Harlow, Lee Tracy.

Not known as a shy and self-effacing enterprise, the movie business has never been reluctant to examine itself on film. Inside Hollywood movies range from celebrated classics like *The Barefoot Contessa*, *The Bad and the Beautiful*, and *A Star Is Born* (so potent it was remade twice) to little-seen gems like Marion Davies's 1928 silent *Show People*. Privileged looks behind the curtain at how the Dream Factory really operates are always welcome, but, except for another favorite, *Sunset Boulevard*, few of them cut so cynically close to the bone, or are as fearlessly caustic about celebrity, as *Bombshell* (1933).

The movie not only stars Jean Harlow in her prime as a movie star named Lola Burns, the blonde bombshell of the title, but smartly pairs her with congenitally fast-talking Lee Tracy, who played Hildy Johnson when *The Front Page* debuted on Broadway. Tracy plays E.J. "Space" Hanlon, the indefatigable head of Monarch Studio's publicity department, whose passion for getting Lola's name in print conflicts with her wistful desire to have even a smidgen of a private life.

No one was more shocked at how inside this high-octane escapade was than a film critic for *Daily Variety*, who called it "the low down on Hollywood . . . a chucklesome morsel for the Coast crowd [that] may be just a little too wise for the mob at large . . . Appeal is strictly to the sophisticated. A fan has to be pretty alert to catch most of the intimate film colony references."

It is fun, even today, to catch the self-referential nods, both large and small, *Bombshell* makes to the contemporary reality of the movie business. There are references to setups and Klieg eye, the glamour photographer George Hurrell and the Coconut Grove nightclub, plus stars of the period like Janet Gaynor and Lewis Stone. Harlow has one of her funniest lines when, delighted by a swain's effusive declarations, she enthuses, "Not even Norma Shearer or Helen Hayes in their nicest pictures were spoken to like this."

It was apparently the notion of coscreenwriter John Lee Mahin to turn a serious but unproduced play by Caroline Francke and Mack Crane about the perils of stardom into an antic comedy. The decision to base it on the life of Clara Bow gained force when the project was joined by director Victor Fleming, who once dated the silent star, and Harlow, who'd had an uncredited bit in *The Saturday Night Kid* (1929).

Yet because Harlow was in the cast, it was inevitable that the film would consciously invite comparisons to her career as well. It was Clara Bow who let her Great Danes have the run of the house (Lola Burns had similarly misbehaving English sheepdogs), but it is Harlow's celebrated platinum hair that's being referenced when an admirer says with a remarkably straight face, "Your hair is like a field of silver daisies. I'd like to run barefoot through your hair."

Bombshell also took advantage of the fact that Fleming had directed Harlow in one of her biggest hits, *Red Dust*. An amusing plot element has Lola Burns doing retakes dictated by the Hayes Office on one of the key *Red Dust* scenes. "Don't think I'm gonna get in that rain barrel," she complains. "Cold as it was last time, a polar bear would've died."

And it is Harlow who comes to mind in the jazzy stardom montage that opens *Bombshell*. We glimpse the glamour queen herself, with a backdrop of fireworks at no extra charge, and watch in awe as copies of fan magazines pour off printing presses with headlines like "The Love Life of Lola Burns" and loyal but dubious fans try out a perfume she's endorsed.

After all this high-energy allure, it's typical of *Bombshell*'s attitude that Lola in private is introduced alone in bed and dead to the world as her loyal maid Loretta (Louise Beavers) wakes her at 6:00 AM for an early morning studio call. "Gee, what a business," Lola unglamorously grouses. "You might as well run a milk route."

Early as it is, Lola and Loretta find time to trade some typically racy pre-Code dialogue when the star complains that the maid is using her evening wrap as a negligee. "I know, Miss Lola," Loretta replies, "but the negligee you gave me got all tore up night before last." Lola, of course, has the last word: "Your day off sure is brutal on your lingerie."

Bombshell portrays Lola as a creature with, as Space Hanlon puts it, "a gorgeous pinwheel personality." She is a sweet-natured and well-intentioned young woman who has a soft spot for her father, brother, and personal secretary, though in cooler moments she recognizes them as "nothing but a pack of leeches." She is a creature of whims, a different one every minute, and she has been shamelessly indulged in as many of them as possible because she is, after all, "the idol of 110 million people."

Though Harlow, who died tragically young at thirty-seven, is best known for her relaxed and natural on-screen sensuality, *Bombshell* showcases other abilities as well, especially her gift for wised-up comic dialogue and a willingness to poke fun at her image. Harlow also brought some unlooked-for poignancy to the trapped-in-luxury predicament of someone who an older woman aptly characterizes with a surprised and sympathetic "you're just a girl."

If Lola is naive, Space Hanlon, the man she shares a love-hate relationship with, is anything but. A self-aware compulsive schemer in a wide-brimmed hat who freely admits "I'm no prize out of a Crackerjacks box," Space is completely amoral in the most cheerful way, caring only about what the public wants to read and willing to do anything to deliver it.

Someone who regularly sends over cases of Johnny Walker Black Label to cooperating journalists, Space is introduced not in relation to Lola but rather trying to hide from another actress whose romantic misadventures he has leaked to the gossip press. Never one to let the truth stand in the way of his relationship with his stars, Space blithely says whatever he feels needs saying, telling the young woman "I wouldn't hurt you any more than I would my own mother" (not true) and "I've got some decency left" (not true either).

Understandably upset that "not one-hundredth of the stories printed about me are true," Lola calls Space on the carpet, but he is not without the resources to reply. No one in sound pictures ever talked faster than Lee Tracy, and this gift for rat-a-tat dialogue comes into play as Space rouses himself to deliver a stirring per-oration about how he and he alone has "seen to it that Lola Burns is a family slogan from Kokomo, Indiana, to the Khyber Pass."

"Strong men," he goes on, "take one look at your picture and go home and kiss their wives for the first time in ten years. You're an international tonic. You're a boon to repopulation in a world thinned out by war and famine." And so on into the night.

There are moments, of course, when Lola wonders if any of this matters if she can't find personal happiness because the stu-dio system subverts her romantic inclinations. As director and former beau Jim Brogan (Pat O'Brien) puts it, "You can't raise a family and make five pictures a year." But *Bombshell*, which cele-brates Hollywood cynicism as much as it mocks it, in effect tells her to get over herself and appreciate what she has.

"Is it any disgrace entertaining people, making them laugh, making them cry?" Lola asks in an apologia that writer/director Preston Sturges would echo nearly a decade later in *Sullivan's Trav-els*. If you can do all that as well as *Bombshell*, it's no disgrace at all.

What to Watch Next:
Show People (1928), directed by King Vidor.

Further Reading:
Pre-Code Hollywood: Sex, Immorality, and Insurrection in American Cinema, 1930–1934, by Thomas Doherty.
Sin in Soft Focus: Pre-Code Hollywood, by Mark A. Viera.

THE DYBBUK

1937

Directed by Michael Waszynski. Starring Leon Liebgold, Lili Liliana.

Though the great works of world cinema have become my solace and my joy, I grew up as a Saturday matinee kid in Brooklyn without any awareness of their existence. One of my paths to knowledge was stumbling on books like Parker Tyler's *Classics of the Foreign Film: A Pictorial Treasury*, and I have not forgotten the shock one particular entry gave me.

This passionate, heavily illustrated book became a touchstone, and I remember reverently turning the pages, looking at the pictures and reading about films I'd never heard of or seen. Then came a when-worlds-collide moment: sandwiched chronologically between Marcel Pagnol's *The Baker's Wife* and Sergei Eisenstein's *Alexander Nevsky* was *The Dybbuk*, a Yiddish language film that Tyler, never one to downplay his enthusiasms, called "one of the most solemn attestations to the mystical powers of the spirit the imagination has ever purveyed to the film reel."

I may not have known from film classics, but Yiddish I knew about. It was the first language of my immigrant parents, who spoke it constantly to each other and everyone they knew. It was a language I loved without reservation, but no one of my acquaintance had ever connected it with anything artistic. A film in Yiddish worthy of being spoken of in the same breath as *Napoleon*, *La Strada*, and *Hiroshima, Mon Amour*? There must be some mistake.

It took some time to experience *The Dybbuk* for myself, but when I did I realized the mistake was mine. This story of love and otherworldly possession was, as Tyler had suggested, a deeply haunting film, a convincing portrait of the existence of a supernatural sphere intimately connected to our own. But it was more than that, considerably more.

Directed by Michael Waszynski (a prolific Polish filmmaker who ended up with associate producer credits on postwar films like *El Cid* and *The Fall of the Roman Empire*), *The Dybbuk* was first and foremost a stylized and sophisticated art film that made use of the tenets of expressionism in set design, music, and dance to create its world and make its points.

But because it was made in 1937, just a few years before the Holocaust would decimate the universe it portrays, the film's re-creation of the culture and civilization of Europe's Hasidic Jews, its depiction of a world that would soon be no more, resonates in a way no one involved in its production could have foreseen.

Another reason *The Dybbuk* is so good is that it's the direct descendant of a pair of culturally significant predecessors, a groundbreaking project of cultural anthropology and a major hit play, both bearing the name of S. Ansky.

S. Ansky was the pseudonym of the writer Shloyme Zanvyl Rapoport, who between 1911 and 1914, when World War I forced a halt to the work, headed an expedition to the Russian Pale of Settlement under the auspices of the Jewish Historical-Ethnographic Society of St. Petersberg. "Armed with cameras and recording equipment," writes J. Hoberman in *Bridge of Light*, his definitive history of Yiddish film, Ansky and his cohorts devoted themselves to "transcribing Jewish legends, noting spells and remedies, collecting songs and proverbs, photographing old synagogues and cemeteries, and purchasing ceremonial objects, jewelry and clothing."

One of the legends Ansky came across was that of the dybbuk, often a demon (as in the writings of Nobel Prize winner Isaac Bashevis Singer) but also a wandering soul who, according to the later screenplay, "returns to the earth so that it may complete the deeds it had left undone, and experience the joys and griefs it had not lived through."

Ansky was so taken with this story that he turned it into a play, *Between Two Worlds*, that is set in an indeterminate past, a time when wonder rabbis regularly performed prodigious miracles, when spirits wandered the earth, and tampering with fate inevitably led to dire results. In this particular story, the soul in question returns to fulfill a love that dared not speak its name while the lover still lived.

Though a number of theatrical impresarios had expressed interest in *Between Two Worlds*, including the Moscow Art Theater's celebrated Constantin Stanislavski, the play was never performed during Ansky's lifetime. It was produced by the Vilna Troupe as a posthumous tribute just a month after the author's death in 1920. Its popularity skyrocketed after that, and as Yiddish language film became a going concern in Poland, a movie version (making use of some of Warsaw's top Yiddish theater talent) was all but inevitable.

The Dybbuk opens with what is essentially a long prologue that sets the film's spectral, otherworldly tone from the opening frames. A long shot of an empty country road suddenly presents a man magically appearing in the middle of the frame, a man walking purposefully with a long staff in his hand.

As his miraculous entry makes clear, this is no ordinary man but a kind of mystical messenger of almost golem-like focus and intensity. A harbinger of destiny who knows what will happen before it happens, the messenger is given to enigmatic pronouncements like "a man must see where he is going" and "a man never knows when it is time to rejoice or time for sorrow," and his somber presence never fails to disconcert whoever he meets on his way.

The messenger (Isaac Samberg) is headed to the court of Reb Azriel, the Tsaddik of Miropole, the head of a Hasidic community whose followers revere him for holiness and wisdom, a man whose grandfather, Reb Velvele the Great, was a student of Hasidism's founder, the Baal Shem Tov, and was said to have the power to resurrect the dead.

As played by Abraham Morewski, who originated the role in the 1920 Vilna Troupe production, the Tsaddik is a wonder rabbi to the core, someone whose faraway look indicates involvement with the higher spheres even as he leads his followers in the singing of evocative *nigunim*, the wordless melodies that are part of Hasidic communion with God.

It is the time of the High Holy Days, and it's not only the messenger who wants to be at the Tsaddik's court. Two good friends from yeshiva days, Sender (Moshe Lipman) and Nisn (G. Lemberger), have reunited here and, discovering that their wives are both pregnant, have made a decision about the future they can't wait to announce to their spiritual leader.

Ignoring warnings from the somber Tsaddik ("man does not make decisions" he cautions them), the two men pledge that should their wives give birth to a boy and a girl, they will marry. The messenger tells them point-blank that "you cannot pledge something as yet unborn," but they are unmoved and begin the journey to their towns with the vow intact. As my mother used to say, no good will come of this.

Things start to fall apart almost immediately, as Nisn dies before reaching home and before telling anyone of the pledge he and Sender have made, a pledge his son Chanon grows up without knowing anything about.

Sender stays alive, but his wife dies giving birth to a daughter, Leah. Partly to deal with his sorrow, Sender devotes himself to his business, coming to care more for money than his lonely daughter.

Eighteen years pass, and the impoverished Chanon (Leon Liebgold) comes to Sender's town of Brinnits to study. Naturally he and the beautiful Leah (Lili Liliana) meet and feel an immediate attraction neither one can explain, as well as a fascination with a grave in the center of town. It's the resting place of a bride and groom who were killed in 1648 by Chmielnicki's murderous Cossacks as they stood under the wedding canopy about to be wed.

Because Sender, having forgotten his vow and having no idea who Chanon is, insists on marrying Leah into a wealthy family, a desperate Chanon abandons study of the cold Talmud for the mystical precincts of Kaballah, which "pulls the soul free of earth to spiritual heights."

The young man fasts, takes ritual baths, mortifies the flesh, and, in his extreme anxiety, even calls out to Satan ("in every sin there is holiness"), all in an attempt to make Leah his own. He dies in the attempt, but when Leah stands under the wedding canopy about to be wed to the young man of her father's choosing, Chanon's spirit enters her body and takes possession of her soul. "Into the bride," says the messenger with terrible and deliberate finality, "has entered . . . a dybbuk." Does anyone, even the great Tsaddik himself, have the cosmic power necessary to sever these bonds?

Several factors make this unnerving and fantastical situation plausible, starting with the film's intense atmosphere, its use of expressionism to create a skewed but compelling world where buildings have a *Cabinet of Dr. Caligari* tilt and Judith Berg's choreography of village dancing, including a pas de deux between Leah and a terrifying figure wearing a death's head mask, is always unsettling.

Equally central, and equally convincing, is the acting in the lead parts, especially Liliana and Liebgold (who costarred with Molly Picon in *Yidl Mitn Fiddle* and with Maurice Schwartz in *Tevye*) as young lovers who create the feeling they must always be together, in death as well as life. In fact the two actors fell in love during the production and remained married for more than fifty years. Such is the power of *The Dybbuk*'s spell.

What to Watch Next:
The Light Ahead (1939), directed by Edgar G. Ulmer.

Further Reading:
Bridge of Light: Yiddish Film Between Two Worlds, by J. Hoberman.

MAKE WAY FOR TOMORROW

1937

Directed by Leo McCarey. Starring Victor Moore, Beulah Bondi.

LOVE AFFAIR

1939

Directed by Leo McCarey. Starring Irene Dunne,
Charles Boyer, Maria Ouspenskaya.

Leo McCarey liked people. More than that, as Jean Renoir once said, he understood them, perhaps better than anyone else in Hollywood. The essence of his success as a director is both that simple and that complex.

Liking people didn't mean that McCarey was fooled by them, because he wasn't. He viewed life whole, recognized the connivers and the charlatans as well as the saintly and the sincere, and accepted it all.

More than that, McCarey's films have an emotional quality that is open and unafraid. The feelings are right out in the open, expressed with a fearlessness that aligns him with Frank Borzage, whose silent films like *7th Heaven* and *Lucky Star* share with Mc-Carey's sound pictures the ability to make what could be the most shamelessly sentimental moments feel natural and inevitable.

McCarey is most often thought of as an expert comedy director, someone who worked with the Marx Brothers (*Duck Soup*), Mae West (*Belle of the Nineties*), and Charles Laughton (*Ruggles of Red Gap*) and received an Oscar for directing Cary Grant and Irene Dunne in the screwball classic *The Awful Truth*.

Before those features, McCarey worked for nearly a decade creating comedy shorts for Hal Roach Studios. The approximately three hundred one-reelers he had a hand in, besides personal favorite *Pass the Gravy*, included the Our Gang series. He's also credited with teaming Stan Laurel and Oliver Hardy and helping secure the place of the slow burn reaction shot in the film comedy lexicon.

Even before that, however, McCarey began his film career with a job that seems completely out of character. He worked as assistant director for master of the macabre Tod Browning, reportedly directing the disturbing Lon Chaney in a scene from *Outside the Law.*

Though they couldn't possibly be mistaken for Browning's work, both *Love Affair* and *Make Way for Tomorrow* have a whiff of that darker side. Because these films are initially open and optimistic, a McCarey trademark, their portrayal of bleak events in good lives has the ability to come out of nowhere and take us by surprise. In this filmmaker's world, only the finest of lines separate joy and sorrow, heartbreak and happiness.

Love Affair (1939), a romantic fantasy with an unusual and unexpected edge, was quite a success in its day, and was such a favorite of actor Cary Grant that he convinced McCarey to remake it as *An Affair to Remember* (1957), which in turn inspired *Sleepless in Seattle* (1993).

The 1939 original was so admired it received six Oscar nominations, including best picture, two acting selections (Irene Dunne and Maria Ouspenskaya), and best original story. Given the almost haphazard nature of the film's origins, that last nomination is something of a surprise.

McCarey was contracted to work with costars Dunne and Charles Boyer in a project that fell apart at the last minute. The new film, which begins on a transatlantic cruise, came together quickly. The brightness and sprightliness of its dialogue in the first half of the movie was to a certain extent improvised, a method McCarey enjoyed, while the screenwriters labored to get the trickier second half in shape.

Dunne later reported that the director "kept handing us pieces of paper all the time with new dialogue. So there wasn't much sense learning anything—you only had to unlearn it." This off-the-cuff quality inspired rather than unnerved the stars, who reportedly felt as let down when the shipboard part of the shoot ended as genuine cruise passengers feel when they reach their final destination.

Before introducing the ship, the SS *Napoli* headed from Naples to New York, *Love Affair* begins with a droll sequence: a British radio announcer reading a news flash announcing that Michel Marnet, "the celebrated sportsman," is sailing for the United States to marry "one of America's industrial nobility: Lois Clark, the rock and gravel heiress. Stone and sand, you know."

So it's no surprise, in a scene reminiscent of what Preston Sturges was to do a few years later with the opening of *The Lady Eve*, that everyone on the boat is agog at the great man's presence and dying to meet him. Except for Terry McKay (Dunne), who almost literally bumps into Michel and is more bemused—"Don't tell me you're the fella"—than impressed by the encounter.

As brought to life by Boyer, Michel, with his dangling cigarette and complete nonchalance toward romantic fidelity, is the epitome of Continental sophistication. But, as played by Dunne in one of her favorite roles, Terry is a woman of wit and style, fully his match, her confident American honesty able to trump his European sangfroid at every turn.

However it was put together, *Love Affair*'s screenplay (written by Delmer Daves and Donald Ogden Stewart from a story by Mildred Cram and McCarey) is wise enough to take its time establishing first the attraction and then the deeper feelings that animate the relationship between these two.

They start by sharing witty lines, then confidences. Terry, it turns out, is engaged as well—to her boss, a man the film hints but doesn't quite say (these are the days of the Production Code after all) she is having an affair with. As their feelings intensify, so does their vulnerability: it's not good for either one of them to be seen together as often and as publicly as they'd like. They know they should resist each other's company, but they can't stay away.

Love Affair's story line starts to pivot to a different tone when the boat stops in Madeira, the home, it conveniently turns out, of Michel's grandmother, played by the great Ouspenskaya, whose career ran the gamut from Stanislavski's Moscow Art Theater to Lon Chaney Jr.'s *The Wolf Man.*

It's from Michel's grandmother that Terry learns that her friend has considerable gifts as an artist he's chosen not to pursue. "Things come too easy for him," she tells the young American in the film's key line of dialogue. "One day life will present a bill to Michel, and he will find it hard to pay."

As the ocean liner nears New York, it's clear to Terry and Michel that transferring their shipboard romance to the hard edges of the real world will be difficult, and the honest and adult nature of their conversation is a mark of a film moving in a new direction.

A penniless marriage, they realize, is a serious step for people "used to lives of pink champagne," and they agree to take six months, as Michel puts it, "to find out if I'm worthy to say what's in my heart." They agree to meet half a year hence, on July 1 at 5:00 PM on the 102nd floor of the Empire State Building, "the nearest thing to heaven we have in New York" (hey, this is a romance after all) and see where they stand.

The second half of *Love Affair* demonstrates the unanticipated obstacles that get put in the way of that plan, obstacles that are best left discovered on the screen. It is enough to say that what Michel's grandmother foresaw was correct: out of nowhere life did present a pitiless bill. But the great satisfaction of *Love Affair* is that by the time that happens the film has involved audiences so deeply in the story of Terry and Michel we feel as disturbed as if that bill had been presented to us personally.

A screen romantic if ever there was one, McCarey believes absolutely in this love, but he refuses to shy away from the difficulties involved, from the heroic perseverance necessary if life's pitiless complications are to be overcome. *Love Affair* can push too hard; it can and does dance on the edge of excessive sentimentality. But while this film may toy with us unmercifully, the payoff is there at the end.

A very different kind of love story presents itself in *Make Way for Tomorrow*, one that remains almost unheard of and even taboo in contemporary movies. This examination of a couple still deeply connected after half a century of marriage is done with a heartbreaking fidelity to the truth of the difficulties that kind of attachment faces in the real world. This is a social problem film that continues to impress decades after its release.

More than *Love Affair*, *Tomorrow* demonstrates the way reality's starkness can assert itself in the unlikely guise of a major studio release. Even for fans of McCarey's innate humanism, this kind of unflinching scenario was something unlooked for and out of the ordinary. This is a film where you can't quite believe what you're seeing, a story that is devastating because, paradoxically, it's made with subtlety and the sweetest possible touch.

The film's original press material tried to square that circle by saying that though "laughter is still first" in McCarey's scale of values, "he is convinced that humor should have significance, that it should spring from something vital in life." Yet this was a director who said, "I want the audience leaving the theater to feel happier than when they came in." How did he end up with his name on a film of which Orson Welles insisted, "Oh my god, that's the saddest movie ever made . . . It would make a stone cry."

Part of the answer was personal. "I had just lost my father and we were real good friends," the director recounted. "I admired him so much." That loss made McCarey especially receptive to the themes of *The Years Are So Long* by Jennifer Lawrence, a successful novel that was a Book of the Month Club selection.

Lawrence's day job was writing an advice column for the *Newark Call* newspaper, and her novel came out of the realization that, next to difficulties involving marriage, "the most frequent questions were, 'Must I support my mother and father?' and 'Is it right for my children to turn their backs on me now that I've grown old?'"

Make Way for Tomorrow's opening title cards, though they end in the standard bromide "Honor thy father and thy mother," lay out the bleak landscape Vina Delmar's script is going to visit: "Few of us pause to consider those who have lost the tempo of today. Their laughter and their tears we do not even understand, for there is no magic that will draw together in perfect understanding the aged and the young."

It is just such a gathering of young and old that begins *Tomorrow*, as parents Barkley and Lucy Cooper (Victor Moore and Beulah Bondi) convene a gathering of their adult children. Unseen daughter Addie in California can't make it ("she never even sent us an orange," someone grouses), but four of the five, led by eldest son George (Thomas Mitchell), show up at the old family home and begin needling and bickering with each other before their parents get a chance to speak.

The news is not good. Unbeknownst to the children, Bark has been out of work for four years and the bank is going to re-possess their home in a matter of days. Throwing themselves on their children's mercy, the parents' only request is that "no matter what happened, we would always be together."

As a temporary measure because of the short notice, how-ever, the parents will be split up. Lucy will go to George in Man-hattan, while Bark goes to daughter Cora (Elizabeth Risdon) who lives three hundred miles away. "It'll be nice living with the chil-dren for a while," Lucy says, but Bark, prophetically, is less san-guine: "It never has worked out for anyone else."

Though George is well-off enough to afford a maid (Louise Beavers), this is Manhattan after all, Lucy has to share a room with her teenage granddaughter Rhoda (Barbara Read). Her huge picture of Bark is as out of place on one of Rhoda's walls as is her noisy rocking chair in the living room, especially on nights when George's wife Anita (Fay Bainter) earns extra money the family needs by teaching contract bridge to a class of elegant couples wearing evening clothes.

One of the great strengths of *Make Way for Tomorrow* is that it doesn't want to take sides in family arguments. It would be good if George's family were happier to have Lucy in their midst, but the film is unsparing in showing how difficult and meddlesome the elderly woman is to have around, and how her unmanageable presence changes the family dynamic, and not for the better.

Yet just when you think you've run out of patience with the old woman, McCarey lets us, as well as the evening bridge class, eavesdrop on a touching phone conversation she has with her far-away husband. "I miss you, Bark, that's the only trouble," she says. "But we'll soon be together for always."

And when a fed-up Rhoda snaps, "Why don't you face facts, Grandma," Lucy responds with one of the film's home truths: "When you're seventeen, facing facts is fun. When you're seventy, about the only fun you have left is pretending that there aren't any facts to face."

Things are, if possible, worse for Bark, so ill at ease at Cora's that he takes daily refuge in a local candy store run by the equally elderly Max Rubens (Maurice Moscovitch), who frankly delights in his independence from his children: "They don't need me and I don't need them."

When Bark gets sick, we see his truculent, even infantile side as he gives the doctor Cora reluctantly calls a hard time. It's his illness that seals the couple's fate: with no child willing to accept both of them, Bark will be shunted off to California "for his health" and Lucy, to assuage George's guilt, pretends to be delighted to be consigned to the ominously named Idyllwild Home for Aged Women. As the Yiddish proverb puts it, one mother can take care of ten children, but ten children can't take care of one mother.

Before this inevitably final parting, however, Bark and Lucy will get to spend five hours together in New York, the site, as it turns out, of their honeymoon fifty years earlier. Lucy, however, has a stipulation: if she agrees to go to the home, Bark must not be told. "It must be handled my way," she says with steely resolve previously unseen, before adding a softer "it'll be the first secret I've ever had from him."

The key thing about that enchanting Manhattan interlude (details are better experienced than described) is that it allows us to see Bark and Lucy at their best. To see them alone together for the first time is to realize they're difficult when apart because this is a couple that really only works for each other. Yet this Babes in Toyland fantasy moves seamlessly to the frank conclusion that put Orson Welles away, and that inspired Kogo Noda to write what many critics consider the greatest of Japanese postwar films, Yasujiro Ozu's *Tokyo Story*.

That concluding section also sees Bark and Lucy clear-eyed about their children for the first time. They are having so much fun with each other they blow off a chance to have a family dinner with the clan. "This is your father, remember me," Bark says sharply when he calls to say they're not coming, and then, in a beautifully done movie moment, puts his hand over the receiver so the audience can't hear exactly what he says when he tells off Nellie and her siblings. There is also the unthinkable implication that as parents they must have had a hand in how their progeny turned out, as even the more forgiving Lucy says, "You don't sow wheat and reap ashes, Pa."

Though all the actors are strong, it is difficult to imagine *Make Way for Tomorrow* without the remarkable performances of Bondi, who was two decades younger than her character, and Moore, who was so well-known as a strictly comedy actor that McCarey had the great makeup artist Wally Westmore change his look so audiences wouldn't immediately recognize him.

Both actors rely on underplaying and delicacy to create performances that are unsparing in their emotionality. Moore later wrote that "I felt my role so keenly that sometimes I couldn't prevent tears from coming to my eyes. 'Barkley mustn't feel sorry for himself,' Leo would say. 'Let the audience do the crying.'"

It is McCarey's all-encompassing spirit, of course, that animates everything, that understands that this is a story that avoids heroes and villains in favor of everyday people with the best of intentions. These are individuals who want to help, want in fact to do the right thing, but find themselves handicapped by self-interest, self-absorption, and lack of empathy. Everyone is human, but the different generations are not speaking the same language, and that's where the tragedy begins.

McCarey never doubted how good his work was in *Make Way for Tomorrow*, believing "if I really have talent, this is where it appears." He worked on the film for a year and resisted pressure from studio chief Adolph Zucker to provide a softer ending, a decision that led to his leaving Paramount and going to Columbia.

It was at that studio later that same year that McCarey teamed Cary Grant with Irene Dunne and made *The Awful Truth*, the film that won him a best directing Oscar. "Thanks," he reportedly said on accepting the award, "but you gave it to me for the wrong picture."

What to Watch Next:
Tokyo Story (1953), directed by Yasujiro Ozu.
An Affair to Remember (1957), directed by Leo McCarey.

Further Reading:
Leo McCarey: From Marx to McCarthy, by Wes D. Gehring.

THE FORTIES

In ways expected and otherwise, obvious and subtle, World War II runs like a bright red line through almost all the films chosen from this decade.

It is easy to see the conflict in the films that use it as a backdrop, whether it's the daring comedy of *To Be or Not to Be* or the paradigmatic romance of *Casablanca*.

On the other hand, it takes a bit of film history to know that Aldous Huxley took on the adaptation of *Pride and Prejudice* only after being convinced that doing so would help the British war effort. Or that *Children of Paradise* was made in France during the last days of the German occupation, with some of its Jewish creators forced to work from hiding.

Both *The Shop Around the Corner* and *The Lady Eve*, each in its own social sphere, show societies that would never be the same after the war. And though it's World War I that figures prominently in *Random Harvest*, thoughts of the current conflict were doubtless on the minds of its creators.

It's also interesting that the trio of postwar films I've chosen—*Great Expectations, Bicycle Thieves, The Third Man*—were all from Europe. Starting with the 1948 Consent Decree judicial ruling that severed movie studios from the theaters they owned, the studio system was starting to crumble. But not before one last hurrah.

PRIDE AND PREJUDICE

1940

Directed by Robert Z. Leonard. Starring Greer Garson, Laurence Olivier.

That *Pride and Prejudice* the Hollywood movie is not *Pride and Prejudice* the Jane Austen novel is another one of those truths that must be universally acknowledged. Yet it is equally difficult to argue with the assertion made by the film's 1940 trailer, which took pains to insist, "One of the most famous novels ever written, now one of the screen's happiest events."

Certainly having Austen's quietly perfect novel about the ease of misjudgment and the difficulty of making amends to use as source material was very much an advantage for this literary romance, which stars Laurence Olivier as the proud Mr. Darcy and Greer Garson as the prejudiced Elizabeth Bennet.

If absolute fidelity to the Austen text was not to be expected, what MGM gave in return was the high gloss of impeccable studio craftsmanship offered by a legendary team that included cinematographer Karl Freund, art director Cedric Gibbons, costume designer Adrian, and hair stylist Sydney Guilaroff.

Always happy to bring literary quality to its projects, MGM approached Aldous Huxley, the famed British novelist then living in Los Angeles, and offered him $1,500 a week to collaborate on the *Pride and Prejudice* script with Jane Murfin, a veteran screen-writer who was known for having introduced the first movie dog, Strongheart, to eager audiences in the 1920s,

In a letter to a friend Huxley sounded ambivalent about the project: "One tries to do one's best for Jane Austen; but actually the very fact of transforming the book into a picture must necessarily alter its whole quality in a profound way." But these qualms notwithstanding, *Pride and Prejudice*'s verbal dexterity, its gift for the thrust and parry of witty dialogue among people who are never at a loss for words, is continually delightful.

Things worked out so satisfactorily, in fact, that it is instructive to look back at the project's history and realize what a near thing many of these choices were. That this film exists at all turns out to be in part due to Harpo Marx, of all people, who back in 1935 attended a Philadelphia preview of a Broadway-bound dramatization of the Austen novel written by an Australian named Helen Jerome.

The very next day, Harpo sent a telegram to Irving Thalberg in Hollywood: "Just saw Pride and Prejudice. Stop. Swell show. Stop. Would be wonderful for Norma. Stop."

Irving Thalberg, the model for sensitive mogul Monroe Stahr in Scott Fitzgerald's *The Last Tycoon*, was at the time head of production for MGM and Louis B. Mayer's right-hand man. Norma was his wife, actress Norma Shearer, who had just been nominated for an Oscar for her portrayal of Elizabeth Barrett Browning in *The Barretts of Wimpole Street* and saw in *Pride and Prejudice* a chance to repeat that success.

So, in January 1936, MGM dutifully bought the rights to the play for $50,000, and Jerome got screen credit in the finished film. Why buy the rights to the theatrical version of a novel that was long in the public domain? Thalberg reasoned that the publicity generated both by the play and by the sale would help sell this rather obscure property to the American moviegoing public.

Thalberg cast Clark Gable, of all people, to appear opposite his wife as Mr. Darcy, but the producer died before filming could begin and the project languished. Actors ranging from Melvyn Douglas to Robert Donat and Robert Taylor were considered for the Darcy role, and nearly a dozen writers tried their hands at the script.

This logjam was broken after Laurence Olivier became a hot screen property courtesy of his performances in *Wuthering Heights* and *Rebecca*. MGM liked the idea of putting him in *Pride and Prejudice*, and he, having recently begun a torrid affair with Vivien Leigh, liked the idea of having her star opposite him as Elizabeth.

The studio, however, had other ideas. Louis B. Mayer, convinced by his son-in-law David O. Selznick that putting Olivier and Leigh in the same movie was chancy commercially because it risked a moral backlash if their affair became public, put Leigh in *Waterloo Bride* instead. Her replacement, recently arrived from England, was Greer Garson.

For a director, MGM now turned to Robert Z. Leonard, nicknamed "Pop," who was one of the most reliable of the studio's contract directors as well as the most senior, having begun in the movie business in 1907 by getting paid $7.50 for riding a horse up a steep hill. A director for twenty-five years and a very capable craftsman, Leonard could be counted on to get the job done efficiently.

As for Huxley, within days of signing his contract on August 30, 1939, World War II broke out, which made him reluctant to go on. He phoned his Hollywood colleague, writer Anita Loos, and according to her reminiscence, the following exchange took place:

"'I simply cannot accept all that money to work in a studio while my family and friends are starving and being bombed in England,' Huxley said.

"'But Aldous,' I asked. 'Why can't you accept that fifteen hundred and send the larger part of it to England?'

"There was a long silence at the other end of the line, and then Maria, Huxley's wife, spoke up.

"'Anita,' she said, 'what would we ever do without you?'"

Though it is tidied up more than Jane Austen would have allowed, the basic plot of *Pride and Prejudice* remains unchanged in the Huxley version. Mr. and Mrs. Bennet, the parents of five unmarried daughters, are cheered beyond measure to learn that the mansion at nearby Netherfield Park has been taken by a wealthy, unmarried man. "It's the most heartening news," says Mrs. Bennet enthusiastically, "since Waterloo."

Irrepressibly played by Mary Boland, Mrs. Bennet is one of numerous supporting roles expertly acted by players—including Melville Cooper as the insufferable Mr. Collins and Edna May Oliver as Lady Catherine de Bourgh—whose ability to make characters comic without becoming caricatures adds polish and pleasure to the proceedings.

What gives this *Pride and Prejudice* pride of place, however, despite all the screen adaptations that have come in its wake, are the interlinked performances of Garson and Olivier, she appealingly high-spirited and he dripping supercilious hauteur while saying things like "I'm in no humor tonight to give consequence to the middle classes at play." Their ability to bring life to both sides of the romantic equation, the repulsion as well as the attraction, shows the advantages of casting one of literature's dream couples with actors who are up to the parts.

Once production started, Olivier, still miffed at not being able to work with Vivien Leigh, was said to be almost as unenthusiastic as Darcy. He did not see fit to mention the film in his autobiography, though he did deal with it in a volume called *On Acting*, in which he said he thought "the best points in the book were missed, although apparently no one else did. I'm still signing autographs over Darcy's large left lapel. MGM always got its costumes right."

Actually Olivier was wrong about the costumes. In its wisdom the studio felt that the actual fashions of the early nineteenth century, what one writer called "the more restrained, classical lines of the Directoire and Empire styles" and costar Ann Rutherford referred to as "the wet nightgown look" were not very much fun. So Adrian gave everyone the much fuller, not to say voluminous clothes that became fashionable decades later.

Helped, presumably, by an ad campaign that announced, "Bachelors Beware! Five Gorgeous Beauties are on a Madcap Manhunt," the film turned out to be a box office success, drawing the largest weekly August audience in Radio City Music Hall's history and inspiring *Variety* to note that its success in Cleveland "overcame all local prejudices against costume drama."

And *Pride and Prejudice* also did the kind of good deeds that film doesn't seem to do anymore. While looking through director Robert Z. Leonard's personal scrapbooks in the Margaret Herrick Library of the Academy of Motion Picture Arts and Sciences, I noticed a tiny envelope tucked between the last page and the back cover. It was addressed to Robert Z. Leonard, Director of Films, Hollywood, California USA. Dated February 10, 1941, it came from one Betty Howard, who wrote the following from Southampton, England·

"My husband is a Naval oficer and a few days ago he had one of his rare afternoons in port and a chance to visit the cinema. We went to see your film made from the book we know and love so well and to our delight were carried away for two whole hours of perfect enjoyment. Only once was I reminded of our war—when in a candle-lit room there was an uncurtained window and my husband whispered humorously, 'Look—they're not blacked out.'

"You may perhaps know that this city has suffered badly from air raids but we still have some cinemas left, and to see a packed audience enjoying 'Pride and Prejudice' so much was most heartening.

"I do thank you very much as well as all the actors and actresses for your share in what has given so much pleasure to us."

Pride and Prejudice does that to people. Its story more than resolves in a classic happily-ever-after way: its Jane Austen insights into character and motivation are so acute it enables us to believe things just might work out that way for the rest of us as well.

What to Watch Next:
Persuasion (1995), directed by Roger Michell.

Further Reading:
Pride and Prejudice, by Jane Austen.

THE SHOP AROUND THE CORNER

1940

Directed by Ernst Lubitsch. Starring James Stewart, Margaret Sullavan.

TO BE OR NOT TO BE

1942

Directed by Ernst Lubitsch. Starring Carol Lombard,
Jack Benny, Robert Stack.

In an irony the man himself would have appreciated, the best-known anecdote about Ernst Lubitsch took place after he died. As the story goes, fellow émigré directors Billy Wilder and William Wyler were walking to their cars after the funeral. "No more Lubitsch," Wilder said, shaking his head. "Worse than that," Wyler countered. "No more Lubitsch films."

It's a shame the director wasn't around to hear that, because in its rueful combination of sadness, humor, emotion, and sophistication it had many of the qualities that are usually referred to as "the Lubitsch touch."

While there are as many definitions of his style as there are critics attempting to define it (maybe more), what the Lubitsch touch essentially comes down to is the ability to convey a complex understanding that the human comedy is not necessarily funny all the time.

A master storyteller who would literally act out the entire film for his cast, Lubitsch could be warm and empathetic without a trace of sentimentality: his sharp, sly wit and the delicacy of his film's dialogue and situations made that kind of backsliding out of the question.

Born in Berlin to Russian Jewish émigré parents, Lubitsch became a cult-of-personality brand name in 1930s Hollywood for the high style Continental sophistication of films like *Trouble in Paradise* and *Design for Living*.

Lubitsch's personal signature, not just his name, appeared on screen to announce whose production this was, and, ever present cigar in hand, he even made a charming appearance in the theatrical trailer for *The Shop Around the Corner*, pointing to his watch to let actor Frank Morgan know that time is money.

In the era before affordable air travel, Lubitsch's films were as close to Europe as many Americans got, and the director himself was fond of saying, "I've been to Paris, France, and Paris, Paramount, and Paris, Paramount is better."

Though, in classic Lubitsch style, both *The Shop Around the Corner* and *To Be or Not to Be* are set in Europe, by the time he made these particular films some things had changed. The high style escapist world of his 1930s efforts was less in vogue, with Lubitsch saying in a 1939 interview, "No one used to care how characters made their living if the picture was amusing. Now they do care. They want their stories tied up to life."

One reason audiences cared was that 1939 was the year conflicts that eventually became World War II began to engulf

Europe. The war was a key player in *To Be or Not to Be* (1942), but it figures as well, though more peripherally, in *The Shop Around the Corner* (1940).

The engaging look back at prosperous prewar Budapest in *Shop* served to remind and reassure viewers of the way things used to be and might be again. In an intriguing prefiguring of a debate that was to engulf the response to *To Be or Not to Be*, film critic John Mosher of the *New Yorker* complained of "an unfortunate choice of setting. Somehow, today it is difficult to accept any capital in Europe as a scene of whimsical romance and humorous enchantment."

Both then and now, that quibble was very much a minority position, because it is difficult to think of a more perfectly constructed studio romance than *The Shop Around the Corner*. Emotionally realistic and deeply satisfying, it is made with such exceptional ease and skill that it can be watched endlessly without any loss of enthusiasm.

Though it is very much a "Paris, Paramount" kind of production, *Shop* takes pains to ground us in its Hungarian milieu. The opening specifically locates the Matuschek & Company leather goods store "on Balta Street, just around the corner from Andrassy Street," customers are told the prices in Hungarian penga, and the word "Raktar" on a door designates a storeroom. All this to counteract the fact that, as the *New York Times* gently put it, James Stewart, "on the face and speech of him, could hardly be called a Budapest type."

Budapest type or not, Stewart is exceptional. Even though the studio press material says *Shop* was his ninth picture in two years, he is anything but worn out. Genuine, honest, and vulnerable, his trademark naturalness has rarely been so well used. The reason is likely rooted in his longtime rapport with costar Margaret Sullavan.

It wasn't just that Sullavan is a singular actress with a lighter-than-air nonchalance that is breathtaking. She and Stewart had known each other as friends for seven years, starting with his undergraduate days at Princeton, and when he came out to Hollywood she helped him find his footing and campaigned for him as her leading man in *Next Time We Love*. Lubitsch had no one but these two in mind for his leads, and when they proved temporarily unavailable, he postponed the project and did *Ninotchka* starring Greta Garbo instead.

Giving the stars splendid material to work with was Samson Raphaelson's beautifully constructed script, which was adapted from a play by Hungarian writer Nikolaus Laszlo that Lubitsch liked so much he had optioned it personally.

Raphaelson's screenplay is a marvelous high-wire act, where the fluid, witty dialogue is so artfully layered that plot complications and coincidences seem perfectly natural. The setup is charm itself as we meet store owner Hugo Matuschek (Morgan) and staff members who worry about the proprietor's whims and try to stay out of his way when he says, "All I want is your honest opinion."

Stewart plays head clerk Alfred Kralik, the boss's calm and competent favorite. His coworkers include the kindly Pirovitch (Felix Bressart), the officious Ferenez Vadas (Joseph Schildkraut), and the live-wire messenger boy Pepi Katona (William Tracy). The shop is mostly empty, the customers never quite ready to buy, and the establishment's ordinariness is beautifully conveyed.

Kralik, as it turns out, is in an especially good mood. "I got a letter from a girl," he confides to Pirovitch. Not just any girl, and not a girl he has actually met. It's a young woman he has connected with after answering a personal ad: "Modern girl wishes to correspond on cultural subjects anonymously with intelligent, sympathetic young man."

"She is the most wonderful girl in the world," Kralik enthuses, so excited at the anticipation of their first meeting that very night that he has not slept for days. His mood is so good it seems unstoppable. Then Klara Novak (Sullavan) walks in the door.

The spirited Miss Novak immediately gets off on the wrong foot with Kralik when he mistakes her for a potential customer when in fact she's an unemployed shop girl looking for a job. Then she undercuts him with Mr. Matuschek by insisting she can sell a musical cigarette box that plays the Russian folk song "Ochi Tchornya" (also featured in *My Man Godfrey*) after Kralik has said sales were impossible. And that's just the beginning.

One of the joys in *The Shop Around the Corner* is the great sparring relationship between nominal coworkers. Not only do these two grate on each other instantly, but every word either one of them says further antagonizes the other. Stewart and Sullavan, such good pals in real life, take to this task with believable fervor. Adding yet another unneeded complication to Kralik's life at just this moment, the usually friendly Mr. Matuschek seems to have inexplicably turned against him.

Simple and straightforward as it is on the surface, *The Shop Around the Corner* has its share of secrets, things the characters don't know about each other and that the audience doesn't know about the characters.

The way all things are gradually revealed to everyone is a pleasure to experience, as is the adroit way Lubitsch and company create gentle comedy from situations of loneliness and occasional despair. It's no wonder that even as gifted a director as Billy Wilder kept a sign on his office wall that simply read, "How would Lubitsch have done it?"

What the director chose to do in *To Be or Not to Be* was not only daring for him, it was also one of the most audacious films to come out of Hollywood. Begun when Europe was fully involved in World War II, still in front of the cameras when Japan's December 7, 1941, Pearl Harbor attack forced America into the conflict, *To Be* brought Lubitsch's classic comic elements to a story involving murderous Nazis and the German occupation of Poland. Considered by Jean-Luc Godard to be one of the ten best

American sound films, it's an endeavor that feels fully as risky today as it did when it was made.

Not a film to hide its intentions, *To Be* (written by Edwin Justus Meyer from a story by Lubitsch and Melchior Lengyel) immerses us in its counterintuitive intentions right from the opening scene, set in the Warsaw of August 1939, when Europe was still at peace. A crowd of citizens looks on aghast as Adolf Hitler walks among them. "Can it be true?" the voice-over narrator asks. "The man with the little mustache in Warsaw while the two countries are still at peace? Can it be? He's a vegetarian but he doesn't always stick to his diet. Sometimes he swallows entire countries."

No, it's not Hitler, at least not yet. It's an actor named Bronski (Tom Dugan) who is playing the German leader in a satirical drama called *Gestapo* being put on at the Theatre Polski, and he's taken to the streets to prove to his director that he is convincing in the part. This melding of serious issues, theatrical ego, and unmistakable comedy characterizes *To Be* from beginning to end.

When the Polish government pulls the plug on *Gestapo* out of fear of offending Germany, the actors return to their production of *Hamlet*, with Joseph Tura (Jack Benny), the self-proclaimed "greatest Shakespearean actor in Poland" in the title role and his wife, the glamorous Maria Tura (Carole Lombard), taking on Ophelia.

A celebrated vaudeville and radio performer, Benny was always the director's first choice to play an actor of colossal self-involvement. As Benny later reported, the director told him, "You are not a comedian. You are fooling the public for thirty years. You are fooling even yourself. You are an actor, you are an actor playing the part of a comedian, and this you are doing very well."

For the beautiful and equally self-centered Maria, Lubitsch had initially wanted Miriam Hopkins, but various ego issues got in the way, and Lombard, an expert screwball performer whose films included *Nothing Sacred* and *My Man Godfrey*, was given the role.

Lombard's confident and disarming Maria, gleefully insincere one moment, a heroine of the Polish Resistance the next, was not only arguably the actress's most intoxicating performance, it was also her last.

For on January 16, 1942, less than a month after shooting wrapped, a plane carrying Lombard back to Los Angeles after participating in a defense bond drive in the Midwest crashed into a mountain near Las Vegas, killing everyone on board and shocking a nation just getting involved in war.

(Lombard's death so unnerved United Artists in particular that when *To Be* was released later that year, the studio created an unprecedented section in its exhibitor press book called "The Proper Selling of the Film Everyone Wants to See" to encourage "the most carefully calculated showmanship" to deal with what it delicately called "a special situation in the merchandising of this great picture.")

The Nazi references in its opening minutes notwithstanding, *To Be* starts out as a recognizable Lubitsch vehicle, exploring the vagaries of a marriage between two supreme egotists equally addicted to the spotlight.

Joseph Tura's always fragile equilibrium is shattered, as well it might be, when a young and handsome airman gets up and leaves his front and center seat for *Hamlet* just as the actor launches into his celebrated "To be or not to be" soliloquy. "Maybe he had a sudden heart attack," someone says sympathetically. "I hope so," is Tura's sincere reply.

That walkout is no accident; it is part of a plan engineered by Maria Tura to receive the dressing room attentions of Lt. Stanislav Sobinski (Robert Stack), an infatuated airman who has been sending her enormous bouquets of flowers. As her droll maid Anna (Maude Eburne) puts it, "What a husband doesn't know won't hurt his wife."

The lieutenant's second walkout comes immediately before news hits that Germany has invaded Poland. In a beautifully choreographed sequence of serio-comic misunderstanding, Tura mistakes everyone's horror at the Nazi invasion ("It's a crime") with sympathy for his plight as a slighted actor.

As that scene indicates, the arrival of the invaders means a partial change of tone, and *To Be or Not to Be* morphs into an unusual combination of thriller and Lubitsch farce, what studio publicity awkwardly called "an exciting romantic comedy keyed to an ever mounting tempo of suspense."

So while the comedy is still there, so is a serious treatment of the destructive horrors of the invasion, including Warsaw in ruins, references to concentration camps, and warnings about being shot on sight.

As Lubitsch explained in an article published in the *New York Times*, "I was tired of the two established, recognized recipes, drama with comedy relief and comedy with dramatic relief. I made up my mind to make a picture with no attempt to relieve anybody from anything at any time; dramatic when the situation demands it, satire or comedy whenever it is called for. One might call it a tragic farce or a farcical tragedy—I do not care and neither do the audiences."

This nervy combination, black comedy decades before the term was accepted, is seen at its most effective in the character of Colonel Ehrhardt, the head of the Gestapo office of occupation, who is simultaneously a dangerous man and, as played by the veteran comic actor Sig Ruman, a figure of fun.

It is the colonel who, in the film's best running gag, revels in his nickname of "Concentration Camp Ehrhardt." He also has the film's most controversial line. After Tura, in disguise, fishes once too often for a compliment for his acting, Ehrhardt replies, "What he did to Shakespeare, we are now doing to Poland."

Once the thriller elements kick in, *To Be or Not to Be* turns out to have a fairly complicated plot which has these Polish actors getting back into their Gestapo costumes and pretending to be Nazis to save the Polish underground from doom. The story is so complex that even the characters themselves don't always follow it. Heading off on a deadly assignment, Tura tells his colleagues, "After I kill him, I hope you'll be kind enough to tell me what it's all about."

But as François Truffaut, a critic before he was a filmmaker, understood, story line was not the point here. "There is no Lubitsch plot on paper, nor does the movie make any sense after we have seen it," he wrote admiringly in *The Films in My Life*. "Everything happens while we are looking at the film. An hour later, or even if you've just seen it for the sixth time, I defy you to tell me the plot of 'To Be or Not to Be.' It's absolutely impossible."

To many of the critics who reviewed *To Be or Not to Be*, especially those in New York, the wisdom of involving Nazis in the plot was very much the point. Eileen Creelman of the *New York Sun* called it "more grim than hilarious. The tragedy of Poland is too close, too immediate to lend itself to joking." And the *New York Times'* Bosley Crowther went even further, asking "where is the point of contact between an utterly artificial plot and the anguish of a nation which is one of the great tragedies of our time."

Lubitsch was taken aback by this criticism and responded in print more than once, most famously in an open letter to Mildred Martin of the *Philadelphia Inquirer*, who took a swipe at *To Be* the following year in her review of the director's *Heaven Can Wait*.

"What I have satirized in this picture are the Nazis and their ridiculous ideology," he wrote. "It can be argued if the tragedy of Poland realistically portrayed as in 'To Be or Not to Be' can be merged with satire. I believe it can be." Even more to the point is what Lubitsch told a reporter that same year about his motivations in making the film: "It seemed to me that the only way to get people to hear about the miseries of Poland was to make a comedy. Audiences would feel sympathy and admiration for people who could still laugh in their tragedy."

Looked at in that way, *To Be or Not to Be* is aligned to Preston Sturges's *Sullivan's Travels* in its belief in the power and validity of the comic impulse. As a creative person, Lubitsch did not want to be pigeonholed, did not want to feel that his way of reacting to tragedy had any less validity than the point of view of anyone more conventionally serious. Comedy could go anywhere and do anything, and who better than he to demonstrate that.

With that in mind, we can find the essence of Lubitsch in some lines near the beginning of *To Be or Not to Be*, where Theatre Polski producer Dobosh (Charles Halton) quashes a brilliant ad-lib by Bronski as Hitler with a curt, "That's not in the script."

"It'll get a laugh," Bronski insists.

"I don't want a laugh," retorts Dobosh, at which point actor Greenberg (Felix Bressart, whose characters often spoke for Lubitsch) gets the last word.

"A laugh," he says, "is nothing to sneeze at."

What to Watch Next:
Remember the Night (1940), directed by Mitchell Leisen.
Ninotchka (1939), directed by Ernst Lubitsch.

Further Reading:
Ernst Lubitsch: Laughter in Paradise, by Scott Eyman.

THE LADY EVE

1941

Directed by Preston Sturges. Starring Barbara Stanwyck,
Henry Fonda, Charles Coburn.

Preston Sturges is to my mind the most gifted writer/director
of sound comedies Hollywood has ever seen. His films combine
bracing verbal wit with unashamed slapstick and completely un-
hinged romantic plots in a way no one else has managed.

More impressive still, Sturges somehow shoehorned eight of
these films into the five year period between 1940 and 1944, getting nominated for three writing Oscars and winning one (for
The Great McGinty). It's a feat that defies belief, which is exactly
what Sturges's masterpiece, *The Lady Eve*, does every time I see it.

For in addition to the trademark Sturges comic virtues, *The
Lady Eve* also takes to heart the advice Ballets Russes impresario Serge Diaghilev famously gave to collaborator Jean Cocteau
when he insisted to the artist, "Etonne-moi." In simple English,
"Astonish me." This is not standard territory for studio comedy,
but Sturges never hesitated to do things his own way.

With writer/directors now thick on the land in Hollywood, it
is remarkable to remember that until Sturges took that role with
McGinty in 1940, no writer had ever directed before. Though he

was at the top of his profession (*The Power and the Glory* preceded the similarly structured *Citizen Kane* by eight years), Sturges burned to become what he called "a prince of the blood." He elaborately courted Paramount executives ("the seduction of a virgin saint would not have been better planned") and when he agreed to sell the McGinty script to the studio for one dollar, they agreed to let him behind the camera.

Though it wasn't released until 1941, *The Lady Eve* was the third film Sturges wrote and directed in 1940, an output studio publicity didn't hesitate to claim as "a record never before accomplished in Hollywood."

Although three films in a year might sound like a recipe for exhaustion, the rush of energy that propelled Sturges into directing showed no signs of abating. *The Lady Eve* was the most antic project he'd yet pulled off, as well as being as beautifully structured as the most elaborate spun sugar confection.

Like most of the writers who followed him, Sturges wanted to direct because he felt he understood his scripts better than the functionaries often assigned to them. In the case of *The Lady Eve* this was especially true. While the film's glamorous setting inside the world of the superrich who crossed oceans on luxury liners wearing tuxedos and alluring gowns was the stuff of fantasy for audiences, for Sturges it was old home week. The man who'd been married to heiress Eleanor Hutton did not direct to achieve wealth and cultural status; that was where he'd come from.

Though he idolized Solomon Sturges, the wealthy Chicago stockbroker who married his mother and adopted him when he was two and a half, the key influence in Preston Sturges's life was clearly his mother. Mary Desti, as she elegantly renamed herself, was a world-class eccentric and free spirit who was, her son recalls, "endowed with such a rich and powerful imagination that anything she had said three times, she believed fervently. Often, twice was enough."

Among the many roles Desti played in her life was proprietor of a successful Parisian perfume house, purveyor of something called "Le Secret du Harem," mistress of noted satanist Aleister Crowley, and, most lasting of all, great friend and confident of dancer Isadora Duncan. Diaghilev and Cocteau were not figures in a landscape to her; she likely knew them.

Sturges's mother met Duncan in 1901, soon after her marriage to Solomon Sturges, and for the next quarter of a century, until the dancer's death (strangled in an auto accident with a scarf that Mary had given her), the two women were as close to inseparable as they could manage. Preston spent much of his youth in Europe in the wake of these two, often parked in some prestigious private school or other until "every so often a beautiful lady in furs would arrive in a shining automobile with presents for everyone. This was Mother, of course."

Though many of today's film directors come to the medium directly from darkened movie houses and claustrophobic screening rooms, without noticeable real-world experience to draw on, Sturges's life, especially his youth, was so much the opposite that he must have viewed living and working in Hollywood as a kind of anticlimax.

In his youth Sturges met everyone from Enrico Caruso to Buffalo Bill, played with L. Frank Baum's children and Richard Wagner's grandchildren, and experienced the greatest restaurants and wine cellars Europe had to offer while still in knee pants. He ran his mother's perfumery in chic Deauville when he was but fifteen, was training to be an American flyer when World War I ended, and only thought of playwriting, his prelude to screenwriting, when an attack of appendicitis combined with a challenge from a girlfriend inspired his first effort.

Perhaps because he felt so at home in *The Lady Eve*'s world, Sturges took what Paramount considered to be inordinate risks in casting what turned out to be one of the great comic romantic couples of the day, Henry Fonda and Barbara Stanwyck.

Fonda, nominated for best actor for *The Grapes of Wrath* (1940), was considered to be such a serious dramatic player after appearing in films like *Drums Along the Mohawk*, *Young Mr.*

Lincoln, and *Jesse James* that studio publicity noted that "not once in the past three years has he worn his own clothes on screen."

Stanwyck, best known for racy pre-Code classics like *Baby Face* and high-class weepies like *Stella Dallas,* also did not seem to have sparkling comedy in her future. But when she starred in the Sturges-written *Remember the Night,* the future director told her, "I'm going to write a great comedy for you."

"I told him I never get great comedies," Stanwyck told Sturges biographer James Curtis, "and he said, 'Well, you're going to get one,' and of course he followed through." Did he ever.

As it turned out, the chemistry between these unlikely co-stars was electric, and, helped by the twenty-five glamorous outfits Edith Head designed for Stanwyck, helped create an on-screen atmosphere that was considered positively racy by 1941 standards. The film's credits focus on a lascivious serpent wearing a top hat while newspaper advertising called this "the vexiest picture of the year" and featured lines like "Eve sure knows her apples" and "Girls, the best way to get a man is to get him bothered" to enhance the point.

That *The Lady Eve* would end up as a film where, the publicity material claims, Fonda so "turns 'great lover' with a bang" that he winds things up with "six torrid, long, crushing clinch-and-kiss moments in the last 500 feet of the film," could not be predicted from the delicately deadpan opening Sturges concocted.

Here we meet timid and scholarly Charles Pike (Fonda), heir to a great brewery fortune ("Pike's Pale: The Ale That Won for Yale") emerging from the headwaters of the Amazon. He's been on a year-long snake hunting expedition and as he bids a regretful farewell to his companions he insists this life of quiet scientific exploration is how he'd love to spend the rest of his life. As if.

Pike is accompanied by William Demarest's Muggsy, a rough-edged valet/bodyguard whose motto is "I look out for the kid." He also has the benefit of a family wealthy enough to convince an ocean liner to stop and pick him up in the middle of nowhere. His affluence and unmarried status has the entire ship atwitter, but no one looks on his arrival with a more calculating eye than Colonel Harrington (Charles Coburn) and his daughter Jean, spectacularly played by Stanwyck.

For the Harringtons, not to put too fine a point on it, are card sharps and grifters, eager for a chance to fleece the new arrival, as long as it can be done with style. "Don't be vulgar, Jean," the Colonel admonishes his daughter early on. "Let us be crooked but never common."

If Fonda's Charles is the ultimate naive stooge, a bookworm whose idea of light dinnertime reading is "Are Snakes Necessary?" Stanwyck is his perfect foil, a glittering conniver who calls him Hopsie and never does the expected. Which is exactly how they meet.

While Sturges's ability to make movies with a fine-tooled precision is visible throughout *The Lady Eve*, it's at its height in the set pieces that bring these two together, first in the ship's main dining room and then in Jean's suite.

We know exactly how eager the other eligible women on board are to make Charles's acquaintance because we see it all reflected in Jean's makeup mirror as she assays the competition's moves and makes snarky comments on their collective feeble attempts, things like "Holy smoke, the dropped kerchief. Hasn't been used since Lily Langtry."

Jean's approach is nothing if not direct. As Charles attempts to leave the dining room, she trips him as he walks past (Fonda apparently had to do twenty-nine takes to get the film's various stunts right), then brazenly accuses him of not watching where he's going. Having broken the heel on her shoe, the unfortunate man is dragooned into accompanying Jean back to her stateroom to get another pair of evening slippers.

Back at the suite, Jean works her wiles on the stupefied Charles, who weakly protests, "I've been up the Amazon for a year, and they don't use perfume." Jean even drapes herself with practiced seduction across her open shoe trunk and asks, "See anything you like?" When the two return to the table and the Colonel remarks, "it certainly took you long enough to come back in the same outfit," Jean snaps back, "I'm lucky to have this on." Nobody could frustrate the era's censors like Sturges in his prime.

The joke, of course, is initially on Jean, who is soon enough telling her father "this is on the up and up, I'm in love with the poor fish." The mayhem that follows, with Jean trying to protect Charles from the Colonel's depredations while counting on the fact that "a moonlit deck is a woman's business office" is captivating, but it turns out to be only a warm-up to *The Lady Eve*'s main course.

For the necessity eventually arises for Jean to fool Charles a second time ("I need him like the ax needs the turkey," she coolly explains) but in a completely different way that is too audacious to be revealed.

The brilliance of *The Lady Eve* is that we get to have it both ways, get to simultaneously bask in the emotional warmth of a storybook romance while being amused by the spectacle of the stuffy Charles getting skewered for not believing such a thing possible. In a triumph of sensibility over sense that Jane Austen might have savored, love manages to conquer all. Even if it does take a double reverse twist ending only Sturges could pull off—or have the nerve to attempt, for that matter—to make it happen.

What to Watch Next:
Sullivan's Travels (1941), directed by Preston Sturges.

Further Reading:
Preston Sturges by Preston Sturges: His Life in His Words.
Five Screenplays by Preston Sturges, edited by Brian Henderson.

STRAWBERRY BLONDE

1941

Directed by Raoul Walsh. Starring James Cagney,
Olivia de Havilland, Rita Hayworth.

No other actor in American film had the combination of pugnacious energy, graceful physicality, and pure charisma that could be called James Cagney's birthright. Whether his films called for strong fists, snappy patter, or soft-shoe dancing, Cagney answered the call.

The actor could do so much so well, I would be hard-pressed to pick one scene from his more than sixty features as a favorite. Cagney dancing down the White House stairs in *Yankee Doodle Dandy*? Going up in "top of the world, Ma" flames at the end of *White Heat*? Convivially conversing in excellent Yiddish in the pre-Code *Taxi*? Choosing only one is more than I can do. But when it comes to the Cagney feature I prefer, it's none of the above but rather *Strawberry Blonde*, a film as difficult to define or pigeonhole as it is a pleasure to enjoy.

Strawberry Blonde was a popular film in its day largely for its evocation of the celebrated Gay Nineties, both with vintage language of the "she's all the fudge" and "23 skidoo" variety and songs like "Wait Till the Sun Shines Nelly," "Meet Me in St.

Louis," and "Bill Bailey" as well as the title tune. It was also a favorite of its two key players, star Cagney and director Raoul Walsh, and largely for identical reasons.

Cagney, who enjoyed making the film so much he invited his mother to the set, and Walsh, who consistently referred to it as his favorite among his sound features, both appreciated that *Strawberry Blonde* helped them escape from being typecast as strictly gangster film material. (In fact, Cagney and Walsh had worked together in just such a guns-blazing venture, *The Roaring Twenties*.)

Strawberry Blonde also gave a young Rita Hayworth one of her first substantial roles and utilized the best of studio talent in other key positions. Its script was adapted from the Broadway play *One Sunday Afternoon* (filmed in 1933 and 1948 to minimal effect) by the twin brother team of Julius and Philip Epstein, who went on to cowrite *Casablanca*. And the cinematographer was the expert James Wong Howe, who made park scenes shot indoors on a sound stage live and breathe like the great outdoors.

But to talk about *Strawberry Blonde* this way is in a sense misleading. For this is no big strapping studio picture but one whose virtues are surprisingly quiet, restrained, and understated. Wise rather than slick, this is a film whose emotional impact is no less potent for sneaking up on you when you're not looking.

Made with an off-hand assurance, *Strawberry Blonde* accomplishes all this thanks to Cagney's manifold gifts, his ability to find the reality in a decidedly quirky story, to bring serious shadings to what is largely presented as comic material with some pleasant musical interludes. Few were Cagney's equal seeing to it that lightness and dark reinforced rather than canceled each other out.

Though the middle of the film takes place in the 1890s, *Strawberry Blonde*'s plot is book-ended by sequences set a decade later. Cagney plays T.L. "Biff" Grimes, a dentist who grouses to his best friend Nick the Greek barber (George Tobias) on a quiet Sunday afternoon that he's only had two patients in the last eight months.

At first Biff seems a standard pugnacious sort, a human firecracker always aching for a fight and often getting one. Biff is such a fountain of cranky notions about anything and everything ("In my opinion no woman can sing, that's the way I'm constituted") that it's a wonder his patient wife Amy (a wonderful Olivia de Havilland) can put up with him and his frequently uttered insistence that, in a line Cagney borrowed from his father, "I take nothing from nobody, that's the kind of hairpin I am." Maybe, he wonders in the film's first hint of darkness, the time he spent in prison is standing in his way.

A snatch of the title song ("Casey would waltz with a strawberry blonde and the band played on") from the house next door gets Biff to thinking of the past he and Nick have in common. "We'll never have those good times again," he says darkly, still furious about an as yet unrevealed evil that was done to him. Then, out of nowhere, a phone call puts his rival in his power.

It seems a man named Hugo Barnstead desperately needs a dentist and Biff is the only one around. This is the same Hugo that Biff, who says he has every right, has thought of going after with a gun. Now, with Hugo about to be an unwitting patient in his chair and potentially deadly gas at the ready, Biff exults that "poetic justice" is just an arm's length away. How seriously should we be taking this threat? With an actor of Cagney's intensity, it is hard to say.

Before Hugo arrives, the film flashes back to *Strawberry Blonde*'s central Gay Nineties section. Walsh immediately indulges a taste for classic Irish types, with Alan Hale as Biff's feckless father Old Man Grimes and the venerable Una O'Connor as the feisty Mrs. Mulcahey.

As for Biff, he is working part-time as a saloon bouncer (a job he soon loses when he gets into a fight with his dad) while taking correspondence school courses on dentistry. In the scene where he practices pulling teeth on the old man, who insists he "won't play favorites" by telling his son which tooth actually hurts, it's hard to know whether to laugh or cry.

The beauty of the neighborhood, and does she ever know it, is Virginia Brush, the strawberry blonde of the title, played by a pleasantly relaxed and radiant Hayworth. Naturally, Biff is mad about her, but so is Biff's friend Hugo (Jack Carson), a hustler who is always working the angles.

Hugo wangles a date with Virginia, but she won't meet him in the park without her girlfriend. So Hugo convinces Biff to come along and he ends up reluctantly talking to de Havilland's Amy. Not only does she look more attractive than the script likely intends (movie stars weren't allowed to be plain), but she ends up being more than Biff's match where cantankerousness is concerned.

Enough of a proto-feminist to cause even Virginia to say "try to be a woman, not a pamphlet," Amy has many of the Epstein brothers' best lines, including describing marriage as an "outmoded, silly convention started by cavemen and encouraged by florists and jewelers."

We know from the opening sequence that these two, joined by having barks worse than their bites, will end up together, but *Strawberry Blonde* is not about the unraveling of the darker strands of its plot, or even about what happens when Biff finally confronts Hugo and Virginia ten years after the fact.

What makes this film so effective is its light touch with weighty matters like the process of discovering what is truly important in life and why. Being passionate about this easy-to-overlook item is like belonging to a secret society: when you meet another member, you know you've met a friend.

What to Watch Next:
Yankee Doodle Dandy (1942), directed by Michael Curtiz.
White Heat (1949), directed by Raoul Walsh.

Further Reading:
Cagney, by John McCabe.

CASABLANCA

1942

Directed by Michael Curtiz. Starring Humphrey Bogart,
Ingrid Bergman, Claude Raines.

Just like Rick, who thought he was over Ilsa, I thought my love for *Casablanca* had run its course.

Not that I didn't remember how overwhelmed I'd been the first time I saw the film. I was a Swarthmore College undergraduate in the 1960s, part of a standing-room-only crowd lured to an off-campus apartment by a friend's promise of something special, and I literally stood spellbound for nearly two hours as *Casablanca*'s pleasures revealed themselves on a small television screen. I felt like I'd never seen anything quite like it, and I was not alone.

Casablanca was nominated for eight Academy Awards and won three, including best picture, best director, and best screenplay. Later, it was runner-up only to *Citizen Kane* in the American Film Institute's top 100 films list and was similarly number 2 behind *The Godfather* in a Zagat survey of "over 17,000 avid moviegoers." More than that, considerable chunks of the film took on lives of their own.

Humphrey Bogart's trench coat–wearing Rick became Woody Allen's alter ego in *Play It Again, Sam* and lots of *Casablanca*'s dialogue entered the popular culture cosmos. Who doesn't know "here's looking at you, kid," "round up the usual suspects," "I think this is the beginning of a beautiful friendship," and "we'll always have Paris." Really, did anyone need to hear more about *Casablanca*? Wasn't everybody already a fan?

So I thought until I started viewing a much admired documentary series on the history of film that immediately sought to establish its iconoclastic bona fides by running down *Casablanca*. The multihour series was not ten minutes old before it spoke unhappily about the way Ingrid Bergman is "lit like a movie star, with highlights in her eyes" and disdainfully insisted that *Casablanca* is "too romantic to be classical in a true sense."

I stopped watching cold turkey at that point and vowed to give *Casablanca* another look. And promptly fell in love with it all over again. As my mother had told me decades before when I said I was thinking of not including a trip to the Eiffel Tower on my first visit to Paris, "If so many people see it, there must be a reason."

Yet for all *Casablanca*'s acknowledged success, however tempting it may be to treat it like a slick product of the Hollywood machine, the reality is that no one expected or even planned for its achievement. As Aljean Harmetz pointed out in *Round Up the Usual Suspects*, her excellent history of the film, "Of the seven (Warner Bros.) pictures being shot during the first week of August, four concerned the underground Resistance." It's as if pure happenstance turned what was envisioned as a fairly standard piece of pre–World War II propaganda entertainment into something a whole lot more.

But if *Casablanca* was born out of a kind of controlled chaos, with writers frequently bringing new pages to the set on the morning of shooting, it was chaos managed by complete professionals at the top of their games at all levels of the production.

It wasn't just the skill of stars Bogart and Bergman, it was the use of name talent—Paul Henreid, Claude Raines, Conrad Veidt,

Sydney Greenstreet, Peter Lorre—far down the cast list. Even the great French star Marcel Dalio, spending the war years in Hollywood, had a small part as the croupier Emile.

The protean Max Steiner wrote the *Casablanca* score, and Don Siegel, who would go on to direct *Invasion of the Body Snatchers* and *The Killers*, created the film's opening montage. Producer Hal Wallis was one of Hollywood's most efficient, and though Michael Curtiz was an arrogant, autocratic director whose on-set empathy was strictly limited, as an immigrant himself he had an innate understanding of the refugee despair that is a key *Casablanca* element.

At least four of Hollywood's best writers worked on the script adapted from Murray Burnett and Joan Alison's unproduced play, "Everybody Comes to Rick's": twin brothers Julius and Philip Epstein, Howard Koch, and, uncredited, Casey Robinson.

As *Casablanca*'s reputation grew in stature over the decades, the writers argued over who did what, but taken as a whole the script is remarkable for the number of different tones and genres it casually masters. The finished film manages the feat of being as political as it is romantic, a story where humor, idealism, cynicism, espionage, melodramatics, and even deadly gunplay all play a part. It's almost like a whole season of films crammed into a single 102-minute package.

Yet the project's extensive reliance on studio skills doesn't account for something inexplicably magical that happens on the screen in *Casablanca*, an emotional and political tone is generated that, against all reason, allows both idealism and personal romance to simultaneously triumph.

More than giving the film its romantic name, Casablanca, a city in French Morocco, becomes a key character in the story. Though Nazis are conspicuously present, it is technically unoccupied French soil, so it is teeming with both European refugees anxious to leave for America and the unscrupulous individuals who prey on their desperation. "The scum of Europe has come to Casablanca," a helpful gentleman tells a new arrival in the film's opening sequence—before lifting his wallet.

The heart of Casablanca is Rick's Café Americain, a nightclub and clandestine gambling establishment that mainlines the cosmopolitanism of wartime despair. "Everyone comes to Rick's," we are assured, which is convenient for the film because it means each important character will walk through its doors at one time or another.

Bogart, of course, plays the American Rick, full name Richard Blaine, and a lot of time and trouble is taken to establish his ironclad character and personality since deviations from it are going to be the heart of what *Casablanca* is about.

Talked about before he is seen, and glimpsed first as a disembodied hand playing chess with himself and writing a firm "okay" on a request of some sort, Rick appears to be, as Peter Lorre's unscrupulous Ugarte says early on, "a very cynical person."

Unsmiling, implacable, oblivious to women who toss themselves at him with regularity, Rick lives by his own set of rules, which include never drinking with his customers and maintaining complete political neutrality. His motto, which he says more than once in case we've forgotten it, is "I stick my neck out for nobody."

As marvelously played by Claude Raines, Captain Louis Renault, the head of the city's Vichy French police, is cynical the way Rick thinks he's cynical. "How extravagant you are, Ricky, throwing away women like that," he says with genuine wit after watching Blaine (no one else calls him Ricky) ignore a mistress. "Some day they may be scarce."

Ruthless and amoral to the point of being eager to prey on desperate females, Captain Renault's mocking and articulate pessimism provides the astringency that keeps *Casablanca* from descending into bathos. Who else would have the sangfroid to say "my heart is my least vulnerable spot" when a pistol is pointed at his chest?

Captain Renault is not only the only man capable of bringing a smile to Rick's lips; he's also the only man who suspects the truth about this American who has run guns to rebels and fought in Spain: "Under that cynical shell," Renault says, "you are a sentimentalist."

The equation between these two, and everything else in Casablanca, changes when Ilsa Lund walks into Rick's in a knockout two-piece white dress by costume designer Orry-Kelly. The simplicity of the costume, which did not come without a battle, was a masterstroke, emphasizing her status as, in Captain Renault's words, "the most beautiful woman ever to visit Casablanca."

Ilsa is there with her husband, Victor Laszlo (Paul Henreid), who just happens to be the world's most eloquent anti-Nazi voice. On the run from the Germans, epitomized by the snarling Major Heinrich Strasser (Conrad Veidt), Laszlo and Lund are frantic to leave the city. But, as the oily Signor Ferrari (Sydney Greenstreet) tells them, "It will take a miracle to get you out of Casablanca, and the Germans have outlawed miracles."

Though Victor Laszlo doesn't yet know it, the famous interchange between Ilsa and Dooley Wilson's Sam over a song ("Play it once, Sam, for old time's sake. Play it, Sam. Play 'As Time Goes By'") has let the audience know that Ilsa and Rick have shared a past that neither one of them has a prayer of forgetting.

How these complicated personal and political dynamics evolve, how they play off each other in continually unexpected ways, is the source of *Casablanca*'s fame and success. Bogart's performance, the way he conveys the pain of love betrayed by suffocating his emotions without quite killing them, is especially strong, but this film is a triumph of the system, not the individual. Hollywood in its prime knew how to put despairing, overpowering, elevating big love on the screen as well as any cinema ever has, and if that isn't enough to make *Casablanca* a classic, I don't know what is.

What to Watch Next:
Pepe Le Moko (1937), directed by Julien Duvivier.

Further Reading:
Round Up the Usual Suspects: The Making of Casablanca,
by Aljean Harmetz.

RANDOM HARVEST

1942

Directed by Mervyn LeRoy. Starring Ronald Colman, Greer Garson.

A standard synopsis of *Random Harvest* will insist it's a film about amnesia, but don't you believe it. This wholly absorbing romantic melodrama, a polished product of MGM at its glossiest, is best viewed as a multi-hanky entertainment about the enduring power of endless love. Rarely revived and not generally considered a great film, it remains irresistible, a can-you-believe-it emotional high-wire act that sustains itself against all logic and probability.

Of course, this kind of filmmaking has never been for everyone. *Random Harvest* received seven Academy Award nominations in 1942, but it didn't win anything and saw its star, Greer Garson, take home the best actress Oscar for her role in another film, the much feted *Mrs. Miniver*.

Critics were also divided on the production. *Daily Variety* was upbeat but the *New York Times'* Bosley Crowther considered it "a strangely empty film." As late as 1951, J.D. Salinger was mocking key elements of its plot in *The Catcher in the Rye*, having protagonist Holden Caulfield insist with typical vigor, "It was so putrid I couldn't take my eyes off it. . . . All I can say is, don't see it if you don't want to puke all over yourself."

Audiences at the time, however, showed no such reservations. *Random Harvest* was the #5 box office hit of the year, bested only by powerhouses like *Bambi*, *Casablanca*, and *Yankee Doodle Dandy*, and it played New York's mammoth Radio City Music Hall for a record twelve weeks, with the 6,000-seat theater even instituting 7:45 AM screenings to meet the crush.

This box office success was not surprising given that the film was adapted from a whopping best-seller—100,000 copies sold in the first six weeks—by the hugely popular novelist James Hilton, whose other credits include the books *Lost Horizon* and *Goodbye, Mr. Chips* and whose screenplay for *Mrs. Miniver* took home an Oscar.

Random Harvest was especially fortunate in the astute pairing of veteran Ronald Colman and relative newcomer Greer Garson. While Colman was celebrated for his mellifluous voice, he'd started in films in 1917 during the silent era and had been a major star for twenty years. Garson, if MGM publicity is to be believed, had only one week left in her studio contract when she was given her very first feature role, in *Mr. Chips* (1939).

That success led her to such a flurry of demure parts, including Elizabeth Bennet in *Pride and Prejudice* and the protagonist in *Mrs. Miniver*, that it was considered newsworthy that Garson's *Random Harvest* role would at one point feature her as a showgirl dancing in an abbreviated kilt. "Star's Shapely Legs to Be Revealed on Screen" headlined a story that quotes Garson claiming, possibly with a straight face, "it's pleasant to be able to prove that I have legs after all."

It is Hilton's story, however, that is the heart of the matter, and the author was so pleased with this Oscar-nominated adaptation (by Claudine West, George Froeschel, and Arthur Wimperis) that he agreed to read the voice-over that starts the film.

The time is autumn 1918 and, Hilton says mysteriously as the camera moves forward, "our story takes you down this shadowed path." The destination is England's Melbridge County Asylum, a grim, remote building that warehouses men whose "minds were shattered by the war that was to end all wars."

One of the most poignant of these cases is Smith, a British army officer who has absolutely no idea who he is. Rumpled, confused, but killingly handsome, Colman plays this role so beautifully that he makes having misplaced your mind look positively attractive. Though Smith can barely speak, everyone tells him he's much improved, and the doctor in charge says that all he needs to recover is to get his confidence back.

Everything changes for Smith on the night the war ends. The asylum guards leave their posts to celebrate and he innocently wanders into the town of Melbridge, where his difficulty with speech makes the local tobacconist (MGM veteran Una O'Connor) suspect he is a dangerous inmate on the loose.

Just at that moment, the warm and luminous Paula Ridgefield (Garson), a vivacious showgirl in town with a traveling revue, comes to the rescue. Taking an immediate liking to Smith, whom she takes to calling "Smithy," she hurries him out of the shop and more or less adopts him. Paula intrepidly finds him a room in her hotel and takes him along as she headlines a rousing version of "It's a Long Way to Tipperary" at the local theater.

"I've lost my memory, I don't even know who I am," Smith confesses, looking truly bewildered. Paula, who has enough life force for both of them, is nothing daunted. "I know who you are," she replies with enviable spirit. "You're someone awfully nice."

Trusting her instincts, Paula is resoluteness itself when Smith's freedom is jeopardized, leaving her life in the theater and relocating both of them in a tiny, quintessentially English hamlet "at the end of the world."

Soon enough (maybe it's all that refreshing country air) Smith has fallen in love as well and proposes marriage. "Never leave me out of your sight again," he says passionately. "My life began with you. I can't imagine a future without you."

Though Paula and Smith think this is their "happily ever after" moment, *Random Harvest* has other ideas. A lot of them. Smith takes a crack at journalism and shows enough promise that a newspaper in Liverpool asks him to come in for an interview. Smith takes the train to the city for what he assumes will be the briefest of separations, but once he arrives in Liverpool nothing is ever remotely the same again.

It goes without saying that *Random Harvest* has surprises up its sleeve, but this film contains more eye-widening, credulity-straining plot reversals than you can easily imagine, even when you think you've imagined them all. Blessed with as many inside out twists and turns—none of which will be revealed here—as a two-lane road through the Italian Alps, *Random Harvest* correctly believes that the power of story trumps any and all logical concerns.

Helping us get comfortable with all these feints and dodges is the soothing polish and professionalism of the MGM studio style, which specialized in the smoothest possible entertainments. Director Mervyn LeRoy, who'd made his reputation in incendiary items like *Little Caesar, They Won't Forget*, and *I Am a Fugitive from a Chain Gang* in the 1930s, had by this time morphed into an all-around filmmaker at ease in multiple genres. Here he's supported by the likes of veteran art director Cedric Gibbons and consummate cinematographer Joseph Ruttenberg, who in the course of a fifty-year career amassed four Oscars and ten nominations.

But more than anything tangible, *Random Harvest* succeeds because of what it believes in, which is first of all itself. Far from being apologetic about its wild improbabilities, this film embraces them wholeheartedly as an exercise in narrative daring as audacious as any avant-garde adventure.

Random Harvest also believes it's the birthright of film to appeal to emotion in general and endless love in particular. An unabashed romance, it focuses on the existential correctness of believing unreservedly in love, insisting that nothing, no amount of success, acclaim, or recognition, is meaningful without it. Which is why, when the *Saturday Evening Post* asked Garson to name her favorite role, she chose not the Oscar-winning *Mrs. Miniver* but this one.

"The screen's main function," she wrote in 1947, "is to give the world beauty and romance—to make us forget our own troubles for a time and send us out of the theater with a lift of the heart. 'Random Harvest,' I like to think, was that sort of picture." Indeed it was.

What to Watch Next:

Mrs. Miniver (1942), directed by William Wyler.

Further Reading:

Ronald Colman: A Very Private Person, by Juliet Benita Colman.

CHILDREN OF PARADISE

1945

Directed by Marcel Carné. Starring Arletty, Jean-Louis Barrault, Pierre Brasseur.

Children of Paradise is a motion picture you experience more than watch. Set in a specific time and place but the product of a quite different one, this film doesn't just contain worlds, but is the world entire recreated on a screen. To see it is to be transported to a state of wonder and appreciation, taken to a time outside of time and a place that exists in the imagination, and in our hearts.

Located in the teeming world of Paris of the late 1820s and early 1830s, shot under chaotic conditions in German-occupied France in 1943 and 1944, released in 1945, scant months after the liberation of Paris, *Children of Paradise* (*Les Enfants du Paradis* in the original French) is characterized by a peerless sense of life in all its richness and improbability, its irrationality and its yearnings. When I'm asked to pick an all-time personal favorite, this is the title I most often cite.

That's because, along with everything else it does, this is perhaps the preeminent examination of the exaltations and mortifications of the romantic impulse. The complexities of love, loss, and longing have rarely been articulated with the sympathy, insight, and specificity brought to the screen by director

Marcel Carné and his frequent collaborator, screenwriter Jacques Prévert, the leading proponents of a French style that was known as "poetic realism."

"Love is so simple," one character says, but the message of *Children of Paradise* is more ambivalent. We see the ennobling and the deranging power of love that is both requited and unreturned, passionate and cool. We witness the devotion and jealousy love inspires, the way its passion changes and morphs, ebbs and flows. And we watch the numberless permutations that result when no less than four men, based to a great extent on real-life characters, come to look on the same enigmatic woman as the exquisite creature of their dreams.

As related by filmmaker Carné in an interview published in 1991, the spark that ignited this endeavor was a modern actor's fascination with a celebrated performer of the 1830s.

When Carné and Prévert met with Jean-Louis Barrault in the early 1940s, he told them of the celebrated mime Jean-Gaspard Deburau, who at the height of his fame murdered a man for insulting the woman he was with. His trial (he was acquitted) was packed with the most fashionable Parisians, all eager to hear this master of silence finally speak.

From this story the idea grew to construct a drama about Deburau (eventually played by Barrault) and two other real individuals: the great stage actor Frederick Lemaitre and Lecenaire, a celebrated French writer and criminal. These were blended with fictional characters and placed in a setting so realistic creating it would have been an accomplishment under any conditions, let alone in occupied France.

That location would be the Boulevard du Crime in the early nineteenth century. The Boulevard du Temple in Paris earned that name because of the lurid melodramas that played in its numerous theaters. When the film opens and the camera pulls back from a close-up on a tightrope walker to reveal the boulevard's vivid, hectic, teeming world, filled at times with as many as 1,800 extras, it is impossible not to gasp. All the more so when we know that the film's production designer Alexandre Trauner, as well as composer Joseph Kosma, had to work clandestinely because they were Jewish. (Kosma and writer Prévert later collaborated on, of all things, the classic pop song "Autumn Leaves.")

A setting is only as good as the characters who inhabit it, and from top to bottom Prévert and Carné created dozens of individuals so deeply etched that we live and breathe with all of them. Ranging from the malevolent rag picker and fence Jericho (Pierre Renoir, the director Jean Renoir's brother) and the softhearted hood Avril (Fabien Loris) to the coquettish landlady Madame Hermine (Jeanne Marken) and Marcel Peres's tirelessly apoplectic theater director, these characters are indispensable in the creation of this romantic tapestry.

For when the humanity and complexity of these relationships are added to the film's visual richness and splendid dialogue, the result is one of the few films that has the durability and emotional texture of a great nineteenth-century novel.

All that is intensified because *Children of Paradise*'s world is the world of the theater. The title itself refers to those who inhabit the highest balconies (and the cheapest seats) in the myriad Boulevard du Crime theaters. These spectators are the equivalent of Shakespeare's groundlings, those whose love of theatrical spectacle is in inverse proportion to their ability to pay for it. "Their lives are small," someone says, "but their dreams are grand."

The woman who becomes the center of all this excitement is Garance (played by Arletty), first glimpsed up to her neck in a tub of opaque water, posing as the Naked Truth in a Boulevard du Crime sideshow. "She will fill your mind and haunt your dreams" the barker says, and that turns out to be as much truth as poetry. Beautiful, unknowable, capricious, and unashamed, Garance is the fulcrum around which the movie's plot turns as we gradually meet the quartet of men she intoxicates.

Encountered first is the chilling Lecenaire (Marcel Herrand), a cold-eyed Nietzschean criminal/philosopher who has declared his own private war against society. When this ascerbic and amoral man says, "I'd spill torrents of blood to give you rivers of diamonds," you fear he is speaking literally. Though Lecenaire is terrifying in his coldness, the cool Garance spends time in his company because she feels that watching him is like watching a play.

Garance is with Lecenaire when he lifts the watch of an unsuspecting citizen outside of the Theatre des Funambules, a kind of vaudeville house on the boulevard. She is almost arrested for the crime when a performer named Baptiste, exiled outside the theater because his father doesn't appreciate his revolutionary gifts, mimes what really happened. She thanks him and in the blink of an eye he is deeply, irrevocably in love.

As Baptiste gradually comes into his own as an unequaled pantomime artist, even those who disparage the art will find their spirit enlarged by the way, in actor Barrault's hands, physical poetry flows out of him like a river. With his completely soulful face, always in classic white makeup when he's on stage, Baptiste is such an otherworldly creature he's aptly described as a man who "fell to earth during a full moon." He's also a pure romantic dreamer whose ideas of love do not take the realities of life into account. "People live that way in books, in dreams, not in real life," an astonished friend tells him, but that is the way he is.

Equally gifted theatrically, though infinitely more pragmatic as far as love is concerned, is Lemaitre (Pierre Brasseur), a practiced seducer and on his way to becoming the preeminent actor of his day. A charming character of colossal but genial ego who is never at a loss for words, Lemaitre talks about making the audience "a gift of my love," but the person he loves most of all is himself.

Equally self-centered is the Count de Montrary (Louis Salou), a man of impeccable posture and untold wealth. Also struck by Garance's magnificence ("beauty is an affront to an ugly world" is how he puts it), the count gives her his card and tells her to call "if misfortune strikes." Not surprisingly, it does, ensnaring all of Garance's admirers in an elaborate web.

In many ways the most classic of classic French films, with a climax that astonishes no matter how many times it's seen, *Children of Paradise* is a miracle many times over. As a piece of romantic/dramatic cinema, its peers are few, its superiors simply nonexistent.

What to Watch Next:
The Rules of the Game (1939), by Jean Renoir.

Further Reading:
Child of Paradise: Marcel Carné and the Golden Age of French Cinema,
   by Edward Turk.

GREAT EXPECTATIONS

1946

Directed by David Lean. Starring John Mills, Valerie Hobson, Alec Guinness.

David Lean may have been the director and Alec Guinness one of the stars, but when *Great Expectations* was released in 1946, the biggest, most significant name attached was also on the title page of the novel: Charles Dickens.

That's in part because both Lean and Guinness were just starting their careers, the director decades away from classics like *Doctor Zhivago* and *Lawrence of Arabia* and the actor no better than eighth billed in what was essentially his film debut.

But that prominence is also a tribute to the powers of Dickens himself, a man who must be considered, despite formidable competition, as the great English-language narrative genius of nineteenth-century fiction.

A writer with a sure touch for the most vivid characters and the idiosyncratic language they invariably use, Dickens is especially celebrated for the crackerjack plots that kept readers desperate for the next installment of his serialized novels.

Dickens's books were so addictive, or so literary historians claim, that when ships bearing the latest installments of *The Old Curiosity Shop* arrived in New York in 1841, frantic fans concerned about the central character stormed the docks screaming, "Does Little Nell yet live?" Fans of *Twilight* or *The Hunger Games* should look to their laurels.

It was not only the skill of Dickens writing at the height of his powers (this was his thirteenth book) that made this film such a triumph but the way Lean transferred the story to the screen. (It was nominated for five Oscars, including best picture and director, and won two, for black-and-white cinematography and art direction/set design.) His *Great Expectations* is a vivid, full-bodied version of the 1861 novel, a film where the director's excitement at the chance to work with a story he could really tear into is unmistakable.

Determining how best to approach this material turned out to be a two-step process that began with Lean (who shares a screenwriting credit with Dickens and four other collaborators) taking the creative initiative after multiple readings of the book.

"I wrote down in a sort of headline from those scenes, or parts of scenes, which I thought would make a good movie," he says in *David Lean: A Life in Film*, Kevin Brownlow's magisterial biography. "And I left out anything I thought was dull."

Though this may sound like the recipe for a disjointed production, the second aspect of Lean's approach prevented that from happening. *Great Expectations* understood that the key to its success would be to completely embrace the eccentricity of its (of course) Dickensian characters.

Determined to do full justice to what makes Dickens Dickens, the film doesn't even consider softening or blanding out the book's numerous disorderly individuals or eliminating such extraneous but delightful characters as the elderly parent fondly known as the Aged P. As Lean himself put it, "What we did, we did proud. If we had a Dickens scene, we gave it full value."

This all-out approach also unexpectedly works with the story's protagonist, the earnest, good-hearted young man named

Pip, who over the course of the film learns the great lesson that emotion and relationships matter more in life than wealth, status, and position.

Casting for true innocence is always difficult, but *Expectations* does it right by selecting thirteen-year-old Anthony Wager for the film's initial sections. Wager's immersion in the role, as well as Lean's expressive filmmaking, enables us to get as fully into the story as Pip does, to feel that we are actually living it along with him.

Setting this in motion is how genuinely scary *Great Expectations* opening sequences play as Guy Green's brooding cinematography deposits us in vast windswept marshes where stark gibbets add to the feeling of the most fantastical danger.

Young orphan Pip is introduced fearfully rushing through this intimidating landscape, headed for the local churchyard to tend his mother's grave. He's about to leave when, in a moment that retains its power in the face of repeated viewings (Kevin Brownlow calls it "one of the most celebrated shocks in all of cinema"), he comes face-to-face with the terrifying Abel Magwitch, clanking chains and all.

Ferociously played by Finlay Currie, Magwitch is a fearsome escaped convict whose first words to Pip, "Keep still, you little devil, or I'll cut your throat," set the tone for their conversation. Desperately in need of food and a file to cut those chains, he does not spare the invective as he commands Pip to bring them to him or else face the consequences: "I'll have your heart and liver out . . . your liver will be tore out and roasted and ate." Lean spends considerable time on these moments because they are crucial in explaining who Pip is and who he becomes.

Living with his termagant of a sister and her kindhearted husband Joe Gargery (Bernard Miles), young Pip gets a shock of a quite different kind when he is called on to visit "a strange lady in an old house," Martita Hunt's one-of-a-kind Miss Havisham.

"Strange," as it turns out, is a mild word for this unnerving woman, who spends almost all of her time in a decrepit, cobwebby room where mice gnaw ostentatiously at what remains of the wedding cake she was admiring when word came to her decades earlier that the man she loved was jilting her at the altar.

Thirsting for revenge on the entire male sex ("Who am I, for heaven's sake," she insists, "that I should be kind"), Miss Havisham turned a broken heart into something sinister. She adopts a young ward named Estella (Jean Simmons, just 17) and raises her to wreak havoc against all men, starting with Pip, whom the young woman mercilessly teases as a coarse and common little monster.

This, in the way of all fiction, causes Pip to fall in love with Estella and yearn to be a gentleman she might fall in love with in return. At least part of this fantasy comes true when, at age twenty (and now played by John Mills), Pip is told by the "deep as Australia" attorney, the imposing Mr. Jaggers (Francis Sullivan in yet another of the film's magnificent Dickensian turns), that an anonymous wealthy benefactor has entered his life and wants him to know that "he has great expectations."

What this means in a practical sense is that Pip is removed from the tranquility of village life, much to the sadness of Joe Gargery (his "what larks, Pip" farewell is heartbreaking), and taken to London. There he shares rooms with Herbert Pocket (Guinness is geniality itself) and soon enough turns himself into one of London's indolent young men, curious about his benefactor and still pining after Estella. "Take nothing on its look, take everything on evidence," the wily Jaggers advises him, but this is advice Pip cannot take until it is almost too late.

Because Dickens himself was a poor boy who made good, some of the power of *Great Expectations* comes from the sense that Pip's lessons were the author's as well. Lean's film wonderfully conveys the book's portrait of what it is like to be who we thought we were before we knew any better. "All other swindlers on earth," Pip says in voice-over late in the film, "are nothing to the self-swindler," a bit of knowledge that, like all the insight in this rich film, was easier to say than to come by.

What to Watch Next:
Lawrence of Arabia (1962), directed by David Lean.

Further Reading:
David Lean: A Biography, by Kevin Brownlow.

BICYCLE THIEVES

1948

Directed by Vittorio De Sica. Starring Lamberto Maggiorani, Enzo Staiola.

If film means anything to you, you've at least heard of the Italian neorealist classic *Bicycle Thieves*, in its time, as the *Village Voice*'s J. Hoberman has written, "surely the most universally praised movie produced anywhere on planet earth."

But even if you watched it way back in the day, it's likely been decades since you've seen it. Directed by Vittorio De Sica and first released in the United States in 1949, *Bicycle Thieves* has become one of those venerable masterpieces, once number 1 on *Sight & Sound*'s critics poll of the best films ever made, that people pay lip service to but never revisit out of fear that it has somehow dated. And that would be a terrible mistake.

To see *Bicycle Thieves* again is to experience what feels like a miracle. Though it sank to thirty-third on the critics' portion of the 2012 *Sight & Sound* poll (the directors, a bit slower to forget, had it as number 10), this film has not lost a step since it won a special Academy Award and helped pave the way for the foreign language Oscar category. In some ways, frankly, it's even more involving now than it was then, an emotional juggernaut that has the kind of power contemporary films rarely match.

Told in brief summation, *Bicycle Thieves* (loosely based on a novel by Luigi Bartolini and written by Cesare Zavattini and several collaborators including Suso Cecchi d'Amico) has a narrative premise that sounds so slight it seems highly unlikely to be made into a film at all, let alone one that would captivate so many for so long.

After being unemployed for two years, Antonio Ricci (Lamberto Maggiorani) finally gets offered a job—putting up movie posters and the like on the walls of Rome—but only if he has a bicycle. Getting his hands on one is difficult, however, so much so that his wife Maria (Lianella Carell) has to pawn the family linen to come up with the money (a neodocumentary shot of a huge room overflowing with similarly pawned sheets underlines the extent of post-war Roman poverty).

But on Antonio's first day of work, ironically just after putting up a poster for the decidedly unrealistic, Rita Hayworth–starring *Gilda*, his bicycle is stolen. There is no dramatic music to heighten the moment. The theft just happens, and the small detail of Antonio taking a moment to touch up the poster before reporting the robbery is priceless.

In truth, he needn't have hurried because the police, indifferent to its devastating impact, are blasé about the theft. It is left to Antonio and his unforgettable young son Bruno (Enzo Staiola) to make their way through the city, scouring markets and alleys in an attempt to find the bicycle before it disappears forever. "If you only knew what this means to me," Antonio tells people, but no one cares, and Antonio's sense of impotence and despair increases until it culminates in a shocking conclusion.

One of the paradoxes of *Bicycle Thieves* is that the tiny bursts of momentary happiness it allows its characters, things like the husband giving his wife a ride on the bike's handlebars or the father and son having a pleasant restaurant meal they can't begin to afford, are unexpectedly difficult to bear because they contrast so vividly with the elements that cause despair.

That this slender tale ends up having the emotional resonance of classic tragedy may sound unlikely, but that is what happens. *Bicycle Thieves* places us right there, allows us to live what turns out to be a shattering experience with these people, lets us feel for them in a deep and profound way that is almost beyond describing.

Making all the difference in this were the tenets of neorealism, a movement that took hold, partly out of ideological conviction and partly out of the necessity of a postwar lack of resources, in Italy in the late 1940s and early 1950s. According to director Federico Fellini, who had early experience with the style, "neorealism is a way of seeing reality without prejudice, without conventions coming between it and myself—facing it without preconceptions, look at it in an honest way—whatever reality is, not just social reality but all that there is within a man."

Neorealist films—others include *Open City*, *Paisan*, and De Sica's own *Shoeshine* and *Umberto D*—were shot on real locations with available light, used nonprofessional actors, and often had socially conscious themes. This may sound like business as usual to young directors trying to get into Sundance, but at that time telling movie stories so far outside the conventions of Hollywood was nothing less than revolutionary.

"We were a little group of friends who just wanted to make films and went out into the streets to do so," screenwriter Cecchi d'Amico has modestly explained. "If we had as many newspapers and magazines back then as we do now, maybe many of us would have become journalists instead of making films. But there weren't many papers and making film was inexpensive and we merely wanted to tell our stories about our experiences of that era."

Shooting on the streets of Rome allowed *Bicycle Thieves* to showcase the vivid street life of this beautiful city and its gesticulating, engagingly verbal inhabitants, a chance to see Italians being intensely Italian at a time before a one-world culture brought people together and softened the edges of traditional differences.

But just because *Bicycle Thieves* cared about reality doesn't mean it was slipshod or improvised. De Sica, who began his career as an actor and eventually appeared in more than 150 films, felt strongly that what he did was "reality transposed into the realm of poetry." So this film is beautifully photographed by Carlo Monturi and features a subtle Alessandro Cicognini score. In De Sica it had a director who put every scene together for maximum effectiveness.

De Sica painstakingly choreographed crowds, even, says critic Robert S.C. Gordon, shooting the scene of the theft "in real time, without stopping the traffic, timing the theft to the traffic lights so that the thief could make his escape." The director had the Rome fire department hose down streets to make them look rain-soaked and even hired forty vendors for a scene where Antonio, his son, and his friends look for the stolen bike in an open-air market. (Future star Alberto Sordi can be heard dubbing one of the marketers.)

An equal amount of care went into selecting key cast members, especially the father-son team. Maggiorani, a factory worker who was selected when he brought his son to audition, has a handsome, almost noble visage that soon becomes a mask of worry and tragedy. And ten-year-old Staiola, whose parents owned a vegetable cart in Rome, has one of the most expressive childhood faces in the history of cinema. (There are stories, says Gordon in his BFI monograph, that the director tricked the boy into crying "by planting cigarette stubs in his pockets and accusing him of theft.")

De Sica's earlier neorealist film, *Shoeshine*, also had success, including a Special Academy Award that came with a citation that could have been written for *Bicycle Thieves*: "The high quality of this motion picture, brought to eloquent life in a country scarred by war, is proof to the world that the creative spirit can triumph over adversity."

As a result of this accomplishment, De Sica was able to pitch his new film to *Gone with the Wind* producer David O. Selznick, who apparently suggested Cary Grant for the lead with De Sica counter-suggesting Henry Fonda. It all came to naught. "I needed the spontaneity of untrained talent," De Sica said at the time of *Bicycle Thieves* release. "There is a freshness in their response to simple realities that was right and valuable to these pictures."

Seen from a contemporary perspective, it is the spareness and restraint of the film in general and the performances in particular that make *Bicycle Thieves* so powerful. That, and something else.

For this film has the gift of meaning more to us as we grow older and experience enough to find life's vicissitudes and tragedies becoming less theoretical and more actual. In addition, the passage of time has only intensified the resonance of something De Sica said sixty years ago: "We are so tired, we have lost any feeling of responsibility toward anyone but ourselves and, when we cut ourselves off from our brother, we prepare our own destruction." See *Bicycle Thieves* and delay that apocalypse, if only for a brief eighty-nine minutes.

What to Watch Next:
Shoeshine (1946), directed by Vittorio De Sica.

Further Reading:
Bicycle Thieves, by Robert S.C. Gordon.

THE THIRD MAN

1949

Directed by Carol Reed. Starring Joseph Cotten, Alida Valli, Orson Welles.

The Third Man dazzles with its structural complexities and mastery of tone. It was the rare film production of Graham Greene's work that the novelist was happy with, the only example of Orson Welles's art that the actor liked well enough to watch on television. A film of brilliant pieces that coalesce into a superb whole, it won the equivalent of the Palme d'Or at Cannes. What Greene biographer Neil Sinyard called its "definitive evocation of . . . decadence, demoralization, and dismay" still enthralls.

It's director Carol Reed (and not star Joseph Cotten, as in the original American release version) who reads the opening voice-over that sets the film's corrosive, casually amoral postwar tone. "I never knew the old Vienna before the war with its Strauss music, its glamour, and its easy charm. I really got to know it in the classic period of the black market. They could get anything if people wanted it enough."

When the camera pauses to reveal an unidentified corpse floating face down in the water, Reed delivers the coup de grace: "A situation like that does tempt amateurs. But they can't stay the course, not like professionals." Clearly not.

Just as much of a character as anyone played by an actor is Vienna itself in those lean and nasty days when the city was divided into sectors run by each of the four great powers: Britain, France, America, and the USSR. *The Third Man* makes excellent use of particular real-life locations, all specified by Greene: the venerable circa 1897 amusement park Great Wheel, the bleak Central Cemetery, or Zentralfriedhof, and a more than slightly seedy nightclub.

Even more evocative are the city's magnificent buildings, often glimpsed half crumbling or standing destitute next to enormous piles of rubble. The atmosphere Reed and company created is as thick as the local coffee, an ideal setting for a world without heroes where everyone is either a fool, a cynic, a criminal, or quite possibly, a combination of all three.

Robert Krasker's Oscar-winning black-and-white cinematography is essential in creating this ambiance. Its use of disconcerting camera angles to depict a nocturnal atmosphere of deep and dangerous shadows, a dark world in every sense of the word, was key to its being named in *American Cinematographer* magazine as one of the ten best-shot films of cinema's first half century.

The film's other sine qua non element is the brisk zither playing of Anton Karas. Though it's often said that director Reed stumbled on Karas playing in a small café outside Vienna and decided to employ him on the spot, Charles Drazin in his authoritative *In Search of the Third Man* says Reed heard him at a welcome party the day he arrived in Vienna.

The director's decision to use Karas for the score was unheard of, Drazin writes, "like Steven Spielberg telling John Williams not to bother turning up and hiring instead a man he'd met on the beach with a penny whistle." But it paid off. Karas's music became a worldwide sensation, selling, in producer David O. Selznick's words, "more record copies than any other record in the entire history of the record business in England," and leading to a US ad campaign that promised, no kidding, "He'll have you in a dither with his zither!"

Into the film's cesspool of casual amorality comes Holly Martins (Cotten), a bumbling, self-righteous, and therefore dangerous American (Greene didn't think there was any other kind) who has naive notions of justice and righteousness plus a great deal of misplaced confidence in his ability to get to the bottom of things. Greene, who believed "innocence is a kind of insanity," returned to this theme in *The Quiet American*, and in his and Reed's hands *The Third Man* is the story of a man's unsentimental education, of the hard road he travels in the getting of wisdom.

A self-proclaimed creator of "cheap novelettes" with titles like *The Lone Rider of Santa Fe* and *Death at Double X Ranch*, Martins, "happy as a lark and without a cent," has come to Vienna at the behest of his oldest friend and possible future employer, Harry Lime. (It's been suggested that Greene based Lime on his devious close friend and Soviet mole Kim Philby, whose middle name was Harry.)

Unfortunately, everyone tells Martins, he has come a bit too late. Lime has been killed, the victim of a random traffic accident, mourned by his girlfriend, Anna Schmidt (Alida Valli), and a pair of epicene Viennese named Baron Kurtz (Ernst Deutsch) and Dr. Winkel (Erich Ponto).

Met at Harry's funeral is the film's ultimate realist, the unemotional Major Calloway (a crisp Trevor Howard), a British military policeman who tells Martins that his lifelong comrade was a trafficker in deadly adulterated penicillin, "the worst racketeer who ever made a dirty living in this city."

Filled with alcohol-inspired righteous indignation and never considering that he might be getting into something considerably out of his depth, Martins is determined to prove the major wrong and find out what really killed Harry, starting with trying to discover who an unidentified third man seen at the site of the accident might be. "Death's at the bottom of everything, leave death to the professionals," the major says but Martins is in no mood to listen.

Director Reed does exceptionally well conveying the topsy-turvy nature of this world of smiling insincerity where a man typically speculates on Lime's afterlife state by saying, "He's either in heaven [pointing down] or in hell [pointing up]." Reed, whose other work includes *Odd Man Out*, *The Fallen Idol*, and *Outcast of the Islands*, was a masterful orchestrator of this kind of off-kilter ambiance, the hopelessness of a universe turned morally upside down.

Reed and Greene also combine to create vivid characters who are very much of their time and place, like the smirking Baron in his enormous fur-collared overcoat incongruously walking through a Viennese café holding a tiny dog and a copy of Martins's *Oklahoma Kid* or the small boy (Herbert Halbik) living in Lime's apartment building who starts to resemble a sinister, malignant dwarf.

The Third Man provides defining roles for all its lead actors, especially Joseph Cotten as the hapless, self-pitying fool who thinks he's a hero in the making, and for Orson Welles in a part that influential French critic Andre Bazin called a milestone in his career. Welles's first on-screen appearance is one of cinema's great reveals and puts the actor's polished nonchalance and world-class enigmatic smile to the best possible use.

Not that the American actor couldn't be fussy: Reed later recalled that Welles so rebelled against filming in underground Vienna ("Carol, I can't work in a sewer, I come from California") that his shots for those sequences were filmed in England's Shepperton Studios. Modern tourists, who've made Third Man tours of Vienna sewers quite popular, are considerably less finicky.

Though Welles wrote parts of his own dialogue, including the celebrated speech comparing the relative cultural merits of peaceful Switzerland and Italy under the bloody Borgias, the key directing choices were all Reed's.

That very much includes the film's somber closing shot and its nervy unwavering camera placement that *Sight & Sound* magazine called a candidate for the greatest film finale ever. This ending was shot even though Greene objected to it, a position the writer recanted once he saw the film. "He has been proved triumphantly right," Greene wrote of the filmmaker. "I had not given enough consideration to the mastery of Reed's direction." No one encountering this film, for the first time or the hundredth, will make that mistake again.

What to Watch Next:
Outcast of the Islands (1952), directed by Carol Reed.

Further Reading:
In Search of The Third Man, by Charles Drazin.

THE FIFTIES

N ever is heard an encouraging word about the Fifties. It's a decade periodically denounced as the epicenter of tedium and conformity, the decade of the country club and the cocktail hour. Yet it placed more films on my list—a full dozen—than any other. What gives?

It turns out that, at least to me, the Fifties were a decade where worlds collided in a most productive way. A resurgence of the optimistic classicism of the prewar years meshed with a kind of honest cynicism—the despairing realization that winning the war did not mark an end to everyone's problems.

As a result you got impeccably made films that were unblinkered and unafraid. Movies like *All About Eve, The Asphalt Jungle, Sunset Boulevard,* and *Vertigo* from the major studios, *Kiss Me Deadly, Seven Men from Now,* and *The Sweet Smell of Success* from smaller entities, all shared this approach.

At the same time, in France, two of the great romances of all time, *Casque d'Or* and *The Earrings of Madame de . . . ,* were produced. And countries like Japan, whose films had not previously gained much traction internationally, were making their presence felt with works like *Seven Samurai.* Reviled though it is, this is a decade that made a difference.

ALL ABOUT EVE

1950

Directed by Joseph L. Mankiewicz. Starring Bette Davis, Anne Baxter, Celeste Holm.

No film has had more Oscar nominations than the fourteen *All About Eve* earned in 1950. No film has equaled its mark of having four stars up for best actress awards, and no other writer/director has duplicated Joseph L. Mankiewicz's feat of taking Oscars in both categories two years running (for *Eve* and the earlier *A Letter to Three Wives.*)

It's ironic that 1950, the year that also saw Gloria Swanson's "We had faces" lament for silent cinema in *Sunset Boulevard,* now looks like a departed golden age of a different sort. They had words then, they had intoxicating language, they weren't afraid of the power of speech. And if Mankiewicz, whose biography is suitably titled *Pictures Will Talk,* was the exemplar of that style, *All About Eve* is his masterwork. If you try to note all the memorable lines, you'll end up with just about every word that's spoken.

A quintessentially adult drama with a fine understanding of the dynamics of personal relationships, a wisdom about what people say and do to each other, *All About Eve* allows us to have our cake and eat it, too. We get to enjoy the bite of Mankiewicz's witty, sophisticated, take-no-prisoners dialogue before coming to appreciate the deeper satisfactions of, for instance, a toast offered to celebrate friendship: "To each of us and all of us . . . never have we been more close—may we never be further apart."

All About Eve is based on a short story by Mary Orr, "The Wisdom of Eve," which appeared in *Cosmopolitan* magazine in May 1946 (itself apparently based on a real-life experience by actress Elisabeth Bergner). This movie is the ultimate backstage story, a look at a calling whose high standards require "a concentration of ambition, desire and sacrifice such as no other profession demands." It's also a delicious portrait of connivance and complicity that is a result of, in costar Celeste Holm's words, the way "Joe was in love with the concept of the theater as a wolverine's lair of skullduggery and bitchcraft."

The younger brother of Herman Mankiewicz, who shared screen credit for *Citizen Kane* with Orson Welles, Joseph L. Mankiewicz was especially adept at writing parts for actresses. If he wrote *All About Adam*, he once said, it would be done as a short film. Both Anne Baxter and Bette Davis were nominated for best actress, Holm and Thelma Ritter for best supporting; a fifth actress, Marilyn Monroe, used the film as a launching pad for a legendary career. Though the competition meant that none of the four won, the ensemble work they did is splendid.

As he did in *Letter to Three Wives*, Mankiewicz smartly employs a flashback structure to tell his tale. *All About Eve* opens at the annual awards banquet of the Sarah Siddons Society, at which this prestigious but fictional organization awards "the highest honor our theater knows" to a deserving actress. On this particular night, it goes to a grateful Eve Harrington (Anne Baxter).

It's the ascerbic, hypnotic voice of Addison De Witt who fills us in on the details of the award and the background of the theater people in the room. As played by George Sanders (winner of the film's only acting Oscar) in a quintessentially urbane performance, De Witt, who later claims he has "lived in the theatre as a Trappist monk lives in his faith," emphasizes here that "in it I toil not, neither do I spin. I am a critic and commentator."

It is Addison (likely named after the eighteenth-century English literary journalist Joseph Addison) who points out the film's dramatis personae, the most celebrated of whom is Margo Channing, the great theatrical diva of her day, played by Davis in perhaps her signature role. Temperamental, not to say tempestuous, even volcanic, Margo, with her big hair, bigger fur coat, and magnificently lived-in face is an unstoppable force, the Broadway star all the others envy.

Though Davis, newly free from her eighteen-year contract with Warner Bros. and thought to be on a career downswing, was a last-minute replacement for Claudette Colbert, who had hurt her back, she completely threw herself into the role of someone who Addison at one point describes as maudlin, full of self-pity . . . and magnificent. As Davis wrote in *The Lonely Life*, her autobiography, "The unholy mess of my own life—another divorce, my permanent need for love, my aloneness. Margo Channing was a woman I understood thoroughly."

The result, in a throaty voice that was partly the result of a vocal injury, is a performance fated to astonish and filled with spectacular lines, from familiar ones like "fasten your seat belts, it's going to be a bumpy night" to lesser-known classics like "I'm still not to be had for the price of a drink like a salted peanut."

Into Margo's realm, which includes playwright Lloyd Richards (Hugh Marlowe) and the diva's director/boyfriend Bill Sampson (Gary Merrill, who fell in love with Davis during filming and was her husband for ten years) comes a younger Eve Harrington, who appeared in a freeze frame receiving the Siddons award.

For weeks on end, six nights a week, always wearing the same worn trench coat and floppy hat, she stands in flashback outside the stage door of the Broadway theater where Margo is starring in Richards's *Aged in Wood*. Finally Karen Richards (Celeste Holm), the wife of the playwright and Margot's best friend, brings her in from the cold to meet the great woman, with results that play out like moves in an especially intricate chess game.

Soft-spoken, well-mannered, and deferential, Eve is more than the individual the film is named after (producer Darryl F. Zanuck chose the title from a line in the script); she is its pivotal person, the driver of all action. Seemingly floored by the company she has been thrust into, Eve has the presence of mind to bring forth an affecting tale of an early life marked equally by tragedy and love for the theater: "Acting and make-believe began to fill up my life more and more. It got so that I couldn't tell the real from the unreal except that the unreal seemed more real to me."

The only person immune to Eve's chronology is Birdie (marvelously played by Thelma Ritter), Margo's fiercely loyal factotum, a former vaudevillian who is part wisecracker, part suspicious detective. Her biting line after Eve's introductory monologue—"Everything but the bloodhounds snappin' at her rear end"—is the perfect counterpoint to what we've just heard, and it sets the tone for what is to come.

For no one divides this group of friends like the presence of Eve, whom people come to depend on or mistrust or sometimes depend on and mistrust. It's one of the keys to Mankiewicz's success that he made Eve into a convincingly contradictory character, someone who is both awe-struck and ambitious, conniving and uncertain, sincere in her goals and gifted in the way she can use people's needs and insecurities to further them. The one trait Eve does share with her new friends is a genuine passion for the theater that's so intense it's almost physical. As *All About Eve* proceeds to demonstrate, there isn't anything she won't do to satisfy a need for the applause she characterizes as "like waves of love coming over the footlights and wrapping you up." (The 1970 Tony-winning musical based on the film was in fact called *Applause*.)

That description would no doubt resonate with the young actress who plays the gorgeous but pliant Miss Caswell, the date

Addison De Witt brings to a party and waspishly introduces as "a graduate of the Copacabana School of Dramatic Arts."

Though she is eighth billed, a young Marilyn Monroe is a standout in that role, even in this heady ensemble, so much so that "an officially authorized stunning hand-painted porcelain collector doll" of the actress in her *All About Eve* party dress now sells for twice its original $195 Franklin Heirloom Dolls price. Cast largely because of the efforts of her mentor, powerful agent Johnny Hyde, Monroe impressed Mankiewicz, he later wrote, as having "a breathlessness and sort of glued-on innocence about her that I found appealing."

Mankiewicz was protective about his language to the point of having one of his characters mock actors who, "under a delusion of literacy, try to tamper with written words," so it's perhaps safest to give his script the final word here. What Addison De Witt says about Eve Harrington is equally true of the film she gives her name to: "There never was and never will be another like you."

What to Watch Next:
Stage Door (1937), directed by Gregory La Cava.

Further Reading:
Pictures Will Talk: The Life and Films of Joseph L. Mankiewicz, by Kenneth L. Geist.
All About "All About Eve," by Sam Stagg.

THE ASPHALT JUNGLE

1950

Directed by John Huston. Starring Sterling Hayden, Jean Hagen, Sam Jaffe.

No movie heist—and likely no real-life one either—has been pulled off with the level of skill and sophistication director John Huston and his team brought to *The Asphalt Jungle*. The same goes for duplicating the narrative line and performances that infused virtuosity onto what could have been a simple genre exercise.

Though it didn't win any of the four Oscars it was nominated for, *The Asphalt Jungle* has been highly influential, not just in terms of the caper films it directly inspired (like Jules Dassin's *Rififi* and Stanley Kubrick's *The Killing*) but also in terms of an entire approach to this kind of crime story filmmaking.

For while a justly celebrated eleven-minute depiction of the late night burglary of Belletier's, a high-end jewelry store, is *Asphalt Jungle*'s meticulous centerpiece, it's the character development that both precedes and follows the crime that set a standard it has been difficult to match.

Cowritten by Ben Maddow and Huston from a novel by W.R. Burnett (an author Huston felt was "one of the most neglected American writers"), this story was unusual at the time in its willingness to invest emotional capital in its criminal protagonists, and, more than that, to treat them with equal measures of empathy and dispassion. *The Asphalt Jungle* both cares deeply about its characters and pitilessly leaves them to their fates.

"The film is chiefly concerned with human relationships, and though melodramatic in form, it's not melodramatic in content," Huston said in a contemporary interview. "You may not admire these people, but I think they will fascinate you." As one of *Asphalt Jungle*'s characters says in a much-quoted line that sums up this inclusive point of view, "Crime is only a left-handed form of human endeavor."

Asphalt Jungle plays so of a piece it feels like it must have revealed itself in a single unified vision to director Huston, but it was the collaborative work of a cadre of individuals that made that success possible, including a subtle dramatic score by Miklos Rozsa and the brooding black-and-white Harold Rosson cinematography that from frame one conveys a mood of bleak urban despair.

The script Maddow and Huston worked on is critical in creating that ambiance. As usual in films focused on crime, *Asphalt Jungle*'s setting is a combustible one, where tempers flare, lies are a way of life, and there is more than enough betrayal and bad faith to go around.

But though the screenplay is laced with underworld slang to give it credibility, it's strongest in its insights into the swirls and eddies of human behavior. As much as anything else, this is a universe of busted dreams, where no one's life turned out as expected but everyone hopes, with increasing desperation, that it's not too late for good things to happen. "The way I figure it," says key player Dix Handley, "my luck just has to turn."

Maddow and Huston are especially good at turning criminal archetypes into memorable individuals by investing them with unblinking realism and originality. The actors, perhaps the premier ensemble in film noir history, are fortunate in having in Huston a director who knew exactly how much weight to give everything that appears on screen.

Each of *Asphalt Jungle*'s fifteen credited actors—from stars Sterling Hayden as Dix Handley and Sam Jaffe as Doc Riedenschneider through eleventh-billed Marilyn Monroe in an early success as the luscious Angela Phinlay—is given the kind of lines and situations that best showcase their abilities.

Advertised as a gritty look at "the city under the city," *Asphalt Jungle* begins with a rare moment of outdoor daylight as a squad car prowls the deserted early morning streets of a Midwestern city (it's an unnamed Cincinnati) as the police radio broadcasts news of a holdup at a local hotel.

Hiding from that car is a tall, haggard man, Dix Handley, whom we instinctively suspect is the perpetrator of the crime. Suspicions are confirmed when Dix slips into a rundown diner and passes his handgun to compatriot Gus Minissi (James Whitmore) just before the police burst in the door.

Hanlon is a small-time criminal or hooligan with a long record and a weakness for playing the horses, a man who radiates such deep and unnerving fury that an eyewitness is too intimidated to pick him out of a police lineup.

Though Cobby, the local criminal middleman (Marc Lawrence, on the nose with his pencil-thin mustache and bow tie), has no respect for Dix, he is underestimating him. Played to the hilt by Hayden (very much the iconoclastic loner in his personal life), Dix is both a southerner who mourns for his family's lost Kentucky horse farm and a man with the inviolable sense of honor of a medieval knight. Always raging about self-respect and throwing himself into lines like "why don't you quit crying and get me a bourbon," Dix towers over *Asphalt Jungle* like a vengeful ghost.

Ironically, the only man who completely understands and values Dix turns out to be someone at the other end of the criminal hierarchy, the legendary mastermind and underworld aristocrat Doc Riedenschneider, a quiet, innocuous Yoda of crime in a homburg and top-coat known among local police as "one of the most dangerous criminals alive."

Played by Sam Jaffe with a slight German accent and a shrewd politeness of manner, Doc is fresh from seven years behind bars, and he has returned with a plan for that robbery at Belletier's, "the biggest caper ever pulled in the Middle West." But to set it up he needs big money, so he uses Cobby to get in touch with Alonzo "Lon" Emmerich (the veteran Louis Calhern), the city's top criminal defense lawyer who dabbles in crime himself when the right opportunity presents itself.

Given its subject matter, it's to be expected that *Asphalt Jungle* is set in an intensely masculine milieu, especially in the taut planning sessions when Doc, Emmerich, and Cobby decide on the personnel they need for the robbery—a boxman or safecracker, a driver, and a hooligan. These associates, Doc says with a chuckle, "will be paid off like house painters. They will be told nothing about the size of the take. Sometimes men get greedy."

Yet despite this emphasis, one of the characteristics of *Asphalt Jungle* is that while the four women in it have smaller roles, each of them—not just the breathless twenty-three-year-old Monroe in her first significant role as Emmerich's mistress—is a striking presence.

Third-billed Jean Hagen, perhaps best known as the talkative Lena Lamont in *Singin' in the Rain*, is quite moving as Doll Conovan, a nervous, twitchy chorus girl type who is hopelessly sweet on Dix. Even the smallest women's roles, like Dorothy Tree as Emmerich's invalid wife and Teresa Celli as the safecracker's spouse Maria, stay with us. Though her time is brief, Maria has one of the film's many unforgettable lines, noting that approaching police sirens "sound like a soul in hell."

This kind of unexpected poetry is one of *Asphalt Jungle*'s trademarks, as it is its theme, as enunciated by Doc, that "one way or another, we all work for our vice." With Dix, it's the horses; with Emmerich, his mistress Angela; with Doc, in a plot line that plays out beautifully throughout the film, it is young women. No matter how painstaking criminal planning is, human weaknesses trump it time after time.

Though we take it for granted, given what comes afterward, *Asphalt Jungle*'s empathy with and even sympathy for its career criminals was something of a departure in 1950, when the moralistic Production Code still held sway.

It's not that the representatives of law and order don't speak loud and clear, especially John McIntire's stern and unbending police commissioner. The law may be upright, but it is also pitiless, and *The Asphalt Jungle* subversively posits that more humanity can be found among those who break the law than those sworn to uphold it.

What to Watch Next:

Rififi (1955), directed by Jules Dassin.

Further Reading:

An Open Book, by John Huston.
Wanderer, by Sterling Hayden.

SUNSET BOULEVARD

1950

Directed by Billy Wilder. Starring William Holden, Gloria Swanson, Erich von Stroheim.

Sunset Boulevard literally starts in the gutter: a close-up of that fabled street name stenciled on the curb is followed by the film's opening credits unrolling on the dirty pavement itself. It was a location some people in Hollywood felt this scathing Billy Wilder film never left. According to costar Nancy Olsen, MGM boss Louis B. Mayer "became absolutely incensed and went up to Billy and said, 'How could you do this to your own industry, to our people?'" A very good question.

It can be truthfully said that of all the inside Hollywood films, a genre I favor, *Sunset Boulevard* may be the bleakest, the most savage. It is as cynical and corrosive as my other favorite, *Bombshell* (a film that gets points for mocking people still in their prime), but it is much less comic and considerably darker in tone. It about the death of a dream, and a dreamer, and it's even narrated by a corpse.

The dreamer is Joe Gillis, persuasively played by William Holden, who sets the world-weary tone in the dead-on voice-over that opens the film, reporting that, as we watch the LAPD scramble on the Sunset Boulevard scene, "a murder has been reported from one of those great big houses in the ten thousand block . . . But before you hear it all distorted and blown out of proportion, before those Hollywood columnists get their hands on it, maybe you'd like to hear the facts, the whole truth."

That opening narration wouldn't be out of place in a standard 1940s film noir procedural, but then the camera shows us something we don't expect: in a shocking moment (filmed with the help of a mirror placed at the bottom of a studio tank), we're looking up at a corpse floating in a swimming pool and realize it is the narrator. "Just a movie writer with a couple of B pictures to his credit," Gillis says about his late self, before adding the coup de grace: "The poor dope. He always wanted a pool."

But what is lasting about *Sunset Boulevard* is not Gillis and his predicament (shown in flashbacks that start six months earlier), not even the darkness of its tone, but rather something more human: the story of the woman who owns that house on Sunset Boulevard, Gloria Swanson's Norma Desmond, the great legend of the silent screen living in delusional splendor years after her prime.

This is not just because Desmond has the film's best lines, even though she does, killer classics like "I am big, it's the pictures that got small" and "we didn't need dialogue. We had faces." It's because it is the gift of *Sunset Boulevard* to turn this strange, desperate, divorced-from-reality sacred monster into an individual we feel for, care about, and remember more than anyone else on screen.

As Charles Brackett, who wrote the Oscar-winning screenplay with Wilder and D.M. Marshman Jr., noted of the writing process, "At first we saw her as a kind of horror woman . . . But as we went along, our sympathies became deeply involved with the woman who had been given the brush by 30 million fans."

Though the casting of Swanson and Holden proved to be ideal, they were not early choices, with Wilder even claiming that he'd pursued Mae West first. As for Joe Gillis, Montgomery Clift had agreed to take the part before backing out because, after *The Heiress*, he feared being typecast as a romancer of older women.

(It is worth noting that though much is made of Norma Desmond's great age, Swanson herself was only fifty-two at the time of the shooting and in fact had resisted being artificially aged. According to Ed Sikov's thorough Wilder biography, *On Sunset Boulevard*, the actress had suggested, "Can't you put the makeup on Mr. Holden instead, to make him look older?" The film eventually did both.)

Once Swanson and, of equal importance, Erich von Stroheim as Norma Desmond's bullheaded, imperturbable butler and factotum Max von Mayerling, were cast, one of *Sunset Boulevard*'s most potent dynamics kicked into gear. By giving two key parts to actors who'd actually lived their roles to a great degree, the film encouraged the real and the imagined stories to echo and feed off each other in a powerful and provocative way.

For Swanson did not just play a retired silent film star of enormous magnitude; she had been one herself. And though she'd done only one film since 1934, her status had been so great back in the day she'd made international headlines by being the first movie star to marry European nobility in the person of Henri, Marquise de la Falaise de la Coudraye.

And von Stroheim not only played someone who turned out to be Norma Desmond's former director, he had in fact directed a younger Swanson in *Queen Kelly* (1929), a clip of which Norma shows Joe Gillis with Max running the projector. The parallels are dizzying, especially when you add in the fact that Joseph P. Kennedy, the future president's father, Swanson's lover, and the producer of *Queen Kelly*, demanded and received $1,000 for use of that clip in *Sunset Boulevard*.

Because it wanted its notions of the soul-destroying nature of the movie business to be taken seriously, *Sunset Boulevard* is careful to get as many small details correct as possible, including the enormous car in Norma Desmond's garage. It's an ultra luxurious Isotta Fraschini, which cost $28,000 back when that was real money, and had been favored by Clara Bow and Rudolph Valentino as well as a dubious character in Raymond Chandler's *Farewell, My Lovely*.

When Norma plays bridge with a group of old movie pals Joe calls "the waxworks," they're played by real-life former silent luminaries H.B. Warner, Anna Q. Nilsson, and Buster Keaton. Cecil B. DeMille also plays himself, riding boots and all (his fee was $10,000 for a day's work), the classic Paramount studio gate plays itself, and when Joe has a conversation with a Paramount executive, names of real actors Alan Ladd, William Demarest, and Tyrone Power figure in the conversation.

But because mood and ambiance were as important as reality to Wilder, when it came to Norma Desmond's house, in Gillis's words, "a great big white elephant of a place, the kind crazy movie people built in the crazy Twenties," nothing is the way it seems on screen.

The driveway Gillis turned into was supposedly at 10086 Sunset Boulevard in West Los Angeles, but the house itself, then owned by J. Paul Getty's ex-wife and torn down in 1957 after use in *Rebel Without a Cause*, was on the other side of town, on Wilshire Boulevard in Hancock Park. It lacked the requisite swimming pool, so the studio had to build one. And though there is no house numbered 10086 on Sunset Boulevard, if you stood today where Norma Desmond's mansion would have been, you would be standing, in a chilly twist of fate, directly across the street from the house where singer Michael Jackson died.

After the shock of Gillis floating in the pool, *Sunset Boulevard* flashes back to another real location, the still-standing Alto Nido Apartments in Hollywood where we see Gillis pounding out unsold scripts in his bathrobe and fencing with repo men who show up looking for his Plymouth convertible, which he's craftily hidden in a nearby lot.

Gillis next finagles a meeting with an executive at Paramount where he encounters studio reader Betty Schaefer (Nancy Olsen) who, not noticing that he's in the room, rips his "Bases Loaded" baseball spec script as "flat and banal."

Things get even worse for the beleaguered writer a few days later when those same repo men spot him in his car on Sunset Boulevard and give chase. A flat tire causes Gillis to pull into the nearest driveway, but instead of the refuge he initially hopes it will be, Norma Desmond's house turns out to be a rabbit hole leading to what might as well be another dimension. When Gillis references Dickens's lost in time Miss Havisham in his initial description of the place, he is closer to the truth than he realizes.

For the past is where Norma Desmond lives, where she is most comfortable. Surrounded by old photographs of herself, freed from pedestrian money worries ("I'm richer than all this new Hollywood trash," she proclaims, "I have oil in Bakersfield—pumping, pumping, pumping"), she favors leopard skin accents, cigarettes in strange holders, and bangles on her wrists. And she certainly knows what to do with her hands. Norma Desmond's dramatic gestures, simultaneously flamboyant and imperious, characterize her as much as the fantastical way she speaks.

For a Hollywood hustler like Gillis, the silent era is as far removed from contemporary moviemaking as the Civil War, but even he recognizes Norma. When he in effect seals his doom by saying so, she launches into the first of the series of tirades that turn her character into a much-quoted legend.

"There was a time," she begins in arch fury, "when this business had the eyes of the whole wide world. But that wasn't good enough. Oh no! They wanted the ears of the world, too. So they opened their big mouths, and out came talk, talk, talk. . . . You've made a rope of words and strangled this business!"

Norma goes on and on, and while it is tempting to quote even more, especially her anger at being accused of contemplating a comeback ("I hate that word. It's a return."), the triumph of this performance is not so much in its anger but in how sympathetically Swanson plays the character's covert desperation, how much the painful poignancy of her position makes her someone whose presence we crave when she's not on the screen. As DeMille accurately says to an underling late in the film, "A dozen press agents working overtime can do terrible things to the human spirit."

When Norma hires Gillis to work on her script—a version of *Salome* of all things—while staying in the apartment over her garage, he admits to feeling "quite pleased with the way I'd handled the situation." His car would be safe, and he'd be well-paid for being a script doctor. He assumes it's Norma who's snapped at the hook, but in reality he's the one who took the bait.

Though Gillis thinks of himself as cynical ("I talked to a couple of yes men at Metro," he reports. "To me they said no."), like all dreamers he is naive, someone with little or no idea how rigged the system is, how much the deck is stacked against him, how doomed he really is.

If *Sunset Boulevard*'s story refuses to allow us even the illusion of a happy ending, the film itself had a similar fate at Oscar time. Though nominated for eleven Academy awards and winner of three, it was overshadowed by *All About Eve*, nominated for fourteen and winner of six, including best picture and best director. But the film's allure, its ability, among other things, to capture something quintessential about the mysteries of Los Angeles, endures.

As British actor Hugh Laurie, the star of TV's *House*, wrote about his time in the city, "Even now, I challenge you to drive west on Sunset Boulevard, peer in through those mysterious shaded driveways, dripping with jasmine and bougainvillea, and tell me that Norma Desmond doesn't—couldn't—live there." I've made that drive many times, and it's the truth.

What to Watch Next:

The Barefoot Contessa (1954), directed by Joseph L. Mankiewicz.

Further Reading:

Conversations with Wilder, by Cameron Crowe.

On Sunset Boulevard: The Life and Times of Billy Wilder, by Ed Sikov.

CASQUE D'OR

1952

Directed by Jacques Becker. Starring Simone Signoret,
Serge Reggiani.

I've seen *Casque d'Or*, French director Jacques Becker's masterful interweaving of love, violence, and fate in turn-of-the-century Paris, more times than I can remember. But not until my last viewing did I discover that Simone Signoret, who gives the performance of a lifetime as the golden-haired beauty of the title, was this close to not being in the film at all.

Speaking in a 1963 French television interview included in the Criterion Collection's DVD release of the film, Signoret candidly spoke of being in the city of Nimes and having a passionate romantic interlude with future husband Yves Montand (who was there making *Wages of Fear*) when the time came for her to board a train for Paris for the first day of *Casque* shooting.

"I went to the station but I didn't get on the train, I went back to the hotel," Signoret recounts. "The next day I got a call from Jacques Becker who said to me, 'You're absolutely right. You're in love and you should embrace that. I respect your choice, you did well.' Then he mentioned two or three other actresses he would be contacting to take my role. I got on the train the next day."

Signoret's role as Marie is not only her personal favorite ("like being in a state of grace") in a long career that included an Oscar for *Room at the Top* and a nomination for *Ship of Fools*, it is the essence of a film so beloved in France they even put it on a postage stamp.

Yet one of the remarkable things about *Casque d'Or* is that it's so strong in so many areas that Signoret's vivid performance as the woman men can't take their eyes off doesn't overwhelm the film. It's simply one of several elements in a balanced whole that wraps you up in its mood, in its ability to present a past world that lives and breathes despite vintage costumes and horse drawn carriages. Becker doesn't so much recreate Paris of La Belle Epoque but, as critic Gavin Lambert wrote on the film's 1952 release in Great Britain, "takes us at once inside the story . . . making the past as continuously alive as the present."

That cross-channel praise was key to the ultimate success of *Casque d'Or* because when it debuted in Paris, the reception was cool at best ("the film was a total flop" was costar Serge Reggiani's pungent recollection), a situation which apparently did not trouble the director.

A traditionalist who friends said never worried about being fashionable, Becker was one of the few from the older generation who impressed the young firebrands of the French New Wave. As Jean-Luc Godard wrote, "Before us, the only person who tried to see France was Jacques Becker."

Becker, who died in 1960 when he was only fifty-four, was a master craftsman who regularly baffled theoreticians. Godard's colleague François Truffaut did not understand why Becker's "simple, vivid, true to life stories" were not more commercial. "There are," he wrote, "no theories about Jacques Becker." Critic Phillip Kemp, writing more recently in *Film Comment*, admitted that while he felt Becker's films had a distinctive quality, "just what that quality consists of isn't easy to pin down."

Perhaps coming closest to defining the director's gift was Marguerite Renoir, who edited Becker's key films, including *Casque d'Or.* The filmmaker, she said, believed in "the continuity of emotions." He was someone who would use ten takes for a scene that could have been done in one, in part because of his complicated approach to editing, using up to a thousand splices per film in a way that was intended to increase complexity without being showy.

Marguerite Renoir had also edited many of Jean Renoir's greatest films (she was his longtime companion and took his name though they never married), and Becker's connection with that director may also have led people to undervalue his work. Becker's family and the Cezannes were friends, and that led to his meeting with the son of painter Pierre-Auguste Renoir. Becker worked as the older man's assistant for seven years in the 1930s (Renoir called him "my brother and my son") and he had cameos in some of Renoir's films, most memorably as an English prisoner of war who destroys a watch rather than turn it over to the Germans in *La Grand Illusion.*

For Renoir fans, *Casque d'Or,* apparently inspired by a true story of the period, opens in a way that inevitably recalls the master's forty-minute short *Partie de Campagne* (A Day in the Country), which both Becker and Marguerite Renoir worked on.

It is a quiet Sunday afternoon on the outskirts of Paris. A cross-section of the city's demimonde, young toughs known as Apaches and their wised-up soiled dove girlfriends, are introduced rowing out to a riverside *boîte* where dancing to a live band is the attraction and the chance to *épate les bourgeois,* shock the middle classes, is part of the fun for the visitors.

The power couple in the group is the irritable, insolent Pretty Boy Roland, the nominal leader of the pack, and his discontented mistress Marie (Signoret), whose piles of blond hair form the "golden helmet" of the film's title. Radiant with frank sensuality and famous for her temper—and for being the best dancer in the rough Belleville neighborhood of Paris—Marie is completely aware of her allure and won't be pushed around by anyone, especially not by Roland.

Before the music can begin, however, the bandstand must be repaired, and on the work crew is Manda, immediately identifiable as a carpenter by his wide sash. This costume, however, doesn't fool one of the gang, who recognizes the dark, intense Manda as Jo, his closest friend during five years spent behind bars who is now attempting to go straight.

Even this early on, Reggiani's character conveys a compelling sense of quiet masculine assurance. He is without doubt a stand-up guy with an unspoken code of conduct, someone who can be pushed only so far without provoking the kind of retaliation it would be best to avoid.

Marie and Manda exchange glances as she dances with Roland—how could they not—and in that *coup de foudre* moment they fall inescapably in love and seal their fates. Manda asks her to dance and she agrees, much to Roland's disgust, and the complex, yearning looks they exchange in that dancehall pierce the heart. (In real life, Signoret had recently broken her fibula and did her dancing with her leg in a cast hidden by her long skirt.)

Not the shy type, Marie tracks Manda to the Paris carpenter shop where he works and pulls him into an embrace. But the sour, severe daughter of Manda's boss comes out of the shop, frankly calls Marie a whore, and reveals that she and Manda are engaged. Feeling scorned and humiliated, Marie slaps Manda and leaves in a cold fury which leads to the kind of complications that put the fatal into fatalistic romances.

One of those difficulties is the oleaginous Felix Leca (Claude Dauphin, far removed from his usual doctors and diplomats), who masquerades as a respectable wine merchant while in fact heading up Roland's gang of thieves. Conniving, malevolent, fussy about keeping his mustache just so, Leca wants to acquire Marie for himself and schemes to use the rivalry between Roland and Manda over her to his advantage.

As these plot dynamics work themselves out, larger themes also come into play. Intense feelings are complicated not only by misfortune, miscalculation, and misunderstanding, but also through the dynamics of crime, jealousy, personal honor, and the implacable code of the underworld.

Finally, though, we have that unforgettable romance, and a closing dance floor scene that is every bit a match for what has come before, an elegiac reverie that's as tender, implacable, and heartbreaking as anything French cinema has to offer. The only thing that survives unscathed through the conflagration these two lives touch off is their love, and its purity and intensity are incendiary.

What to Watch Next:

Touchez Pas au Grisbi (1954), directed by Jacques Becker.

THE IMPORTANCE OF BEING EARNEST

1952 ·

Directed by Anthony Asquith. Starring Michael Redgrave,
Edith Evans, Joan Greenwood.

Engagingly subtitled *A Trivial Play for Serious People*, Oscar Wilde's 1895 tour de force is the most enduring of the writer's works. Transforming it into one of the wittiest of British films involved not the usual stratagem of opening the play up but rather emphasizing its theatricality. It's a paradox the author himself would have relished.

A wild farce about identity, impersonation, and love, *Earnest* is chockablock with the kind of brilliant banter and immaculate bon mots that were Wilde's specialty, including classic epigrams like "the good end happily and the bad unhappily, that is what fiction means." Or this piece of touring advice: "I never travel without my diary. One should always have something sensational to read on the train."

Trusting in the play's legendary strengths and understanding that any attempt to unduly widen its horizons would be ruinous was director Anthony Asquith. (In an odd twist his father, the politician and Prime Minister H.H. Asquith, had a hand in the arrest for homosexuality that would savage Wilde's career.)

The younger Asquith, as it turns out, had a penchant for turning dramas into film. His excellent 1938 *Pygmalion*, from the George Bernard Shaw play, makes a fascinating companion piece to *My Fair Lady*, and his versions of a pair of Terence Rattigan plays, *The Winslow Boy* and *The Browning Version*, are also well thought of.

But what makes *Earnest* effective is the way it points up its dramatic play within a film roots instead of fleeing from them. The first image we see is of a fashionable couple in an elegant box in the theater. The lady leans forward, moves her opera glasses into position, and we watch as a curtain goes up on a card that reads, "Act I, Scene 1. Ernest's Room in the Albany." Even the film's supportive *Variety* review noted that it was "not setting new standards in filmcraft."

But despite this theater-forward structure, it soon becomes apparent that *Earnest* is going to marshal considerable cinematic resources to create a version of the play that is more vibrant and more memorable than one you could see from a theater seat, even that lovely box. This is going to be a moviegoing experience after all, albeit a very particular one.

Initially most noticeable (in part because *Earnest* was the rare British film to be shot in three-strip Technicolor) is the unparalleled vividness of the film's costumes. Decked out by Beatrice Dawson (whose later work included the Joseph Losey films *The Servant* and *Accident*), *Earnest*'s key characters are very much dressed to kill, in wild tweeds, paisleys, and pastels—including hats to match—all executed in a flamboyant color scheme that can best be described as late Victorian psychedelic.

Wearing those clothes was a superlative collection of British acting talent, led by Michael Redgrave (paterfamilias of the celebrated family) as put-upon protagonist Ernest Worthing and Joan Greenwood (*Kind Hearts and Coronets, The Man in the White Suit*) as Gwendolyn Fairfax, the bewitching woman he is desperate to marry.

Each of the ten actors who have speaking parts of any size in *Earnest* is exactly cast, each primed to take advantage of their lines even if they have only a few. Key to this are effective use of cinema's great weapons, the close-up (which allows for full appreciation of raised eyebrows and facial gestures) and editing that ensures we're always looking exactly where we should be.

Even in this group of actors, however, a pair of veterans stand out: Margaret Rutherford (*The Lady Vanishes*) as the mysterious Miss Prism, tutor to Cecily Cardew, Ernest Worthing's innocent young ward, and, very much first among equals, Dame Edith Evans as Lady Bracknell. Evans had so triumphed with this role on stage that director Asquith said in the original press notes that it would have been "treasonable" to even consider casting anyone else.

Lady Bracknell, much to Ernest's distress, is Gwendolyn's implacable, gimlet-eyed mother, of whom the exasperated suitor says, "She's an absolute Gorgon, a monster without being a myth, which is rather unfair."

In typical social dragon fashion, when Ernest admits he knows nothing, Lady Bracknell is much pleased. "I do not approve of anything that tampers with natural ignorance," she proclaims. "Ignorance is like a delicate exotic fruit; touch it and the bloom is gone. The whole theory of modern education is radically unsound. Fortunately in England, at any rate, education produces no effect whatsoever."

Conveying stylish dialogue this potent and pungent in a natural manner requires skilled actors completely at ease with its clockwork precision. More than that, the actors are called on to make the story's preposterous goings-on, its genially savage satire on the Kabuki-like rituals of British high society, seem like the most ordinary situations in the world.

Earnest certainly starts out ordinarily enough, with a chat between Ernest and his best friend Algernon Moncrieff (Michael Denison), who also happens to be Lady Bracknell's nephew.

A little snooping on Algernon's part soon reveals that his friend has two identities: he is Ernest is town but his real name, so to speak, the name under which he sets the proper high moral tone for ward Cecily while he is in the country, is Jack.

What seems like an innocent bit of playacting turns serious when Gwendolyn tells Jack with utter sincerity, "We live in an age of ideals and my ideal has always been to love someone with the name of Ernest. There is something in that name that inspires absolute confidence."

Telling Lady Bracknell soon after that he has lost both his parents creates further distress for the young man when she thunders, "To lose one parent, Mr. Worthing, may be regarded as misfortune. To lose both looks like carelessness."

Taking advantage of all the chaos, Algernon sneaks down to the country and presents himself to Cecily as the Ernest Worthing she has never met. The young lady promptly falls in love with him but, like Gwendolyn, absolutely refuses to marry a man who is not an Ernest in earnest. What to do, what to do?

Though Wilde's play has been presented countless times all over the world and tried more than once on film, this continues to stand as the definitive production. Its theatrical roots are undeniable, but that never stands in the way of the tremendous cinematic fun it provides.

What to Watch Next:
Pygmalion (1938), directed by Anthony Asquith, Leslie Howard.

Further Reading:
The Importance of Being Earnest, by Oscar Wilde.

SINGIN' IN THE RAIN

1952

Directed by Stanley Donen, Gene Kelly. Starring Gene Kelly,
Donald O'Connor, Debbie Reynolds.

On the night of September 11, 2001, scant hours after the bleakest
day in recent American history, Frank Pierson, Oscar-winning
screenwriter of *Dog Day Afternoon* and president of the Academy
of Motion Picture Arts and Sciences, was looking for a film to
watch with his wife to take his mind off catastrophe.

The choice, as Pierson revealed to an Academy audience a
few years later, was a snap: *Singin' in the Rain*. A film guaranteed
to lift your spirits even if you're facing what looks to be the end
of the world.

Codirected by Gene Kelly and Stanley Donen and starring the sun-kissed trio of Kelly, Debbie Reynolds, and Donald
O'Connor, *Singin' in the Rain* has always had that tonic effect on
people. With the exuberance and joy of performance as one of its
themes, it has proved to be the most durable example of the Hollywood musical, the real tinsel underneath all the fake stuff.

Yet though actors' good spirits have never looked so effortless or felt so genuine, the production of *Singin' in the Rain* had
its unexpected and even arduous aspects, which may be why its

preeminent status continues to surprise the people who made it. "No one had the slightest idea," costar Reynolds has said, "that this would ever be listed as one of the greatest films ever made."

And so listed it has been. *Sight & Sound* magazine's prestigious international critic's poll had it tied for third with *Seven Samurai* in 1982, with just *Citizen Kane* and *The Rules of the Game* ahead of it. Despite the changing tastes thirty years brings, it is still the seventh highest ranking American film in the current 2012 poll, an impressive number 20 overall.

(By contrast, the prestige musical of its day, *An American in Paris*, which was nominated for eight Oscars and won six, including best picture—*Singin'* could only manage two nominations and zero wins—has not aged nearly as well: it placed an unhappy 588th in the 2012 poll.)

On paper, *Singin' in the Rain*'s accomplishments are surprising even today because this film did not begin with a story anyone was burning to tell. Quite the opposite: it was a film unapologetically written to order for strictly commercial reasons. But once the top professionals of the Freed Unit got behind the scenario, there was no stopping it.

That Freed team, headed by producer Arthur Freed, was the production group behind all the classic MGM musicals. Its roots at the studio dated back to the beginnings of the sound era, when Irving Thalberg hired then-lyricist Freed and his composer partner Nacio Herb Brown to work on the studio's hugely successful first musical, *The Broadway Melody*, which was also the first sound film to win the best picture Oscar.

Freed wanted to produce, and after his success with Judy Garland (whom he had a hand in signing) in *The Wizard of Oz* he pretty much wrote his own ticket. Studio head Louis B. Mayer "thought Arthur Freed was a god," codirector Donen observed, "and in fact he was a god."

In 1950 Freed called to Hollywood the superb New York–based screenwriting team of Betty Comden and Adolph Green, who'd previously done *On the Town*. He wanted them to write what was known as a catalog musical, a show that would include as many as possible of the songs he'd cowritten with Nacio Herb Brown the way *Easter Parade* had used Irving Berlin's works and *An American in Paris* George Gershwin's.

The duo was given no more to start with than *Singin' in the Rain* as the film's title, and the final credits in fact read "Suggested by the Song." The venerable tune, written for a 1927 stage show and debuting on film in *Hollywood Review of 1929*, has remained widely popular. According to Earl J. Hess and Pratibha A. Dabholkar in their authoritative *Singin' in the Rain: The Making of An American Masterpiece*, when monsoons soaked India in 2007, the *Times of India* listed it as "number one among its choice of five best 'rain songs.'"

"There's nothing more difficult," Green later said of the kind of creative challenge a catalog film represented. "It's like higher mathematics." It was Comden and Green, inspired by the era many of the songs were written in, who came up with the key idea of setting *Singin' in the Rain* in that turbulent period in Hollywood history when silent films gave way to sound.

That setting not only worked for the songs, it enabled *Singin'* to have a pair of focuses that expertly complemented each other. The film's comic examination of the movie business in turmoil is completely wised up, poking smart fun at the tropes of silent movie history, while the story's inevitable sentimental romance is treated with the utmost seriousness and respect.

This combination of cynicism and innocence proved difficult to resist, especially with the casting MGM came up with. While Gene Kelly, the studio's musical actor of the moment, was a given if he was available and interested (he was), the other two choices were a bit outside the box.

For Kelly's inevitable sidekick, the studio, never shy about repeating itself, wanted sardonic pianist Oscar Levant, who'd had that role in *American in Paris*. But codirectors Kelly and Donen were insistent on a dancer, and the acrobatic Donald O'Connor, who grew up in a circus family that had segued to vaudeville, got the part.

Though Kelly's concluding balletic "Broadway Melody/ Broadway Rhythm" number with Cyd Charisse is more often written about, the synchronized tap dancing he does with O'Connor, so joyous it seems like they're making it up on the spot, is the film's energy source. The old-fashioned tapping also highlights *Singin' in the Rain*'s embrace of tradition, one of the main reasons it remains so popular.

When it came to giving O'Connor a number of his own, the filmmakers asked Freed and Brown to write a new song, something in the vein of Cole Porter's "Be a Clown." What resulted, "Make 'Em Laugh," was so close to the original that Donen called it "100 percent plagiarism," but the number expertly suited O'Connor's show-stopping talents and was so close to berserk in its inventiveness that the actor himself later worried that "by the end I might have to commit suicide on screen."

By choosing eighteen-year-old Reynolds for the romantic lead, MGM went for someone who didn't have to act the fresh-faced young ingénue; she was one. Though Reynolds had a background in gymnastics, the actress had never seriously danced until this movie. She pushed herself for eight hours a day for two months—"the university of hard work and pain," Kelly called it— and got good enough, after fourteen hours of rehearsal that led to bleeding feet, to finally dance seamlessly over a sofa with her two costars in the first number she shot, "Good Morning."

Singin' in the Rain opens with the silent era at its height. It is 1927 and Monumental Pictures is premiering Don Lockwood and Lena Lamont in "The Royal Rascal" at Grauman's Chinese Theater in Hollywood. A radio gossip columnist corners Lockwood (Kelly, resplendent in white topcoat and matching hat) and asks him to tell the fans the story of his life.

Though Lockwood talks of a privileged background and a lifelong motto of "dignity, always dignity," the visuals we see tell a different, more harum-scarum story. Lockwood and boyhood pal Cosmo Brown (O'Connor) start out dancing in pool halls and bars and segue to collaborating on "Fit as a Fiddle" in vaudeville towns with delicious names like Dead Man's Fang, Arizona, and Coyoteville, New Mexico, before using stunt work as a way into the movies.

One of Comden and Green's great notions was having Don's elegant-looking perennial costar Lena Lamont talk with an awful adenoidal Bronx cheer of a voice. Judy Holliday was thought of for the part, but when her success in *Born Yesterday* made her too big for a supporting role, MGM contract player Jean Hagen took it and made it her own.

Not only did Hagen brilliantly nail Lamont's voice in scenes like her attempts to bring proper diction to "I can't stand him," she also captures the pleased-with-herself princess who gloats "I make more money than Calvin Coolidge put together." Once the transition to sound mandates that Lockwood and Lamont's next picture, "The Dueling Cavalier," will be turned into "The Dancing Cavalier," that voice—and that attitude—will create problems.

Though Lamont thinks she and her costar are an item, Lockwood's heart is in short order won by Reynolds's Kathy Selden, a love match he joyously celebrates by dancing through the best downpour MGM money could buy in a justly celebrated scene that is movie artifice at its most commanding. "The purpose of a musical," Kelly said years later, "is to make people happy," and in *Singin' in the Rain* he showed just how it should be done.

What to Watch Next:
Band Wagon (1953), directed by Vincente Minnelli.

Further Reading:

The World of Entertainment: Hollywood's Greatest Musicals, by Hugh Fiordin.

Singin' in the Rain: The Making of an American Masterpiece, by Earl J. Hess, Pratibha A. Dabholkar.

THE EARRINGS OF MADAME DE . . .

1953

Directed by Max Ophuls. Starring Charles Boyer,
Danielle Darrieux, Vittorio De Sica.

Max Ophuls's elegant and opulent *The Earrings Of Madame de . . .*
is intoxicating enough to make you swoon. A bittersweet love
story set in a morally corrupt world where pure and innocent passion is the only unforgivable sin, it uses Ophuls's ravishing technique and a superb cast to turn a slight story into an indelible
French romance.

Ophuls was German, not French, born Maximilian Oppenheimer in 1902. He fled his homeland in 1933 and ended up making more than twenty films in five countries (France, Italy, the
Netherlands, the United States, and his homeland) and, someone
once wrote, "could have made a film in Japanese without understanding a word of the language." Such was his mastery of visual
storytelling in general and camera movement in particular. "The
pleasure of seeing," he said, "should be the moving force behind
my film story," and so it always was.

Ophuls admitted he was attracted to the slight novella by
Louise de Vilmorin that is the basis for the film by the twist at
its narrative center: "There is always the same axis around which

the action continually turns, like a roundabout. A tiny, scarcely visible axis: a pair of earrings."

Before we see the earrings, however, or even the face of their owner, the beautiful and pampered countess (played by Danielle Darrieux) whose name we never learn, we see her most intimate possessions. Clearly a creature of luxury who leads an unapologetically superficial life, Madame is introduced with just her elegant arms in camera range as she rifles through her furs, even her jewels, desperate for something to pawn to cover her extravagant bills.

Working with frequent collaborators cinematographer Christian Matras, set designer Jean d'Eaubonne, and costume designer Georges Annenkov, Ophuls does not stop at presenting this rich boudoir; he brings to life an entire physical world so tangible you feel you could step right into it. More than the gorgeous clothes, the gowns, evening clothes, and uniforms the characters wear, it's the spacious rooms and the graceful mansions they inhabit and the paintings, lamps, mirrors, chandeliers, and curtains that fill them. These all combine to create a rich, languid Belle Epoque atmosphere that holds us absolutely.

Ophuls and cowriters Marcel Achard and Annette Wademant also duplicate the moral code of this particular universe. Not surprisingly, it's a place where form is everything and emotion nothing, a cynical world of complete artifice and insincerity, where revealing how you truly feel is an unforgivable breach of protocol.

It is also a world where Madame de's husband, a prominent general as well as a count, is completely at home. Impeccably played by Charles Boyer (whose Hollywood career started as one of Jean Harlow's lovers in *Red-Headed Woman* and went on to include *Gaslight*, *Algiers*, and *Love Affair*), the general is a decisive man of command—"what's done is done" is one of his favorite phrases—who does more than embody patrician hauteur, he makes it real and human. Casting his cool inflexibility against the soft and feminine Darrieux, whose character is a self-described "frivolous liar," is an example of how the restraint of the film's acting effectively plays against the lushness of its setting.

After a bit of indecision, Madame decides to pawn a pair of earrings with diamond hearts, an expensive wedding present from her husband. The jeweler she turns to promises complete confidence—"We only sell to men because of women," he tells her, "discretion is part of our profession"—but, in a turn of affairs that sets the tone of the film, a change in circumstances forces him to betray her confidence and reveal the truth to her husband.

That duplicity sets the earrings on a journey that takes them first to Constantinople and then back to Paris, where each change in ownership symbolizes the ebb and flow of love from one character to another.

Bringing the jewels back is Baron Donati, an Italian diplomat stationed in France who's played with appropriate cheeriness by Vittorio De Sica, a veteran actor as well as the celebrated neorealist director of *Shoeshine* and *Bicycle Thieves*.

Donati is immediately attracted to Madame when he sees her at a border crossing in Bern but has no idea who she is or how to find her. The fates, who soon enough will try to separate them, initially conspire to bring them together. For not only do they move in the same circles, the general counts the baron as one of his friends.

Everyone imagines that the notoriously fickle countess will ensnare the baron in the superficial flirtations she has made a way of life. "Each a bore," the general says dismissively of her legion of admirers, "together they are insufferable." Her method, Donati is told, is "torture through hope," and even she offers him a word of friendly advice: "I'd hate to see you caught in my game."

What develops instead is a kind of love that is new for both of them. The countess and the baron find themselves in danger of committing the ultimate sin in their heartless world: genuinely caring for each other and allowing true feeling to penetrate into their luxurious, suffocating lives. The countess, especially, is the last person you expect to fall heedlessly in love. When, in an attempt to convince herself it isn't happening, she tells the baron over and over "I don't love you, I don't love you," it is devastating..

Ophuls's lifelong fascination with camera movement bears exceptional fruit here, especially in *Earrings'* visual centerpiece, a montage of a series of gliding, gilded balls in which the countess and the baron gradually realize they are intoxicated with each other, a sequence which has to be one of the most visually sublime ever put on film.

The costumes change, the dialogue indicates the passage of time, the waltzes blend gloriously into one another as onlookers gossip about this unavoidably public courtship. "They're seen everywhere," says one, while another replies, "because they can meet nowhere." As critic Phillip Lopate has written, "no other director in the history of movies wrung so much emotional resonance from cinematic technique."

For who else could replicate the sensual, caressing nature of Ophuls's camera movements, or the unself-conscious ease with which they're executed? Though the director moved the camera whenever possible—he has the jeweler forget first his hat and then his cane just for that pleasure—Ophus's technique never feels showy for the sake of being showy, and his shots feel so natural that you're often enjoying the move before you even realize it's happening.

"The highest reaches of the actors' art begin, I believe," Ophuls famously said, "at the point where words cease to play a part." Nowhere are those particular words made flesh more eloquently than they are here.

What to Watch Next:
General Della Rovere (1959), directed by Roberto Rossellini.

SEVEN SAMURAI

1954

Directed by Akira Kurosawa. Starring Takashi Shimura,
Toshiro Mifune.

The great German composer Richard Strauss was conducting his three-hour-plus *Der Rosenkavalier* when, or so the story goes, he turned to his concertmaster and said, "My, this is a long opera."

"But maestro," the man replied, aghast, "you wrote it."

"Yes," the imperturbable Strauss answered, "but I never thought I'd have to conduct it."

In artistic matters, as in many things, length is relative. Clocking in at three hours and twenty-seven minutes, *Seven Samurai* was to be the longest—and arguably most popular—film in director Akira Kurosawa's extensive career, one of the works that led Steven Spielberg to call him "the pictorial Shakespeare of our time," but that didn't stop it from making people uneasy.

In fact Toho, the studio that made it, cut fifty minutes before so much as showing the film to American distributors, fearful that no Westerner would have the stamina for the original length. And the *New York Times'* Bosley Crowther did contend that "it is much too long for comfort or for the story it has to tell." Yet, paradoxically, more than any other kind of cinema, long films done right have the potential to envelope you completely in character and experience.

The longest audience film since the three-hour, forty-two-minute *Gone with the Wind* (1939), *Seven Samurai* came by its length honestly. The script took six intense weeks to write, with the screenwriters cloistered at an inn and forbidden visitors and even phone calls for the duration. Preproduction lasted three months, and the film's 148 shooting days were spread out over an entire year, four times the time span that was originally budgeted.

Unlike the at times self-indulgently long films of today's auteurs, *Seven Samurai* uses its length creatively, not merely to burnish egos. Confident of his powers and in no rush, Kurosawa functions as a master slow-cook chef, allowing his ingredients to simmer and become tastier, tastier, and tastier still. "An action film is often an action film only for the sake of action," the director said. "But what a wonderful thing if one can construct a grand action film without sacrificing the portrayal of human beings." Which is what Kurosawa has accomplished here.

This particular story, the tale of a group of masterless samurai coming together to defend a village of farmers against the depredations of roving bandits, takes full advantage of its allotted time. It mixes the broad canvas of epic action with intimate personal details, finding time not only for movement and drama but also comedy, young love, and even poetic visuals.

That mixture may seem more Western than Japanese, and in fact Kurosawa, though often accused by his fellow countrymen of being too Western, is more accurately seen as an adroit mixer of both cultures. "I was able to harmonize the two strands without any contradiction," he said, because that's the way they blended in his own psyche.

Seven Samurai unrolls naturally and pleasurably, like a beautiful scroll. Rather than ignore time, the film luxuriates in it, emphasizing its passage and even underlining key scenes with a quiet but insistent drumbeat that could almost be a clock ticking off the inexorable seconds.

The setting is one of Japan's numerous sixteenth-century civil wars. A fierce outlaw leader with a patch over one eye looks over a village and promises to return with his thieving hoard "when their barley is ripe."

This message terrifies the peasants, who fear they have nowhere to turn. Advised by a wizened elder to recruit masterless samurai, the villagers feel it's beyond their means. "Even bears," the elder replies, sending them off to a nearby city, "come down from the mountain when they're hungry."

Given that the satisfactions of doing for others is one of *Seven Samurai*'s themes, it's no accident that the villagers' first recruit comes to their notice through an act of self-sacrifice. That would be Kambei Shimada, played by Kurosawa veteran Takashi Shimura (star of the earlier *Ikiru*), who is introduced shaving off his topknot, a mark of status, in order to rescue a kidnapped boy. "By protecting others," he says at one point in the film, "you save yourself."

Under the leadership of this canny strategist, the other samurai, both experienced and novice, come into the fold, an unhurried process that takes a full hour of screen time and includes Gorobei, the skilled archer, and Kyuzo, the master swordsman with impeccable form.

Most memorable is Kikuchiyo, a would-be samurai with more energy than sense who, as played in an exuberant, star-making performance by Toshiro Mifune, was a late addition to the story. As Mifune related in a 1993 interview, the script was originally going to be called "Six Samurai" until the writers had a change of heart. "Finally it dawned on them that six sober samurai were a bore—they needed a character that was more off-the-wall," he said. "So I had complete freedom to do whatever I felt like."

Once in the village, the samurai have two parallel tasks. They have to simultaneously reassure the villagers, who fear their impressionable daughters will lose their heads, and mold them into an acceptable fighting unit before the bandits return. Once again, it's all about time.

The film's length works in its favor in ways large and small. It allows Kambei, the samurai leader, to gradually grow his hair back. And it allows the uneasy bond that grows between the samurai and the villagers, as well as the villagers' martial confidence, to seem more believable as we watch both increase over time.

Three hours plus also allows us to observe each of *Seven Samurai*'s many characters in the round, to view them as individuals with their own back stories, philosophies, martial arts skills, and reasons for being there. We get to know them naturally, the way we get to know our friends, by putting in the time. We get to experience the emotional arc of the youngest samurai and understand where the fury of Mifune's ragtag battler Kikuchiyo comes from. When the bandits finally do attack, our hearts are in our throats because we know the defenders so well, and because we can sense not everyone will survive.

It's fitting that *Seven Samurai* ends not with a quick battle but a complex, extended combat sequence that plays out over several days, an astonishing clash that lasts more than half an hour on screen and culminates with six full minutes of fighting in a sea of mud. Filmed in a driving rainstorm using multiple cameras and telephoto lenses, it was shot in January and February, when the actors didn't have to pretend to be frigid.

The passage of time has one final advantage: it shows us the entirety of the agricultural year, from planting to gorgeous blossoming to final harvesting. That's critical because the film's final message is to applaud the endurance of that kind of life. "In the end we lost this battle, too," one of the survivors says, "The victory belongs to the peasants, not to us." By showing us nature's time in the round, Kurosawa's humanistic epic ensures that the message comes through loud and clear.

What to Watch Next:

The Magnificent Seven (1960), directed by John Sturges.

Throne of Blood (1957), directed by Akira Kurosawa.

Further Reading:

The Films of Akira Kurosawa, by Donald Richie.

The Emperor and the Wolf: The Lives and Films of Akira Kurosawa and Toshiro Mifune, by Stuart Galbraith IV.

KISS ME DEADLY

1955

Directed by Robert Aldrich. Starring Ralph Meeker,
Maxine Cooper, Gaby Rodgers.

Something there is that does not like Los Angeles, that does not
wish it well on screen. The famously bleak, despairing film noirs
that came out of Hollywood in the 1940s and 1950s insisted on a
corrosive darkness lurking below the surface in perpetually sunlit
LA, a spiritual malaise that made the city rotten to the core, a
place where bad people came to do worse things and lived to tell
the tale. Or did they?

Even among these films, Robert Aldrich's 1955 *Kiss Me
Deadly* stands out from the crowd. Strident yet poetic, a highly
stylized vision of breathtaking savagery and nuclear hell, it's film
noir pushed to the limit and beyond, a borderline irrational version of an already extreme genre.

On one level, the fiercely independent, go-his-own-way Aldrich did to noir what novelist Mickey Spillaine had previously
done to the hard-boiled fiction genre on the page, adding explo-
sively high levels of sex and violence to novels like *I, the Jury*, *My
Gun Is Quick*, and *The Big Kill* and gaining international sales that
rose to the hundreds of millions.

· 156 ·

But while the violence in *Kiss Me Deadly* seemed extreme back in the day—a network TV censor insisted the film "has no purpose except to incite sadism and bestiality in human beings"—the point was always something much more subversive.

Working with screenwriter A.I. "Buzz" Bezzerides, Aldrich took little more than the title and Spillaine's Mike Hammer private eye from the original novel and constructed a kind of ultimate 1950s paranoid epic that tells you to be very afraid without revealing until the very last moment what that fear is all about.

Handsomely shot with a feel for the genre by Ernest Laszlo, *Kiss Me Deadly* uses odd camera angles and deep shadows that make even full sunlight seem tainted to create unease so strong you can taste it. There is no sense of the quotidian anywhere in this film; even what seems ordinary is anything but. Add in elliptical dialogue, edgy characters, and intentionally disorienting situations, and you understand why Martin Scorsese called this "a key film of the modern era and as ferocious a movie as has ever been made in America."

Kiss Me Deadly's disorientation starts with the film's opening credits, huge letters that do the unheard of and crawl across the screen from the bottom to the top instead of the usual top-to-bottom way. Pay close attention, this unsettling design choice says, whatever you're expecting, this isn't going to be it.

Aldrich chooses to begin *Kiss Me Deadly* with the equally disconcerting image of a terrified, barefoot woman, naked under her trench coat as it turns out, running down a highway. Running out of a terrible blackness directly at the camera, directly at us.

After a few desultory attempts at flagging down passing cars, the woman steps in front of a sporty roadster that has to swerve off the road to avoid hitting her. The driver: LA private detective Mike Hammer (Ralph Meeker), who casually says, "Get in," like this kind of thing happens to him every day. Maybe it does.

The woman is Christina (a memorable Cloris Leachman in her film debut), named after the poet Christina Rosetti she tells

Mike, who likely wouldn't know a poem if it hit him over the head. Christina is also an escapee from an upstate mental hospital who's been held against her will because of what she knows. Fearful, for good reason as it turns out, that her future is about to become all used up, she implores Mike to "remember me." How could he forget?

Mike's rare good deed nearly gets him killed, but when he wakes up in the hospital with his adoring secretary Velda (Maxine Cooper) by his side, his immediate thought is to play the angles. As Christina accurately surmised about the man in their brief time together, "you have only one lasting love: you. You never give in a relationship, only take."

Interviewed by a shadowy group called the Interstate Crime Commission, Mike clams up about what he knows even as his evasiveness is met with complete contempt by his questioners, who mock him as a low rent divorce specialist who gets most of his business by compelling the devoted Velda to do his dirty work. "Open a window," one of the feds says as Mike's amoral modus operandi is revealed. The man himself could care less.

Intrigued that Christina's fate and his accident "rings bells all the way to Washington," Mike decides there's got to be some money for him somewhere in this business. All he needs to do is figure out what's going on and what "the Great Whatsit" everyone is after actually is. As Velda sarcastically describes his technique, "first you find a little thread, a little thread leads you to a string, and the string leads you to a rope, and from the rope you hang by the neck. . . ."

Cockiness itself, a hit-first-ask-questions-later type accustomed to being top dog in his underdog world, Mike thinks there's nothing he can't handle. So off he goes on a series of string-gathering interviews, prowling around LA's brooding and bygone Bunker Hill neighborhood, disregarding frequent warnings to back off and meeting a series of inexplicably terrified individuals.

These include a science writer with mysterious burns who says "if you knew, you'd be afraid like I'm afraid;" a twitchy neurotic who says she was Christina's roommate; an opera singer who clams up until the ever sadistic Mike breaks one of his prized records, even a wheezy morgue attendant played by B picture stalwart Percy Helton.

Unlike most movie detectives, who painstakingly make their way to the center of the mystery, the more Mike finds out, the less he knows. Unsure of what he is getting into, he is always a step behind the truth, always getting his few friends into trouble, more over his head than he realizes until it is way too late.

Kiss Me Deadly is celebrated among film buffs for having two endings, a vivid truncated version and the sixty-four-seconds-longer original that dropped from sight for decades. Either way you look at it, this is a film that will shake you up and disturb your sleep. It was made that way.

What to Watch Next:
Pickup on South Street (1953), directed by Sam Fuller.

Further Reading:
The Film Noir Encyclopedia, by Alain Silver, Elizabeth Ward, James Ursini.
Art of Noir: The Posters and Graphics from the Classic Era of Film Noir, by Eddie Muller.

SEVEN MEN FROM NOW

1956

Directed by Budd Boetticher. Starring Randolph Scott,
Gail Russell, Lee Marvin.

As indispensable to the Western genre as the Ring cycle is to grand opera, the films known as the Ranown cycle are the essence of the cowboy film. If you have a passion for that setting and that style, the Ranown films are a recurring vision of the mythic West that repetition does nothing but improve.

Elegant and economical, with plot, action, and character precisely balanced and pared down to iconic essentials, this legendary series of low budget B Westerns directed by Budd Boetticher, mostly written by Burt Kennedy and always produced by Harry Joe Brown and starring the irreplaceable Randolph Scott (the Ranown production company combines both their names) are as good as their reputation, which is saying a lot.

Released in 1956, *Seven Men from Now* is not technically one of the five Ranown films (it came first and someone else produced), but it is indisputably the template from which the series was struck. It is brief—only seventy-eight minutes long—but its focused filmmaking packs in an extraordinary amount of action and its incidents and themes recur throughout the entire series.

Unsentimental films streaked with unexpected humanity, they came to be made because of a favor from one actor to another.

John Wayne, whose production company had commissioned the script from Kennedy (who, the story goes, was given no more than the title to work with), decided against starring in the film himself. So, as director Budd Boetticher recalled in his memoir, *When in Disgrace*, "I said, 'Who do you want to play the lead, Duke?' and he said, 'Well, let's use Randolph Scott, he's through.'" Maybe, but maybe not.

With a face as chiseled as any stone idol and a harsh but resonant voice, Scott's ability to define implacable, to bring tension into every frame because he's compelled to do what he thinks is right, no matter what the situation or the consequences, turned out to embody what *Seven Men* has in mind. Something has all but died inside this man, and we are going to find out why.

First visible from the back, illuminated by the lightning of a torrential Arizona downpour, Scott's aptly named Ben Stride is introduced walking resolutely toward a campfire and the two nervous men huddled around it. On foot because starving Chiricahua stole and ate his horse, he remains unwaveringly on a mission.

A man who wastes few if any words and never says anything he doesn't mean, Stride's idea of an extended speech is "I'd be obliged for that cup of coffee." In short order we discover that he's come from Silver Spring, where seven men recently robbed the express office and took a Wells Fargo strongbox with $20,000 in gold. And one more thing. In the course of the robbery a woman was killed.

We don't get to see what happens next, but the following morning finds Stride riding one horse and leading another behind him. In short order he runs across a married couple from the East, the attractive Annie Greer (Gail Russell) and her garrulous but inept husband John (Walter Reed), travelers whose wagon is stuck in a mud hole on the way to California.

Though you might not guess it, Stride is the kind of man who tips his hat to women and religiously calls them "ma'am," so it's no surprise that he makes it possible for the couple to free their wagon with a laconic "Glad to be of help." When John Greer insists on taking a route that Stride considers unsafe, his sense of duty—and a muted attraction to Annie Greer—doesn't allow them to go alone.

One of the unlooked-for strengths of Scott's performance is that his stoic face is also one on which pain, regret, and humanity show themselves from time to time. The unexpressive Stride turns out to be not someone without feelings as much as an individual who feels too much, who is in so much torment he can't really talk about it.

Stride and the Greers are not alone for long. At a deserted stagecoach relay station they are joined by a pair of bad men, most prominently the oily, insinuating Masters, flamboyant down to his brightly colored bandana and played with perfect cock-of-the-walk insolence by Lee Marvin (cast at Kennedy's suggestion.)

All Westerns have bad men, but Masters breaks with tradition. As Boetticher wrote in his memoir, "Burt and I agreed that the western heavies over the years had been portrayed as much too heavy. They rode black horses and wore black hats. You never saw anything good about any of them. Well, we set out to make our villains extremely attractive . . . We wanted our audiences to really love 'em while they were still kickin'."

Though the best of the Ranown villains is conceded to be Richard Boone's self-possessed and cerebral Usher in *The Tall T*, Masters gives him—and the hero—a run for his money. Masters and Stride share not only a past acquaintance but mutual respect, fearlessness, and the determination to live by a code. When Stride tells him "I'd hate to have to kill you," Masters's unflappable response is, "I'd hate to have you try."

Masters also does the audience a favor by filling us in on the details of Stride's life that the man himself is too terse to reveal. Stride turns out to be the former marshal of Silver Spring whose wife was the woman who died in that express office robbery. Though he no longer wears a star, Stride is determined to track down and kill every one of the seven men responsible.

Ever the unapologetic outlaw, Masters is equally determined to tag along and abscond with the stolen $20,000 once Stride eliminates the perpetrators. But, bad guy though he is, Masters has a code of his own and there are lines he won't cross—like killing Stride from behind a rock—to get the money: "I couldn't enjoy spending the $20,000 if I did."

Masters also set the trend for Renown villains by having an eye for the woman in the film, and by being able to express that attraction in more sensual, almost romantic terms. "You move like you're all over alive," he says to Annie Greer before wondering aloud about her marriage: "Why would a full woman settle for half a man?"

Kennedy and Boetticher do more than set this complex plot in motion; they ensure that it's worked out with unforeseen twists and reversals that also manage to play fair with genre constraints and expectations, something that's by no means easy to do.

This combination of familiar and unfamiliar also characterizes the film's visuals, which were often shot among the stone monoliths of the legendary Alabama Hills outside of Lone Pine, California, the site of many a B Western scenario.

All the Ranown films ended up being photographed near Lone Pine, often with top-of-the-line cinematographers like Lucien Ballard or Burnett Guffey. William Clothier did the honors in *Seven Men* and his unforced, lyrical visuals captured the aridness, desolation, and strange beauty of an area a character in another Ranown film characterizes as "nothing but empty."

Though Budd Boetticher liked to say "the Western has no message," the Ranown films inspired by *Seven Men from Now* unabashedly admires the way their protagonists chose to live their lives. These masculine codes were mostly unarticulated, but every once in a while one of Scott's characters would say "a man has to draw the line somewhere if he's going to live with himself" or, more laconically, "there are some things a man can't ride around."

As a Western motto, it doesn't get any better than that.

What to Watch Next:

The Tall T (1957), directed by Budd Boetticher.

Further Reading:

When in Disgrace, by Budd Boetticher.
Horizons West, by Jim Kitses.

SWEET SMELL OF SUCCESS

1957

Directed by Alexander Mackendrick. Starring Burt Lancaster, Tony Curtis.

"Match me, Sidney."

It sounds like a simple request from Burt Lancaster's omnipotent Broadway columnist J.J. Hunsecker to Tony Curtis's hustling, conniving press agent Sidney Falco that he strike a match and light the great man's cigarette.

But on another level, that iconic line from *Sweet Smell of Success* plays like a challenge, a call to combat from a confident film in effect saying, "Match this dialogue. Write talk that's as alive and electric as these arias of angst and desperation. If you think you can." Few films have taken up that challenge, and even fewer have succeeded.

Justly acclaimed today, in Martin Scorsese's summation, as "one of the most daring, startling, savage films ever made about show business and power in this country," *Sweet Smell of Success* was not always perceived that way. Or maybe it was but what people saw made them uncomfortable enough to treat the film, to borrow another memorable Hunsecker phrase, "like a cookie full of arsenic."

Written by Clifford Odets and Ernst Lehman from a Lehman novella and directed by Alexander Mackendrick, *Success* always had its staunch defenders but it was mostly dismissed in its day, a viewer at an advance screening going so far as to write on the preview card, "Don't touch a foot of this film. Just burn the whole thing."

Critics of all stripes were equally unhappy: Manny Farber derided it in *The Nation*, the *New York Times* concluded its plot "had holes large enough to be seen even by the myopic," and the *Saturday Review* said it conveyed "the taste of ashes." Even its director was publicly unhappy.

"I cannot recommend the film for student study on aesthetic grounds," Mackendrick wrote years later. "It is a film I have mixed feelings about today." Just because he was writing about it, the director took pains to point out, didn't signify that "I mean to claim that it is an important work. It isn't."

In many ways Mackendrick seemed an unlikely person to have made this ultimate Manhattan melodrama in the first place. Born in America but raised in Scotland, he made his reputation directing daft Ealing comedies like the Alec Guinness vehicles *The Man in the White Suit* and *The Ladykillers*. A key reason Mackendrick took this assignment was because it was "a chance to get out of a reputation I had for small cute British comedies."

Screenwriter Lehman, by contrast, was so immersed in this particular world that he initially intended to direct his original script himself. Lehman had at one time worked for press agent Irving Hoffman, a key source for the terrifying Walter Winchell, the syndicated newspaper columnist and radio broadcaster who was the model for J.J. Hunsecker. When Hunsecker says that a detractor "wiped his feet on the choice and predilection of 60 million men and women in the greatest country in the world," it is Winchell's voice he is channeling.

Perhaps one reason that Mackendrick was less than enthusiastic about *Success* was that the production was so troubled there apparently never was a final shooting script. First Lehman was eased out as director, then Burt Lancaster, whose production company financed the film, got intrigued by the Hunsecker role (Lehman had envisioned Orson Welles). Finally Lehman became ill and had to be replaced by Clifford Odets, who famously typed a constant stream of rewrites from inside a prop truck parked near the production's Manhattan locations.

The way those New York after dark locales were shot in black and white by cinematographer James Wong Howe, one of the first times night scenes were shot on location in the city, is one of *Sweet Smell of Success*'s greatest and at times most over-looked assets.

Right from its opening sequences, featuring wave after wave of Broadway neon, *Success* glories in its ability to capture the cel-ebrated street energy of Manhattan, the tremendous excitement that draws people to the city no matter what. The film's look, which involved starting scenes with New York exteriors and fin-ishing them on studio sound stages, is at once mythic and realis-tic, an effect Hunsecker, master of all he surveys, sums up when he looks around and says simply, "I love this dirty town."

The great advantage of Lehman's Broadway background was that it gave his original script the frisson of a forbidden glimpse into privileged territory, a sense that we are being allowed behind the scenes of an ostensibly glamorous world that is in reality a cesspool of power, ambition, desperation, and drive.

Giving that world much of its energy was the rewriting done by Clifford Odets. As the socially conscious playwright best known for such Group Theater efforts as *Waiting for Lefty* and *Awake and Sing*, Odets was, like Mackendrick, not the most obvious match for this material, but his ferocious, even exagger-ated dialogue turned out to be exactly right. After a little writer/director conversation.

As Mackendrick remembered the encounter, "Clifford sensed, I think, that I was concerned about the problem of style and explained to me: 'My dialogue may seem somewhat overwrit-ten, too wordy, too contrived. Don't let it worry you. You'll find that it works if you don't bother too much about the lines themselves. Play the situations, not the words. And play them fast.' When it came to the highly stylized, almost preposterous lines the actors had to speak, I found this to be a marvelous piece of advice."

The dialogue is also successful because it doesn't exist for its own sake but to delineate a pair of scathing, way larger-than-life characters who take up all the air in *Success*, leaving everyone else gasping for breath and scrambling to get a word in edgewise.

J.J. Hunsecker arrives first, but not in person. It's his all-seeing eyes and eyeglasses we initially encounter, part of a delivery truck poster reading "Go with the Globe: Read J.J. Hunsecker, The Eyes of Broadway."

Even when Hunsecker arrives in person, we hear him before we see him, a menacing monolith so powerful even United States senators feel the need to kiss his ring. It's the restrained ferocity of Lancaster's performance that makes the character unnerving, the sense that it takes an enormous effort of will on Hunsecker's part to keep from literally tearing everyone he meets limb from limb.

"Hunsecker would almost inevitably be a man rotted away with contempt for the world in which he lives," Mackendrick wrote in an annotated script memo that's part of Lehman's archive in the University of Texas Harry Ransom Center. "Hunsecker is a monster, certainly. But in order to be truly terrifying, he should be a monster that we understand and believe; a monster all the more impressive because he makes appalling, cynical sense."

Then there is Curtis's Sidney Falco, a small-time press agent who lives in a bedroom behind his office and is involved 24/7 in planning, scheming, manipulating, and conniving, mostly with an eye toward achieving the holy grail of getting his clients into J.J.'s column. Only, for the last five days, his batting average has been zero. "You're dead, son," the great man himself tells him. "Get yourself buried."

The problem is that J.J. has given Sidney an assignment that is proving difficult to accomplish: he's been told to break up the budding romance between J.J.'s young sister Susan (Susan Harrison) and her jazz guitarist boyfriend Steve Dallas (*Route 66*'s Marty Milner). It's dirty work, but someone has to do it.

Having a teen heartthrob like Curtis (the script knowingly calls him "the boy with the ice cream face") play so amorally against type was a shock to the actor's fans (as was Harrison Ford similarly going from *Indiana Jones* to *Blade Runner* decades later) and likely contributed to the film's initial lack of box office success. But it remains one of Curtis's best roles at least in part because it's not that dissimilar from the scrambling, hustling kid from New York he had been in the first place.

The focus of *Sweet Smell of Success*, obviously, is not what happens to those bland youngsters Susan and Steve but what goes down in the tricky, anxious, unholy relationship between Sidney and J.J., the twin titans of duplicity. They're the reason the film's advertising line—"The Motion Picture That Will Never Be Forgiven, Or Forgotten!"—turns out to be less hyperbolic than it sounds. Match me, Sidney, indeed.

What to Watch Next:
Citizen Kane (1941), directed by Orson Welles.

Further Reading:
On Film-making: An Introduction to the Craft of the Director, by Alexander Madkendrick.

VERTIGO

1958

Directed by Alfred Hitchcock. Starring James Stewart, Kim Novak.

Proof of the variability of film critics is as close as the reviews that greeted Alfred Hitchcock's *Vertigo* when it opened in 1958.

"'Vertigo' Induces Same in Watcher," headlined the *Los Angeles Times*, *Time* magazine mocked this "Hitchcock-and-bull story," and the *New Yorker* said the director "has never before indulged in such farfetched nonsense." Partisans, too, conceded that this was no more than "middling Hitchcock."

Even seven years later, when iconoclastic British critic Robin Wood nervily described *Vertigo* as "one of the four or five most profound and beautiful films the cinema has yet given us," he made sure to follow his statement with the acknowledgment that "this is a claim that may surprise, even amuse, the majority of my readers."

That kind of disclaimer is no longer very much in evidence, as *Vertigo* is acknowledged to be, in the words of Hitchcock biographer Donald Spoto, the director's "richest, most obsessive, least compromising film." More than that, by 2012, when *Sight & Sound* magazine did its once a decade survey of the world's film critics to compile an all-time ten best list, *Vertigo*, which hadn't even been listed in 1962 or 1972, put an end to the fifty-year run of Orson Welles's *Citizen Kane* and took first place.

What's going on here? How has a film dismissed in 1958 become the paramount icon of modern cinema? Were they crazy, or are we? Or is it simply that *Vertigo* defines the concept of art that was ahead of its time, a motion picture whose virtues resonate much more strongly with contemporary viewers than they could have done in the past.

I was one of the 191 critics worldwide who put *Vertigo* on their 2012 list (*Kane* came in second with 157 votes), and my own experience with the film paralleled the larger world's. When I first saw it at a college screening in the late 1960s, introduced by a student who considered it a masterpiece, it unnerved me so much that I almost didn't know what to think except that I very much wanted to see it again.

Now, after multiple viewings spaced out over decades, *Vertigo* stands out in my mind as what it probably always was, an audacious, brilliantly twisted movie, infused with touches of genius and of madness. A disturbing meditation on the interconnectedness of love and obsession disguised as a penny dreadful shocker, a Tristan and Isolde–style romance of lovers doomed by their passion for each other, it's more impressive today than when it debuted because of several interconnected factors.

For one thing, the combination of the 1960s New Wave, the rise of the auteur theory, and the emergence of American independent film have given considerable cachet to the notion of individual movie making. And though it was made in the heart of the studio system, *Vertigo* is as intensely personal as any entry at Sundance, with some of the biggest stars of the day helping Hitchcock work through the nakedest version of his perennial obsession with glacial blonds and the ghastly jokes of fate.

Hitchcock was able to get away with the private nature of this psychological horror story because as usual he worked within the context of a thriller plot. *Vertigo* started out as a novel called

D'entre les Morts (Between the Dead) by the French team of Pierre Boileau and Thomas Narcejac, the same pair who had written the book on which Henri-Georges Clouzot's *Diabolique* was based. Though Hitchcock didn't find out about the possibility until his celebrated series of interviews with François Truffaut years later, the authors may have concocted their new novel specifically to get the director's attention.

Hitchcock chose to open *Vertigo* on a pure thriller moment, a close-up of an outdoor ladder and then a hand grabbing it in the midst of a rooftop chase as two uniformed San Francisco policemen and a plainclothes detective scramble after a fugitive.

That plainclothesman is John "Scottie" Ferguson (James Stewart), soon to be forced into early retirement by the sudden onset of acrophobia, a fear of heights leading to intense dizziness or vertigo, brought on by the particulars of that chase. Only another emotional shock, he's told, could end his affliction.

Reduced to spending his spare time with Midge, his sensible former fiancée (played by Barbara Bel Geddes, later known as Miss Ellie on *Dallas*), Scottie chafes at the inactivity and at being called "Johnny-O" by Midge, whose work as a ladies underwear designer hints at the film's voyeuristic themes.

Then, out of the blue, comes a welcome call from an old college buddy named Gavin Elster (Tom Helmore), now a wealthy local shipbuilder. Elster is concerned about his wife, Madeline. Though he knows it sounds far-fetched, Elster (in a plot device that uncannily echoes S. Ansky's *Dybbuk*) feels something or someone has taken possession of Madeline, quite possibly from beyond the grave, and because he fears for his wife's safety and sanity, he wants her followed by someone he knows and trusts.

Scottie, who prides himself on his hardheaded practicality, is dubious at first, but his first glimpse of the blond and ethereal Madeline, breathtaking in a black evening gown with a brightly colored, almost fluorescent wrap, changes his mind. He is almost afraid to look at her, because that one stunning moment reveals what Scottie himself is not ready to admit: he's intoxicated enough to follow this woman anywhere.

Where anywhere turns out to be is one of the many shocks this famously unpredictable plot has in store. Yet, difficult though its twists are to anticipate, *Vertigo* is also admired for the way, in vintage Hitchcock fashion, it gets its strongest effects not out of surprise but from the more satisfying notion of suspense. The idea is to let the audience in on things the characters don't know and exploit our anticipation of how they'll react when they find out.

Helping to unnerve us is Bernard Herrmann's otherworldly score, justly considered one of the pinnacles of modern film music, filled with haunting, yearning violins that unsettle with insistent hints of something evil this way coming.

But if we know more than the characters, we don't know as much as Hitchcock, and one of the most notable things about *Vertigo* is the elegant, effortless way it plays with the audience, manipulating our reactions to situations from the smallest (a sinister alley leads to a cheery flower shop) to the most significant. And just as the screenplay features dialogue we don't fully understand till later in the story, the camera work encourages us to notice what Hitchcock wants us to notice, not what turns out to be truly important.

What we notice most of all is Madeline Elster, played, in one of her strongest and most persuasive performances, by Kim Novak. Frankly gorgeous in a series of Edith Head costumes, projecting vulnerability, hauteur, and a powerful, otherworldly sensuality, she underlines Truffaut's comment to Hitchcock that "very few American actresses are quite as carnal on screen." It's hard to imagine *Vertigo* without her, yet that's what the director was determined to do.

Hitchcock had initially preferred Vera Miles, who had co-starred in his 1957 *The Wrong Man* with Henry Fonda. But Miles became pregnant, and the director was not amused. "It was her third child," he explained to biographer Spoto, "and I told her that one child was expected, two was sufficient, but that three was really obscene. She didn't care for this sort of comment."

Although he was too upset with Miles to use her even when *Vertigo*'s shooting ended up starting so late that she became available again, Hitchcock was far from keen on Novak. She was a top box office draw who had come to the project as part of a deal engineered by agent Lew Wasserman that had Novak and costar Stewart then segue to *Bell, Book, and Candle*.

For one thing, the actress was independent-minded and had her own ideas about things like wardrobe, a stance the director had little patience with. "My dear Miss Novak," he is famously said to have replied, "you can wear anything you want, anything— provided it is what the script calls for." Said the actress years later, "When I played it I felt absolutely stripped naked. I felt so vulnerable. He knew exactly what he wanted."

Hitchcock, who could be something of a sadist on the set, is said to have insisted on multiple retakes (one estimate is 24) of a scene that called for Novak being dunked in a studio tank. Still, the actress apparently didn't hold a grudge, telling another reporter years later: "Hitchcock was dictatorial, but at heart he was a sweet, charming man. He didn't know how to relate to actors as people. He could put you into his plots, but it was a chess game. You were just a piece."

Equally problematic for a long time was how to turn the novel's plot into an acceptable script. Playwright Maxwell Anderson did a first draft with the unpromising title "Darkling I Listen." Alec Coppel did a second version and ended up sharing screen credit with Samuel Taylor, who also wrote *Sabrina* and came up with the key element that made everyone happy.

Taylor, who never read the original novel, explained in a later interview that he had told Hitchcock that the problem with the Coppel script was "'a matter of finding reality and humanity for these people. You haven't got anybody in this story who is a human being; nobody at all. They're all cutout cardboard figures.' I told him immediately that I would have to invent a character who would bring Scottie into the world, establish for him an ordinary life, make it obvious that he's an ordinary man. So I invented Midge." Stewart, for one, was so delighted he charged into the director's office and said, "Now we have a movie, now we can go ahead!"

Once Hitchcock began to work, another of the qualities that make him a figure of increasing interest came into play: the amount of craft he brought to the table, almost unheard-of today because it can only be acquired by directing more than fifty features over three decades. Hitchcock was a master of every detail of the filmmaking process, meticulous enough to have Novak practice some of her movements to a metronome and to use the unhealthy green glow of a based-on-reality neon sign to cast a disturbing light on a hotel room. His solution to simulating Scottie's vertigo, done by having the camera simultaneously track backwards and zoom forward, was the result, he told Truffaut, of fifteen years of thinking about how best to show dizziness on screen.

So strong was Hitchcock's control of the medium that, working with cinematographer Robert Burks, he was able to bend busy San Francisco to his will. In place of the bustling reality, *Vertigo* creates a dream state city, a calm and ghostly metropolis, nearly deserted and not of this world, for the wealthy Madeline to solemnly drive around in her enormous Jaguar.

Hitchcock also shrewdly combined studio shots with location work, recreating in carefully measured detail on Hollywood sound stages such San Francisco landmarks as Ranshohoff's department store and Ernie's restaurant. The director even flew the establishment's co-owner and the maitre d' down from San

Francisco to appear in the scene and had real Ernie's food prepared for the extras to eat.

The mission at San Juan Bautista, ninety miles south of the
city, is a key *Vertigo* location, but in real life it doesn't have a critical bell tower. So Hitchcock constructed one in the studio and
superimposed it on the shot. His pure skill as a director is crucial
to making the story plausible and shows why screenwriter Taylor
later said, "I don't believe there's anybody who in purely cinematic terms is Hitchcock's equal."

Finally, more than Hitchcock's ability, what connects most
impressively to contemporary audiences is the strange fever
dream darkness of *Vertigo*'s themes, its moments of obsessive
eroticism, its tipping of the hat to sadism, masochism, fetish-
ism, necrophilia, and more garden-variety neuroses. The film's
continued ability to unsettle and disconcert without resorting to
graphic visuals underlines how modern and timeless its themes
and execution remain. And the fact that those themes were so
personal to the director create a told-from-the-inside feeling that
makes *Vertigo*, despite all its artifice, feel more real than Hitchcock's films usually do.

Interestingly enough for a film that became so celebrated, all
of *Vertigo*'s creators had problems with the finished product. Not
only had Hitchcock wanted Vera Miles, but he grumbled later that
the film had done poorly at the box office because Stewart looked
too old. Screenwriter Taylor said he would have preferred Ingrid Bergman for the female lead, and composer Herrmann said:
"They never should have made it in San Francisco and not with
Jimmy Stewart. I don't think that he would be that wild about any
woman. It should have been an actor like Charles Boyer. It should
have been left in New Orleans, or in a hot, sultry climate."

Yet despite all this carping, *Vertigo* continues to have the
strongest possible effect on audiences. Because Alfred Hitchcock
put so much of himself into the film, *Vertigo* plainly demands an
equally strong and personal response, and it invariably gets one.

What to Watch Next:
North by Northwest (1959), directed by Alfred Hitchcock.

Further Reading:
Hitchcock, by François Truffaut.
Hitchcock's Notebooks: An Authorized and Illustrated Look Inside the Creative Mind of Alfred Hitchcock, by Dan Aulier.

THE SIXTIES

T his is the rebellious decade, the years of turmoil and rev-
olution, and for once the image fits the films chosen. Up
to a point.

Only five films from this decade made the list, and taken as a
group they have something very particular in common: they start
with a familiar genre and fearlessly go their own way with it.

The Man Who Shot Liberty Valance is a Western where what's
right and true matters not. *The Gospel According to St. Matthew* is
the story of the life of Jesus as it had never been told before. Both
Point Blank and *Le Samouraï* are gangster films from a nightmar-
ish, nihilistic perspective. And *Kes* is a coming of age story that
never blinks. A new age was upon us.

THE MAN WHO SHOT LIBERTY VALANCE

1962

Directed by John Ford. Starring James Stewart, John Wayne, Lee Marvin.

The Western is not considered an especially poignant genre, a place where melancholy, regret, and even sadness can find a home alongside the cowboy, the six-shooter, and the plow that broke the plains. But it can be, if you know where to look.

If, for instance, you understand the reason John Wayne's Ethan Edwards slowly moves his left hand to cradle his right arm at the close of John Ford's *The Searchers*—it's a subtle but affecting tribute to the actor's mentor and friend, silent Western star Harry Carey—you can't watch that scene without being moved. And the same is true for *The Man Who Shot Liberty Valance*.

Starring Wayne, James Stewart, and Lee Marvin as a holy trinity of Western archetypes who jostle for supremacy in the wretched town of Shinbone, *Liberty Valance* reveals unexpected depths of emotion and even despair. It's a film of missed opportunities and lost illusions where, as British director and critic Lindsay Anderson neatly encapsulated, "the hero does not win and the winner is not heroic." Even director Ford, invariably dismissive about his own work, broke with form and called it "a story full of pathos and tragedy."

Liberty Valance is also a film that tells you everything you think you know is wrong, both in terms of the immediate plot laid out before you and the bigger picture clash of forces that created the modern West. It's a subversive film about the questionable nature of heroism that introduced the "when the legend becomes fact, print the legend" philosophy into the modern movie lexicon. So it's more than ironic that the driving force behind its creation should be John Ford.

For it was Ford, in films like *Stagecoach*, *My Darling Clementine*, and the cavalry trilogy (*Fort Apache*, *She Wore a Yellow Ribbon*, *Rio Grande*) who practically defined the dashing bravado of the Western genre. In *Liberty Valance* it's as if he uses the very icons he created to undermine the system he brought into being.

And this is Ford not going off on some avant-garde tangent (as if that were even possible); it's the director using the most classical means at his disposal to tell his image-busting story. Pared down with a vengeance and told with a simplicity that feels almost like ritual (imagine Carl Theodor Dreyer or even Robert Bresson directing a Western), *Liberty Valance* unfolds seamlessly, with not a frame wasted or out of place.

The actors Ford used were the best traditional Hollywood could provide, starting with Wayne at the peak of his influence, Stewart and his five Oscar nominations, and Marvin as the malefactor of the moment. They were joined by a luminous Vera Miles and a wide range of familiar faces as supporting actors, including Edmond O'Brien, Andy Devine, Woody Strode, Ken Murray, Strother Martin, Lee Van Cleef, and John Carradine.

The source material for *The Man Who Shot Liberty Valance* was a narrative of the same name by highly regarded Montana author Dorothy M. Johnson, named "the best short story writer of the century" by the Western Writers of America, a woman who also wrote the tales behind two other Hollywood movies, *A Man Called Horse* and *The Hanging Tree*.

The film was written by Willis Goldbeck and James Warner Bellah, who had previously combined on Ford's *Sergeant Rutledge*.

They kept the core of Johnson's unnerving story of crucial secrets long withheld, added supporting characters like Dutton Peabody, inebriated editor of the *Shinbone Star* (a scene-stealing O'Brien), made protagonist Ransom Stoddard more agreeable (something the casting of Stewart further emphasized), and placed the events in the broader context of a political battle for the soul of the West.

The film begins and ends with a framing sequence set in an unnamed state in what is meant to be the early modern West, the year 1910 by Dorothy Johnson's reckoning. A special train is headed for the town of Shinbone, and ancient lawman Link Appleyard (Devine) waits nervously at the station for it to arrive.

Who wouldn't be nervous with Ransom Stoddard—the state's first governor, multiterm senator, former ambassador, and potential vice presidential candidate—on board. The senator and his elegant wife Hallie (Miles) have made the special trip to attend the pauper's funeral of a man no one in town much remembers, a man named Tom Doniphon.

The trip is meant to be incognito, "purely personal," but once Stoddard is recognized, the polished politician in him takes over and he agrees to be interviewed about the issues of the day by the *Shinbone Star*. In the meantime Appleyard takes Hallie on a buckboard ride around a pleasant town that has changed mightily in the decades since she last was there.

A sense of regret suffuses these early scenes, an affecting air of what might have been. Hallie and Appleyard speak almost in code as he knows without her having to tell him where she wants to be taken, what she wants to see. It's an old crumbling ranch house surrounded by blooming cactus roses. If you've viewed the film before and know what's coming, the delicacy of these moments is enough to make you cry.

The scene shifts to a makeshift mortuary, where a handful of old-timers wait around for Tom Donophon's service. Asked point-blank by the newspapermen, "Why did you come all the way down here to bury a man," the senator attempts to avoid the question. But a nod from Hallie changes his mind, and the film flashes back to the early days of Shinbone as brawling frontier hamlet where the law of the gun ruled with no questions asked.

It's a much younger, fresh out of law school Stoddard we see now, a passenger on a stagecoach headed to Shinbone with $14.80 in his pocket and a pile of law books as his luggage.

But before he can get to town, the stage is robbed by a group of armed desperados. Outraged by their rude conduct toward a woman on board, Stoddard shouts, "What kind of men are you?" only to be beaten savagely with a silver-handled whip by the bandit leader (a marvelous Lee Marvin) who then rips his lawbooks in half and screams, "I'll teach you law, western law." The bandit's psychotic rage is so unnerving that even his men, deranged in their own right, feel the need to pull him off before he does too much damage.

Everyone in Shinbone, including the timid marshal, know that it was Liberty Valance—as fully a creature of the id as the monsters that devastated the Krell in *Forbidden Planet*—who did this terrible deed. But in this quasi-lawless era no one seems to have the jurisdiction—or the nerve—to bring him in. This outrages Stoddard, the first man in the place ever to speak up for law and order, and he wonders, "Is everyone in this country kill crazy?"

Stoddard is discovered half dead and brought to town by a very different kind of man, Tom Donophon. Played by Wayne with an easy charisma and supreme unconcern that is almost regal, Donophon believes in what's right but is in no way bothered by the fact that out here, "rights have to be defended by a gun." His description of Valance is apt and to the point: "He's the toughest man south of the Picketwire—next to me."

Archetypes both, Donophon and Stoddard stare at each other across a gulf of incomprehension and genial contempt as wide as the different worlds they represent. The only thing they have in common is their interest in Hallie, who has been Donophon's girl, the recipient of frequent gifts of cactus flowers from his ranch, until Stoddard comes to town and turns her head with his youthful idealism and determination to teach her how to read and write.

Director Ford and his screenwriters have shrewdly set all these conflicts against a backdrop of a battle for statehood between the farmers and townspeople of Shinbone, who want it because it promises order and security, and the state's cattlemen, who fight it because it threatens the future of the open range that makes their way of life possible. It's a conflict where the dark power of Liberty Valance, a hired gun for the ranchers, is fated to play a key role.

We know all about this clash over the future of the West, we know the way it turned out, with civilization triumphing over savagery, and we know that we're supposed to feel that it was all for the best. Yet if *The Man Who Shot Liberty Valance* is about anything, it is about delicately questioning aspects of that bit of received wisdom. The victory may have been inevitable, but is it just possible that something was lost along the way, that the price paid for advancing civilization was steeper than anyone anticipated? When John Ford and company ask a question like that, you have to listen.

What to Watch Next:
Stagecoach (1939), directed by John Ford.

Further Reading:
Searching for John Ford, by Joseph McBride.
Company of Heroes: My Life as an Actor in the John Ford Stock Company,
    by Harry Carey Jr.

THE GOSPEL ACCORDING TO ST. MATTHEW

1964

Directed by Pier Paolo Pasolini. Starring Enrique Irazoqui.

The Gospel According to St. Matthew is an acknowledged spiritual masterpiece from a completely unlikely source, the controversial Italian director Pier Paolo Pasolini. When veteran British critic Alexander Walker says it "grips the historical and psychological imagination like no other religious film I have ever seen," he is not alone in his belief.

And there have been other New Testament films. Many others. According to Roy Kinnard and Tim Davis in *Divine Images: A History of Jesus on the Screen*, some forty-seven actors have played Christ between 1897 and 1989, everyone from Jeffrey Hunter and Max Von Sydow to Zalman King and Willem Dafoe. And that's not even counting a beleaguered Jim Caviezel in Mel Gibson's *The Passion of the Christ*. Yet none of these films reached the heights that Pasolini's film did.

A Catholic turned atheist and a committed Marxist who got into trouble with both the party and the church for his unapologetic homosexuality, Pasolini was indicted for blasphemy and later made films like *Salo* that were declared obscene by Italian courts. His brutal murder at the age of fifty-three likely came at the hands of a seventeen-year-old boy he picked up in a bar. Not the expected biography for the creator of this kind of film.

Yet Pasolini's *St. Matthew* is justly considered to be one of the most spiritual films ever made. It won the grand prize of the International Catholic Film Office (as well as two awards at Venice) and was one of forty-five films recommended by the Vatican in 1996 in honor of the centenary of cinema.

It was an action that fellow director Franco Zeffirelli (whose films did not make the list) angrily condemned because the director was "not only mediocre but also an atheist." Yet no zealous true believer could have made a more effective work on the subject than this dynamic and respectful film.

For not only was Pasolini an implausible filmmaker for the subject matter, his film is an unlooked-for amalgam of disparate elements and influences not guaranteed to blend together smoothly. Yet—one is tempted to say miraculously—they do.

In the beginning were the words. The lines from Pasolini's spare Italian language screenplay are all from Matthew, and the director has found ways to make sentiments like "man shall not live by bread alone" and "the poor shall you always have with you" resound with the power of something potent being spoken for the first time.

If the words are traditional, the music is not. Yes, there is Bach, but there is also the forceful African Missa Luba and the blues of Son House. Odetta's version of "Motherless Child" makes an unexpected appearance, and the music Prokofiev wrote for the German slaughter of babies in Eisenstein's *Alexander Nevsky* fits perfectly behind Herod's massacre of the innocents. Even more nontraditional is the bleak setting of Calabria in southern Italy, which Pasolini chose after scouting and rejecting locations in Israel. Stunningly photographed in black and white by Tonino Della Coli, the parched hill towns and ruined buildings of the area seem to be part of the same universe as ancient Palestine, donkeys and all.

Pasolini's key decision was to shoot this story in the Italian tradition of neorealism, using nonprofessional actors for all the roles and selecting a young Spanish student named Enrique Irazoqui to play his charismatic Christ, a figure always on the move.

Determined to give Christ's words their full weight, Pasolini had Irazoqui's voice dubbed by actor Enrico Maria Salerno. And while the director did give cameos to people he knew—the novelist Natalia Ginzburg played Mary of Bethany and Pasolini's own mother played Mary grieving at the cross—what stays with you more are the marvelous faces of local people. Each one a book in itself, taken together they give this story exceptional resonance.

Because simplicity is his watchword, there is something elevating about Pasolini's conception, something of the deeply moving nature of the great silent films in what he has done. Everyone in the narrative seems to sense without coming out and actually saying it that they are part of what believers will come to call the greatest story ever told.

As Christ's life unfolds from a clearly surprised Joseph learning that his wife is pregnant to the crucifixion and resurrection, Pasolini does not shy away from unusual choices. His Angel Gabriel is a young girl and his Salome is an innocent rather than a practiced temptress. The director treats Christ's miracles with an effective, almost journalistic matter-of-factness and the film is aware of, yet finally indifferent to, the involvement of the Jews in Jesus' fate. That is simply not the story it wants to be telling.

The story *St. Matthew* does want to recount is of an activist, liberation theology–influenced Christ, always moving swiftly perhaps because he was conscious of how short his time was. Looking both ethereal and real, this Christ is an uncompromising idealist with burning eyes and an intense gaze, an enemy of hypocrisy and cant who furiously drives the moneychangers out of the temple. When he says "he that loves his mother and father more than me is not worthy" and insists "he that loseth his life for me shall find it," his presence is so forceful he all but compels agreement in his listeners.

Because he wanted to, in his own words, "remythicize" the events of Christ's life, because of the paradox that "I, a non-believer, was telling the story through the eyes of a believer," Pasolini ended up giving this tale an unshakable sense of actuality. We experience that much recounted life as if we were watching it for the first time, almost in newsreel format, as if it was something that happened to real people at a real moment in time. Pasolini may not have believed, but the dynamic power of belief is behind the work he does here.

Unwilling to be pigeon-holed either aesthetically or philosophically, Pasolini had a thoughtful response when asked how a Marxist could make a film like *The Gospel According to St. Matthew*. He called it "a reaction against the conformity of Marxism. The mystery of life and death and of suffering—and particularly of religion . . . is something that Marxists do not want to consider. But these are and always have been questions of great importance for human beings."

What to Watch Next:

Jesus of Montreal (1989), directed by Denys Arcand.

POINT BLANK

1967

Directed by John Boorman. Starring Lee Marvin, Angie Dickinson.

When John Boorman's *Point Blank* went public in the fall of 1967, the critics agreed on at least one thing: this was the most violent film anyone had ever seen.

"Sado-masochistic," said *Time* magazine, "a textbook in brutality," added *Variety*, with the *New York Times*' Bosley Crowther going one step further: "Holy Smokes, what a candid and calculatedly sadistic film it is! What a sheer exercise in creeping menace and crashing violence for their surface shock effects!"

Though current on-screen violence has escalated to a point where the havoc caused by the film's unstoppable Walker, played by Lee Marvin, seems almost clean and bloodless, watching *Point Blank* remains a disorienting experience. The film's edginess and unnerving style, the way it encroaches on our comfort zone, retain the ability to stimulate and disturb.

To understand how *Point Blank* does what it does, it's essential to start with the novel it's based on, a startling work in itself. That would be *The Hunter*, the first of more than twenty small gems the prolific Donald Westlake turned out under the Richard Stark pseudonym. The books center around a completely amoral antihero, known only as Parker, and memorably described by paperback blurb copy which reads, "Parker steals, Parker kills, it's a living."

As introduced in *The Hunter*, Parker is recovering from a double cross in which a business partner named Mal left him for dead. Even though Mal is now part of a complex and sophisticated criminal organization called The Outfit, Parker is determined to extract both his money and his revenge. *The Hunter* details how he methodically goes about doing this by acting tough and saying things like "I'd touch you once and you'd be dead. Look at me. You know this isn't a bluff."

Point Blank opens not with any tough behavior but with a fragmented and intentionally off-balance series of images. Lee Marvin's character, name changed from Parker to Walker, is lying on his back in a deserted Alcatraz, gunned down by the treacherous Mal (John Vernon) after robbing a syndicate money drop. In an intense, claustrophobic flashback, Walker remembers a reunion of sorts where Mal had wrestled him to the floor amid a flood of people and screamed in his ear, "You're my friend, Walker, I need your help, trust me, trust me."

Though the Alcatraz scenes don't take up much screen time, they are essential in establishing mood, which was why considerable efforts were made to shoot, for the first time ever, on location on what the publicity material called "the most feared, most mysterious, most famous prison in the nation, if not the world."

Five loads of moviemaking equipment had to be trucked to San Francisco from the MGM studios in Culver City and then barged to Alcatraz. Two miles of cable strung throughout the prison gave it temporary lighting and some heat, but that didn't lessen the feeling of dread enhanced by real life memento mori like a slogan penciled on a wall of the prison morgue: "Bob's Mortuary. You stab 'em. We slab 'em."

Despite being badly wounded, Walker somehow drags himself into the waters off Alcatraz, and the very next shot has him on a tour boat circling the place, listening to a guide saying that swimming into shore from there is impossible. On the boat Walker is approached by Yost (Keenan Wynn), a bullet-headed man who for unspecified reasons of his own offers to help him locate Mal, his wife, and the $93,000 that Walker insists is his share of the stolen money.

At every stage of the journey, however, Walker finds himself overmatched in ways he didn't anticipate. He finds his wife but cannot control her behavior. He shoots holes in empty mattresses. He is clumsy, prone to breaking things unintentionally. He is even made to look silly, sitting in a woman's bathrobe touching up a black eye with makeup.

The crime conglomerate Walker is up against is the opposite of all this. It is run by svelte, well-tailored men operating out of posh suites, one of whom tells Walker, "Things aren't done this way anymore, I assure you." Walker's response when another higher-up insists that "no business corporation in the world would honor a debt like that" is a taut "if you don't, you're dead."

Walker's only human contact for much of his quest is Chris, his wife's sister, played by Angie Dickinson, a character invented to give the film a quasi-love interest the book did without.

To further emphasize how cut off Walker is, he and Chris have one of the oddest, most provocative of screen fights. She gets angry and begins battering him about the head and shoulders. At first, by instinct, he attempts to cover up. But then he suddenly stops, standing immobile as she hits him over and over again. Instead of doing any damage, Chris only succeeds in exhausting herself, collapsing at Walker's feet as he turns to impassively flick on the remote control TV.

Walker finally works his way up to Brewster, an organization kingpin played by Carroll O'Connor in a wonderful pre-Archie Bunker turn. Their critical confrontation was described by director Boorman as the only problem that had to wait until after the script was written to be solved.

"I wanted to suggest in this scene that Walker was never going to get what he wanted—that the money he was seeking was merely a symbol of revenge," Boorman explained. "And we never determined precisely how to do the scene until I got Marvin and O'Connor together in my house one weekend and we rehearsed the confrontation in different ways.

"They improvised, and gradually the tension increased until it grew so great that suddenly O'Connor burst out laughing. And that was so wrong, it was right. And he did it again, and this time he said, 'Don't ask me for money, I never carry any with me. I only use checks. I've only got eleven dollars on me.' That's what we used in the completed film," where the exchange causes Walker to slump into a sofa, realizing finally that he is out of his depth, that the rules have been changed.

One of the secrets of *Point Blank*'s success is that it showcases genre material presented by a resolutely non-genre director who is at least as much at home with unconventional films like *Zardoz*, *Excalibur*, and *Leo the Last* as he was with this film and the triple Oscar-winning *Deliverance*.

Boorman made *Point Blank* in an indirect, highly stylized manner that gave Walker's world an air of spooky not-quite reality. The plot, the director insisted, was not permitted to "get in the way of other things."

"Watching film is very like dreaming," Boorman has said. "There's a mystical quality that's very exciting. So I try to make my films in a way that will touch the spectator's dream world: to use areas of uncertainty, touching the twilight of people's thoughts—because this is where communication takes place."

Working with editor Henry Berman, Booman opted for some very audacious cutting, often intermixing dream, memory, and reality. As the director has explained, "The fragmentation was necessary to give the character and the situations ambiguity, to suggest another meaning beyond the immediate plot."

Especially chilling is a scene that starts with Walker rolling over and over in bed in an embrace with Chris and then moves seamlessly to Walker embracing his ex-wife, his ex-wife embracing Mal, Mal embracing Chris, and finally back to Walker and Chris.

"The elliptical cutting is from Renais and especially the time-juggling of '*Hiroshima, mon amour*,'" Boorman told an interviewer. "A lot of Hollywood directors and writers have told me that they were influenced by the techniques of 'Point Blank,' but they were unfamiliar with the *nouvelle vague* directors and they didn't know that I had taken the technique from someone else."

Also helping set the mood was *Point Blank*'s impeccable sense of place. Though the film begins and ends in San Francisco (at Alcatraz and Fort Point specifically), Boorman chose Los Angeles for his prime location because "we wanted a modern city."

Beautifully photographed by the veteran Philip Lathrop (who also shot Walter Hill's *The Driver* and Sam Peckinpah's *The Killer Elite*) *Point Blank* is a classic daylight noir, flooding the frame with sharp, almost blinding sunlight. Using previously ignored locations like the Los Angeles River's concrete flood channels and the massive support columns that hold up the city's freeways, the film has a great eye for the beauty inherent in emptiness and sterility, presenting an LA that is removed and distant but still undeniably striking. The end of the road for the American landscape.

More impressive than the setting is Lee Marvin. Handsome, magnetic, and undeniably rugged, the actor pours himself into this role in a controlled, focused performance as a man both implacable and unreachable. Nothing moves him, nothing human makes a dent in his quest.

The character's name change from Parker to Walker is key here: this is a man who is always relentlessly moving forward, most memorably in a scene where he strides tirelessly through an empty Los Angeles airport hallway, his shoes making insistent clicks on the hard floor. Every step he takes has the inexorable quality of legend, even of fate.

Remarkable for a film so hard-edged, *Point Blank* never loses its aura of ambiguity, its ability to make us question what we've seen. There is even an argument, encouraged by lines of dialogue like "didn't he die or something," "you're supposed to be dead," and Chris's angry "you died at Alcatraz, all right" which posits that Walker may in fact have died, that this entire story may be a kind of last gasp vision that unfolds in the moments before his death on the Rock. Serene, mythic, redolent of existential despair, *Point Blank* never gives its secrets away.

What to Watch Next:
Bad Day at Black Rock (1955), directed by John Sturges.

Further Reading:
The Hunter, by Richard Stark.

LE SAMOURAÏ

1967

Directed by Jean-Pierre Melville. Starring Alain Delon.

With a Parisian hit man less emotional than a clock for a hero, Jean-Pierre Melville's *Le Samouraï* is an austere poem of crime, a fatalistic exercise in mythmaking and transcendent style.

A pivotal modern director, Melville, who died in 1973 at age fifty-five, is considered one of the spiritual fathers of the French New Wave and is perhaps best known to American audiences for his cameo role in Jean-Luc Godard's *Breathless* as the literary celebrity interviewed by Jean Seberg at Paris's Orly Airport. "What is your greatest ambition?" she asks. His reply: "To become immortal and then to die."

Among the filmmakers who admire Melville is action impresario John Woo, who says the director "has always been my spiritual idol" and calls *Le Samouraï* "the closest thing to a perfect movie that I have ever seen."

On the surface, Woo's explosive bloodbaths couldn't be further from a crime film that is as precisely cut as a diamond. What is shared, however, is a passion for the genre, a compulsion to romanticize, and a feeling for antiheroes who live according to their own austere codes.

The director, born Jean-Pierre Grumbach in 1917 and a fanatical film buff from his youth, was so passionate about things American that he changed his name to honor the author of *Moby-Dick* and never looked back.

Melville directed thirteen films, including classics about the French resistance like *Army of Shadows*, but he had a particular affinity for his half dozen or so gangster films where fate decides everything and everyone is complicit in evil to one degree or another.

Melville used actors ranging from Jean-Paul Belmondo to Lino Ventura for his trench-coated, cigarette-smoking anti-heroes, but Alain Delon, with his icily beautiful blank face and the dead eyes of a killer angel, perfectly suited the director's style, especially here.

As British critic Tom Milne wrote in a widely quoted essay, "the impossibility of love, of friendship, of communication, of self-respect, of life itself: all the themes from Melville's work are gathered up in one tight ball in 'Le Samouraï.'"

The film opens with a stark, monochromatic image of Jef Costello (Delon) lying on the bed in his barely furnished room on rue Lord Byron. A chirping bird is his only companion, stockpiles of Vitel water and Gitanes cigarettes his only provisions, and the smoke he blows into the air and the rain coming down outside are the only things that move.

Once Jef does get moving, it's first to set up an elaborate alibi that involves his selfless girlfriend Jeanne Legrange (Nathalie Delon, the actor's wife at the time). Then he pulls off a smooth hit on a nightclub owner after the most minimal of verbal exchanges: "Who are you?" "It doesn't matter." "What do you want?" "To kill you."

Well-planned as this crime is, the walls start to close in on Jef, starting with his coming face-to-face with a potential witness, the club's beautiful pianist (Cathy Rosier). Then a crack police inspector (Francois Perier) has Jef trailed despite a lack of evidence, and the people who hired him show signs of breaking faith. How can Jef, the lone wolf who says without bragging or exaggeration, "I never lose, not really," retain control of his destiny? Just wait and see.

Never an effusive director, Melville pared his style down as far as it could go in *Le Samouraï*, muting the colors to the point where he chose the female bullfinch as the bird that is Jef's only friend because of its simple black-and-white plumage. And Delon, who says fewer words in the entire picture than some actors say in a single scene, is just as he should be as The Ghost Who Walks, a bloodless criminal obsessed with giving his hat brim just the right turn.

Melville focuses on favorite themes here, on his view of crime as simultaneously theater and poetry. His criminals so share a secret behavioral code that almost no dialogue is necessary between them: when Jef drives into a clandestine garage with a stolen car, the license plates are immediately changed without anyone saying a word. When he wants a weapon, he snaps his fingers and one materializes.

The director was also fascinated by the links between criminals and those who enforce the law and the intricate mechanics of their parallel operations. When Jef steals a car, he uses a massive key ring that mimics official equipment, and the standoff between Jef and the police's intricately organized attempts to trap him on the Metro, a system he knows as intimately as the Phantom knows the space under the Paris Opera, is one of *Le Samouraï*'s most bravura sequences.

Yet despite this attention to detail, Melville was the first to almost brag in Rui Nogueira's book-length interview *Melville on Melville* that "I am careful never to be realistic . . . What I do is false. Always." Stylization was his overriding concern, down to the film editor's white gloves he has all his protagonists, Jef Costello included, put on before committing crimes.

Equally artificial is the quote from *The Book of Bushido* that starts the film: "There is no greater solitude than the samurai's unless it be the tiger in the jungle." It sounds too perfect to be real, and in fact Melville claimed he made it up. However what is genuine about *Le Samouraï*, the passion that Melville felt for this quintessentially American genre, is strong enough to make this one of the glories of the modern gangster film, elegant, romantic, and unforgettable.

What to Watch Next:
Le Cercle Rouge (1970), directed by Jean-Pierre Melville.

Further Reading:
Melville on Melville, by Rui Nogueira.

KES

1969

Directed by Ken Loach. Starring David Bradley.

Starting in the late 1950s, inspired by the Angry Young Men of their own theater as well as the cinematic ferment in France, the filmmakers of the British New Wave created a series of socially conscious movies that made a name for themselves because of the honest way they dealt with working-class life.

But while films like *Room at the Top*, *Saturday Night and Sunday Morning*, *This Sporting Life*, and *The Loneliness of the Long Distance Runner* were winning praise around the world for their grittiness, they were irritating a pair of younger British filmmakers who felt they weren't realistic enough, that the compromises these pictures made, including the use of professional actors in starring roles, kept them from having the complete ring of truth.

Determined to get closer to real experience, director Ken Loach and producer Tony Garnett left the protective environs of their work at the BBC and formed Kestrel Films to turn the Barry Hines book *A Kestrel for a Knave* into a theatrical feature called simply *Kes*.

It was only Loach's second theatrical feature (he'd previously done *Cathy Come Home* and others for the BBC and *Poor Cow* for the big screen). And though he was to direct dozens more, including *Raining Stones, My Name Is Joe, Land and Freedom,* and the Cannes Palme d'Or–winning *The Wind That Shakes the Barley, Kes* remains Loach's standout film, a perennial on ten-best-British-films lists and a favorite of thoughtful directors like the Dardennes brothers and the late Krzysztof Kieslowski.

As with all of Loach's films, *Kes* has a socially conscious aspect, a desire to point out society's flaws with an eye toward correcting them, which in this particular case meant what Loach saw as the failures of Britain's callous, unfeeling educational system to deal with bright young people in dire economic straits.

But what makes this film stand out is that those concerns are never allowed to overwhelm *Kes*'s human dimensions, its personal, heart-piercing story of a young boy's passion for a kestrel falcon, a particular tale that tellingly illuminates the overall theme of the stifling of souls.

It is in *Kes* that Loach's longtime watchwords of "observation not manipulation" and his frequent use of nonprofessional actors (in a way that echoes Vittorio De Sica's earlier *Bicycle Thieves*) find their most effective expression. "You let something happen and evolve, to me that's the key to it," he said in an interview recorded for the film's first American DVD release in 2011. "Just give people the space to be who they are."

Flowering most under Loach's philosophy was David Bradley, a natural actor completely at ease in front of the camera who gives a fine performance as Billy, the film's fourteen-year-old protagonist. Bradley not only lived in Yorkshire's Barnsley, the coal-mining town in the north of England where *Kes* was filmed, he went to the same school where Barry Hines set his original book. More than that, as Loach recognized, he had "the ability to make you weep for him simply by doing what he's doing."

Kes starts with an early morning scene of Billy sharing his bed with his older brother Jud. The alarm clock goes off— Jud, like almost every other adult male in town has to report to deadening work in the coal pits—and the two boys lapse into the hostile bickering, inevitably initiated by the thuggish Jud, that characterizes their relationship.

Barely visible in what must be hand-me-down clothes, scrappy ragamuffin Billy, ignored as much as possible by that brother and a single mother who's been abandoned by her husband, is keenly but nonjudgmentally observed as someone who is barely holding his own in his own life.

Billy, however, is no martyr but a difficult handful in his own way, an amoral sneak thief who takes chocolate from the local newsdealer as well as milk off a passing truck. Not for nothing does the newsdealer say to him, "I wouldn't be your teacher for all the coal in Barnsley" and "God help your future employer." The story of *Kes* is the story of how this boy, the product of an everyone-for-himself world and no better than he should be, learns how to care about another living creature and what the benefits as well as the ultimate cost of that caring can be.

Though Barnsley itself is blighted with factories and those coal pits, it is next door to a forested area that cinematographer Chris Menges, the future two-time Oscar winner (*The Mission*, *The Killing Fields*) making his feature debut, brings to sun-dappled life with a series of fluid images.

It's here that Billy catches a glimpse of a kestrel in flight, a sighting that, like any *amour fou*, strikes him to the quick in an instant. Maybe it's the bird's sense of ease, maybe the freedom of movement that the boy conspicuously lacks, but whatever it is Billy is hooked.

Tracking the kestrel to its nest in the wall of a ruined monastery, he makes off with one of the chicks, names it Kes, and, ignoring his brother's "you couldn't train a flea" taunt, vows to master falconry as soon as possible. When the library insists he has to wait for borrowing privileges, impatient Billy promptly lifts a volume on the subject from a secondhand bookshop.

Billy is soon obsessed in the best possible way with his bird, eager to find out all there is to know about its care and feeding. A boy who instinctively resists rules and discipline of every sort turns patient and purposeful, following the book's every instruction with a careful precision. When the bird flies to Billy's fist for the first time, it's impossible not to feel as exhilarated as he does.

In order for audiences to completely understand what this bird means to this lonely boy trapped in a world not of his making, the film devotes considerable time to showing us that environment, not only Billy's meager home life but also how he is systematically brutalized by authoritarian teachers. Plus a delusional physical education coach who fantasizes that he is Bobby Charlton playing for England in the World Cup. Even the fate of leaving school for deadening work is an improvement simply because it means getting paid for another experience you hate.

Perhaps the high point of *Kes* is the classroom moment when Billy, encouraged by his school's only involved teacher, reveals himself to his classmates and talks about his enthusiasm for falconry in general and Kes specifically.

"It ain't a pet, it can't be tamed, it's wild, that's what makes it great," Billy says, his words coming out all in a rush. Billy's pride, his passion, his ability to find joy in the midst of desperation, is mesmerizing. His goal, he says, is to have the bird "fly free," without a tether, a kind of metaphor for what we of course wish for him. *Kes* cuts too close to the bone to allow for that kind of ending, but when that teacher sees Billy fly Kes and calls it "the thrill of a lifetime," only the most hard-hearted will not agree.

What to Watch Next:
Sweet Sixteen (2002), directed by Ken Loach.

Further Reading:
A Kestrel for a Knave, by Barry Hines.

THE SEVENTIES

N o one is more surprised than I am to realize that I found room for only two films from the 1970s among my favorites. Wasn't this decade supposed to represent one of the great flowerings of cinema, a time when independent voices and different ways of doing things changed everything? To quote Evelyn Waugh's *Scoop*, "Up to a point."

I was certainly excited at the time to have the great Seventies classics arrive on screen, films like *Jaws, Dog Day Afternoon, All the President's Men, Taxi Driver, Star Wars, Annie Hall, The Deer Hunter,* and *Apocalypse Now.* In fact, now that I'm listing them all, I wonder if I haven't made a terrible mistake in not including more of them on my list.

But the truth remains that as much as there is to admire in these films, as much as I enjoyed them at the time of release, I have not felt the pull to revisit them or, when I have done so, I've not found them as compelling as the two films that are on the list, *Chinatown* and *The Godfather,* movies I can see again and again without loss of interest or enthusiasm. That's what makes them my favorites.

THE GODFATHER

1972

Directed by Francis Ford Coppola. Starring Marlon Brando,
Al Pacino, James Caan, Robert Duvall.

It starts with sad notes on a trumpet and an undertaker's shaky credo, "I believe in America." It ends as a critical and popular sensation, the first motion picture to take in a million dollars a day, nominated for ten Oscars and the opening salvo of a trilogy that has taken in something like a billion dollars in revenue worldwide. It could only be *The Godfather.*

Francis Ford Coppola's dark side of the American dream story of Michael Corleone's rise to power as the modern successor to his aging father, Don Vito, is a two hour and fifty-five minute epic that's as great and lasting an American film as the past half century has produced. As its outline emerges gradually from a welter of incident, a thrust and parry of action and reaction, what we have is a tale of betrayal, disappointment, and revenge that demands to be described as Shakespearean.

It's not only that this film, like those sixteenth-century dramas, can be watched repeatedly without loss of interest. It's that *The Godfather* is overflowing with life, rich with all the grand emotions and vital juices of existence, up to and including blood.

And its deaths, like that of Hotspur in *Henry IV, Part I*, continue to shock no matter how often we've watched them unfold.

Yet though its characters are as outsized as any of Shakespeare's nobility, *The Godfather* also benefits by the attention it pays to softening detail, to small moments like a little girl dancing on hulking Tessio's shoes at Connie Corleone's wedding or its authentic sense of Italian family dining.

Excessive but natural, larger than life yet always lifelike, *The Godfather*'s people are grounded in an underlying everyday reality that is completely recognizable and in effect vouches for the verisimilitude of the film's more baroque Mafia sequences. Because Coppola is so familiar with the Italianness of this family-centered world, because he knows it so intimately, he's able to convincingly humanize its operatic, occasionally grotesque characters.

A different kind of duality was expressed via the collaboration between director/cowriter (with novelist Mario Puzo) Coppola and meticulous cinematographer Gordon Willis, dubbed "the prince of darkness" by his colleague Conrad Hall for his preference for the blackest hues.

Both literally and metaphysically, *The Godfather* alternates between darkness and light, between the don's funereal study and his daughter's sunlit wedding, between the pure love of Michael for his Sicilian bride and the mess his siblings make of their marriages. And, most famously, in the intercutting between the baptism of Connie's son (played by the infant future director Sophia Coppola) and Michael Corleone's brutal assumption of power.

None of this, of course, would succeed without the exceptional ensemble acting. Included were familiar faces like Sterling Hayden as a corrupt police captain and Richard Conte as a rival mobster, the brilliant John Cazale as haunted brother Fredo, and veteran character performances like Abe Vigoda's Tessio and Richard Castellano as Clemenza, a workaday mobster with a "leave the gun, take the cannoli" attitude.

And when it comes to stars like Al Pacino, James Caan, Robert Duvall, and Diane Keaton, it's almost shocking to realize how early in their careers this film caught them, at a time when they were light on their feet and the characters they played had yet to turn into Mafia clichés. Here is Duvall's impeccable gravitas as consigliere Tom Hagen, Keaton's unmannered freshness as WASP princess Kay Adams, Caan's volcanic, hand-biting energy as Sonny Corleone, and, most of all, Pacino's core unknowability as Michael Corleone.

For if Caan's Sonny telegraphs every action, Pacino's Michael works so much under the surface he could be thinking anything, which makes his transition from war hero and outsider to his father's ruthless successor so compelling. It's a transition, interestingly enough, that the don, like many another immigrant father, is strikingly ambivalent about. "I never wanted this for you," he says to Michael in their celebrated garden tête-à-tête near the film's conclusion. "I thought that when it was your time that you would be the one to hold the strings."

Looming above all these players, even for the long stretches when he's not on screen, is Marlon Brando as Don Vito Corleone. It's a commanding performance in every sense, part realistic, part theatrical, filled with showy gestures and real artistry. For every scene that skirts the edge of excess, there are beautiful, almost unnoticed moments, like the magisterial way the don plays with a kitten while conducting business. And it's in his foibles, his fondness for fresh fruit and his family, that we come to feel the essential humanity of the man.

The wonder of *The Godfather* is not only how undated it remains, it's that, given the chaos that attended every step of its creation, this film turned out as well as it did.

For almost every creative decision, even the ones that seem obvious now, was taken in the face of intense opposition by someone. Even the original novel, which ended up on the best-seller list for sixty-seven weeks and sold tens of millions of copies worldwide, was unlikely. Its author, Mario Puzo, had never known a real gangster when he began to write a book that he initially called "Mafia."

Starting the movie train rolling was Peter Bart, later the editor of *Variety* but in 1967 a key executive working under Paramount head of production Robert Evans. It was Bart who bought Puzo's novel on the basis of an outline and one-hundred-plus pages of manuscript. Al Ruddy was brought in to produce, though his best known credit was the TV series *Hogan's Heroes*. Directors Fred Zinneman, Richard Brooks, Costa Gavras, and Peter Yates turned the project down, and when it was offered to Francis Ford Coppola, he initially said no as well.

In his early thirties, Coppola was better known as a screenwriter (a shared Oscar for *Patton*) than as the director of *You're a Big Boy Now* and *The Rain People*. Wanting independence from Hollywood, he'd started American Zoetrope in San Francisco, but deepening financial troubles made him agree to deal with a book he had at one time dismissed as "cheap and sensational."

Though it's difficult to think of the film without him, Puzo and Coppola's first choice for the don, Marlon Brando, nearly didn't get the part. Paramount president Stanley Jaffe was against the idea until, in a situation that has since crept into Hollywood legend, Brando agreed to do a screen test in makeup.

Given that the studio had made a fuss about casting unknowns, *Variety* couldn't resist a needling headline when the lead role was announced: "No Stars for 'Godfather' Cast—Just Someone Named Brando."

For two other key roles, Coppola turned to Caan and Duvall, actors he'd worked with before in *The Rain People*. He also pushed for Pacino, then mainly known as a New York stage actor who'd debuted against Patty Duke in *Me, Natalie* and gone on to the little-seen *Panic in Needle Park*.

Some of the other casting choices seemed equally eccentric. Gianni Russo, a nonprofessional with an unlimited supply of nerve, talked himself into the role of Connie's husband Carlo Rizzi. And Lennie Montana, a professional wrestler who was serving as a bodyguard when producer Ruddy met him, was cast as Luca Brasi. According to Harlan Lebo's *The Godfather Legacy*, Montana "used muscle-tensing tricks learned in his days as a wrestler to make his face purple and his veins swell" in his death scene.

Just as interesting were the people who didn't get parts. Robert De Niro was an unsuccessful candidate for Sonny Corleone and was actually cast as Paulie Gatto, the don's bodyguard. If he hadn't left the picture to take the role Al Pacino vacated in *The Gang That Couldn't Shoot Straight*, De Niro wouldn't have been able to play the young Vito Corleone in *Godfather II*.

Though Paramount toyed with the idea of shooting the film in Cleveland, Cincinnati, and even Kansas City, Manhattan proved to be the inevitable choice, though coping with 120 locations was one of the several stressors on director Coppola. He also had to deal with lobbying from the Italian-American Civil Rights League (which led to the removal of the few uses of "Mafia" and "Cosa Nostra" in the script) and pressures from the studio to keep costs low.

Rumors were rife that director Elia Kazan, who'd worked with Brando with great success, was going to replace him. "He even dreamed," writes Lebo, "about Kazan coming up to him on the set and taking over the reins—a director's equivalent of the student nightmare about missing final exams." Coppola did get help, but it was from Robert Towne, who wrote that key garden scene between Brando and Pacino and was publicly and generously thanked by Coppola when he picked up his screenwriting Oscar.

Once it opened, *The Godfather* became an enormous success, and the public's will to know focused on all kinds of unlikely areas, including the horse's head (a real one that was obtained from a rendering plant in New Jersey) that ended up in studio head Jack Woltz's bed. "There were many people killed in that movie," the fed-up director was quoted as saying, "but everyone worries about the horse."

Bringing everything full circle, the movie *Godfather* led to the publication of books about the intersection of truth and fiction. Puzo himself, in a collection called *The Godfather Papers and Other Confessions*, wrote of an encounter he had in a Los Angeles restaurant with Frank Sinatra, often mentioned as a possible model for singer Johnny Fontane.

Sinatra, Puzo wrote, "started to shout abuse . . . The worst thing he called me was a pimp, which rather flattered me. But what hurt was that there he was, a northern Italian, threatening me, a southern Italian, with physical violence. That was roughly equivalent to Einstein pulling a knife on Al Capone."

What to Watch Next:
Godfather II (1974), directed by Francis Ford Coppola.

Further Reading:
The Annotated Godfather: The Complete Screenplay, by Jenny M. Jones.
The Godfather Legacy, by Harlan Lebo

CHINATOWN

1974

Directed by Roman Polanski. Starring Jack Nicholson,
Faye Dunaway, John Huston.

Roman Polanski remembered. So did Robert Towne, but not always the same things. It was the fusion of their memories and sensibilities, sometimes divergent, sometimes in sync, that made *Chinatown* and its depiction of mendacity, amorality, and despair in 1930s Los Angeles so compelling.

A native of Poland who didn't move to California until he was in his thirties, director Polanski remembered back to a time, he confessed at the film's 1974 release, when "as a kid you are into a detective book and mother is calling you to table and you call, 'One more moment, one more page.' . . . Why do you love them, why is Raymond Chandler so terrific? Because he won't let you rest."

Decades later, talking to author James Greenberg for a book-length study of his career, Polanski returned to the theme of Chandler, one of the writers whose work defined modern Los Angeles, saying that "in 'Chinatown' what I was trying to create was this Philip Marlowe atmosphere, which I'd never seen in the movies the way I got it in the books of Dashiell Hammett or Raymond Chandler."

Screenwriter Robert Towne, who grew up in Los Angeles, remembered not only what he had read but what he had seen and experienced. His influences were those of the native, starting with Carey McWilliams's often forgotten account of the real life California water wars in his classic *Southern California Country: An Island on the Land.*

Also an influence for Towne was a cover story and photo essay in *West*, the long-gone *Los Angeles Times* Sunday magazine, titled "Raymond Chandler's L.A." It wasn't necessarily Chandler's stories that intrigued the writer, but the memories those pictures evoked.

As Towne wrote in an introduction to a private press printing of his *Chinatown* script, "The photos in *West*—a Plymouth convertible under an old streetlight in the rain outside Bullock's Wilshire, for example—reminded me there still was time to preserve much of the city's past on film, just as McWilliams had shown me that it was my past as well." Towne started working on the screenplay almost immediately.

What makes *Chinatown* so exceptional is not only how many things it does but how it does them, how its multiple influences nourish each other. Though it's a tale squarely in the dark tradition of film noir, it manages to combine a serious historical theme detailing the story of water use in Los Angeles with the character-driven narrative drive it has in common with the best of Chandler's detective stories.

But even *Chinatown*'s nods to the film noir frame prove to be deceptive, because this is a highly modernized noir, using plot elements like a prominent bandage on detective J.J. Gittes's sliced nose as well as an unexpected ending (which Towne and Polanski strongly disagreed about) that would have been scandalous back in the day.

"I wanted the style of the period conveyed by a scrupulously accurate reconstruction of decor, costume, and idiom," Polanski told Greenberg, "not by a deliberate imitation, in 1973, of thirties film technique." In fact, that traditional look, extending to the film's sepia-tinted credits, lulls us into thinking that nothing seriously out of the ordinary is going to happen on screen, when the reality is just the reverse.

To make that reconstruction a reality, Polanski was able to call on the cream of 1970s below-the-line talent, many of whom were among *Chinatown*'s eleven Oscar nominees: cinematographer John Alonzo, production designer Richard Sylbert, editor Sam O'Steen, costume designer Anthea Sylbert, and composer Jerry Goldsmith. (In a year dominated by *Godfather II*, only Towne's original screenplay was a winner.)

The director, picking up on Towne's originating thought, was equally determined to use real Los Angeles locations, places like the Echo Park Lake and the Los Angeles City Council chambers, whenever possible. He adroitly repurposed real buildings for fictional purposes, for instance using what is now the Archer School for Girls on Sunset Boulevard in West LA for the Mar Vista rest home where a fast getaway on a circular driveway was the order of the day.

Notoriously meticulous about everything, Polanski, aided by casting directors Mike Fenton and Jane Feinberg, also made sure the casting choices were exactly right down to the smallest speaking parts. Their names are not always familiar, but selecting actors like Rance Howard (Ron's father) for an irate farmer, Charles Knapp for a mortician, and Allan Warnick for a snippy Hall of Records clerk adds considerably to *Chinatown*'s overall effect.

Chinatown's plot is intricacy itself, beginning with a highly unlikely premise for a hard-boiled tale: who is playing games with the water system of Los Angeles and why. More conventional themes like solving a murder and understanding the motivations of a mysterious woman, are carefully woven around this central core, but though these are genre staples Towne has structured things so adroitly that we don't see the whole picture even when we think we do.

The private eye determined to solve these mysteries, the individual through whose eyes everything in *Chinatown* unfolds, sounds like a version of Raymond Chandler's Philip Marlowe, but this proves to be one of the film's numerous departures from tradition.

Because if Chandler's idealistic tarnished knight was, in the author's words, "a man of honor . . . the best man in his world and a good enough man for any world," Jake Gittes is anything but. His quest may be lonely and his determination to find the truth just as intense, but his morals and his empathy leave a lot to be desired.

Towne wrote the Gittes role with his friend Jack Nicholson in mind, and the actor's impeccable presentation shows why. With his slick suits, slicker hair, and great cat-who-swallowed-the-canary look, Gittes is a cocky, unscrupulous know-it-all who's got all the angles covered. Or so he thinks.

For it is the business of the personal and political complexities of *Chinatown*'s plot to turn Gittes into the mark, someone who is more of a fool than he thought possible. From the first moment he meets Faye Dunaway's faultlessly presented Evelyn Mulwray, a woman who is hiding more than Gittes can imagine, he falls into a rabbit hole of corruption and venality that swallows him whole.

The key player in all of this is Evelyn's father, the shadowy power broker Noah Cross, persuasively played by John Huston. Screenwriter Towne has said he considers the selection of Huston to be the film's key piece of casting, and the actor's ability to marry garrulous geniality with lurking malevolence is irreplaceable. To hear Noah Cross caress lines like "politicians, ugly buildings, and whores all get respectable if they last long enough" and "I still got a few teeth in my head and a few friends in town" is to shiver despite yourself.

It is inevitable, of course, that this film will end up in LA's Chinatown, the location that is Gittes's nightmare, the place where his good intentions as an idealistic young police officer went bad once upon a time.

The film's closing line—"Forget it, Jake; it's Chinatown"—is justly celebrated, but there is another piece of dialogue that best encapsulates the spirit of this thrilling and disturbing film, and, not surprisingly, it's spoken by Noah Cross. "Most people," he says, "never have to face the fact that at the right time and right place, they're capable of anything." Anything at all.

What to Watch Next:
Criss Cross (1949), directed by Robert Siodmak.
Los Angeles Plays Itself (2003), by Thom Anderson.

Further Reading:
Roman Polanski: A Retrospective, by James Greenberg.
Southern California Country: An Island on the Land, by Carey McWilliams.

THE EIGHTIES

Of the three films from this decade, two of them are documentaries and the third, *Distant Voices, Still Lives,* is a memory film of such fierce specificity it could almost double as a documentary on British working-class life during and just after World War II.

Documentaries had of course been a part of film since the very beginning. The Lumiere brothers' *Workers Leaving the Factory* was the first film ever shown theatrically, and *Arrival of a Train at a Station* was perhaps the first to cause panic in the seats with audiences unused to seeing reality duplicated on a screen.

In some ways, both *The Day After Trinity* and *First Contact* shocked me as those first docs had shocked audiences back in the day. Each of these films reshaped my view of the world, the former by showing me how much I'd misunderstood the people behind the first atomic bomb, the second by allowing me to eavesdrop on a historical phenomenon I would have thought had vanished centuries before. You can't ask more of documentaries than that.

THE DAY AFTER TRINITY

1981 ·

Directed by Jon Else.

For drama, pathos, and potentially catastrophic effect on the world we live in, no modern story quite compares to the one behind the creation of the atomic bomb. And *The Day After Trinity* tells it in a way that has the power to completely turn your head around, to change the way you view both history and personal psychology.

Directed and cowritten by Jon Else, nominated for the best documentary Oscar and winner of a Peabody Award, *Trinity* does more than detail the astonishing story of how a group of scientists uncovered one of nature's deepest secrets and constructed the most destructive weapon the world had ever seen.

Equally absorbing, if not more so, is the human story, the revelation of exactly who made the bomb and why they made it. *Trinity* poses and answers the provocative question asked by physicist Hans Bethe early on: "You may well ask why people with kind hearts and humanistic feelings would go to work on weapons of mass destruction."

For while it may be logical to assume, given the savage and irreversibly destructive power of nuclear weapons, that only the coldest, most inhuman and unemotional of scientists would consider working on it, the reverse was the case. The bomb wasn't constructed by unfeeling robots who were human in name only. It was conceived of and executed by warm, cultured, empathetic individuals. It was made, in short, by people like us.

This was the case in spades with J. Robert Oppenheimer, the brilliant theoretical physicist who spearheaded the Manhattan Project that built the first bomb. It may seem inconceivable that a man educated by New York's Ethical Culture Society, someone who devoured sixteenth-century French poetry as well as physics, who knew six languages and learned Sanskrit so he could read the *Bhagavad Gita* in the original, could have been the driving force behind a weapon that could end up obliterating the world as we know it, but this was in fact the case.

Else, a veteran documentarian whose numerous credits include *Eyes on the Prize: America's Civil Rights Years*, uses both unnerving, recently declassified archival footage and piercing, to-the-point interviews with some of the world's smartest, most articulate talking heads to tell his story.

Working with co-screenwriters Janet and David Webb Peoples (David was simultaneously writing what later became Clint Eastwood's equally disturbing *Unforgiven*), Else explores events that were for many of the scientists interviewed, including Nobel Prize–winners Bethe and I. I. Rabe, the best and worst memories of their lives.

If these men were smart, they all thought Oppenheimer was smarter. Bethe calls him "a tremendous intellect," the quickest man he'd ever known, someone who at the remarkably young age of twenty-five received a dual professorship at UC-Berkeley and Cal Tech.

Oppenheimer flirted with communism but, unlike his brother Frank, never joined the party. Yet his intellect was so impressive that when Gen. Leslie Groves, the head of the Manhattan Project, was looking for someone to be scientific director, he overruled security concerns as well as his personal dislike of liberals to put Oppenheimer in charge. Though it initially seemed an improbable appointment, the irresponsible bohemian intellectual emerged as a formidable administrator.

The most joyous parts of *The Day After Trinity* are participant descriptions of the heady early days of the marvelous adventure that was the Manhattan Project. Chosen from universities across the country, the youthful elite of the physics, math, and chemistry worlds (average age 29) agreed to go to an undisclosed place (a former boys school in Los Alamos, New Mexico, as it turned out) to work on a top-secret project. The sense of excitement, exploration, and privilege was as potent as any drug. It was, says physicist Freeman Dyson, "the most marvelous time of their lives."

The reason why the search for the ultimate weapon was initially so intoxicating was that when the Manhattan Project began the German military juggernaut looked all but unstoppable, a prospect that was especially horrifying to the many Jewish scientists, including Oppenheimer, who were part of the team. As Bethe says, everyone involved understandably thought what they were doing was "necessary to save Western civilization."

The first Faustian twist in this story came in the spring of 1945, when once-powerful Germany, the country whose war aims were the ostensible rationale for the project, surrendered to the Allies. But as Los Alamos physicist Robert Wilson reports, "No one walked away, no one even thought of it." The momentum of scientific discovery, the urgent need to solve the problem so much effort had been expended on, trapped everyone and made stopping impossible.

Instead of walking away, the scientists at Los Alamos moved inexorably forward. A location called Trinity Site was selected in a remote part of New Mexico prophetically named Jornada de Muerto (Journey of Death). In July 1945, the bomb was assembled at a ranch house and, as home movie footage chillingly illustrates, moved ever so gingerly to the site.

The Trinity blast, when it happened on July 16 at 5:29 A.M., was like nothing ever seen before. The light was so strong that a blind person saw it, the heat was so intense it was felt five miles away, the fallout was so potent it burned black cattle nearly white. And the scientists involved, as their body language as well as the words of their interviews emphasized, went from fear that the device wouldn't work to horror that it did. "I was a different person from then on," says Robert Wilson simply, his face a mask of despair.

After the bomb was dropped on Hiroshima on August 6, creating a flash that could have been seen from another planet and destroying the city in nine seconds, these powerful misgivings got even more intense. "They'd made a Faustian bargain, they'd sold their souls to the devil for knowledge and power," Freeman Dyson sums up. "And once you sell your soul to the devil, there is no going back on it."

No one was more distraught at what had been done than Oppenheimer. Once famously jaunty, he is painfully haggard in interview footage where he says, "I remembered the line from the *Bhagavad Gita*, where Vishnu says to the prince, 'Now I am become death, destroyer of worlds.'"

Worse, if possible, was yet to come for Oppenheimer. In 1954 his old communist sympathies were made much of; he was stripped of his security clearance and not allowed to work for the government on nuclear issues again. "He was never the same person afterwards," says his brother Frank, with colleague Rabe adding, "it almost killed him spiritually. It destroyed him."

Though he lived until 1967, Oppenheimer could not escape the memory of what had gone before. Asked during the Lyndon Johnson era about talks to stop nuclear weapons, he replied with the phrase that gives this devastating film its title: "It's twenty years too late. It should have been done the day after Trinity."

What to Watch Next:

Barefoot Gen (1983), directed by Mori Masaki.

Further Reading:

American Prometheus: The Triumph and Tragedy of J. Robert Oppenheimer, by Kai Bird and Martin J. Sherwin.

FIRST CONTACT

1983

Directed by Bob Connolly and Robin Anderson.

Lon Chaney unmasked in *Phantom of the Opera*, Buster Keaton unmoved as a house collapses around him in *Steamboat Bill Jr.*, Orson Welles bemused as a kitten plays at his feet in *The Third Man*: these are movie looks you never forget. But none of them are stronger, or stay with you longer, than the amazed and bewildered looks you see in *First Contact*.

A groundbreaking 1983 Australian documentary, *First Contact* was the earliest of three films, known collectively as the Highlands Triology, that were made over more than a dozen years by the husband and wife team of Bob Connolly and Robin Anderson.

All three films (which have won more than thirty awards worldwide) are set in Papua New Guinea, the large island nation just north of its former colonial master, Australia. One of the last places on earth to be impacted by Europeans, Papua New Guinea was largely untouched until 1926, when the discovery of gold brought the inevitable invasion of outsiders. Still, because the interior highlands of the island looked to be one continuous and impenetrable mountain range, no one thought to search inland. Until the Leahys.

Lead by Michael, the eldest, and joined at varying times by brothers Patrick, James, and Daniel, the Leahy mining expeditions, which took place between 1930 and 1934, were in many respects typical of prospectors looking for the big strike.

As Connolly and Anderson wrote in a thorough and thoughtful companion book to the film, Micheal Leahy "was the archetypal white adventurer—ruthless and determined, searching for riches in an alien landscape among alien people, driven on by the lure of gold, sustained by an unshakable conviction in the validity of his presence and purpose—a twentieth-century conquistador, arriving just as Europe's great colonising explosion had all but subsided."

But as the Leahys ventured farther inland, the reality they found confounded everyone. Those supposedly impenetrable mountains turned out to contain huge and fertile hidden valleys, valleys inhabited by close to a million people who had never seen, heard, or so much as imagined the existence of white people. Remembered one highlander, "We thought that, apart from our world, there was nothing."

Encounters like this had been taking place for hundreds of years, ever since Columbus, Cortes, and Pizarro came to what they called the New World. What made the situation in Papua New Guinea different was a simple quirk of fate. Michael Leahy was a photography buff, someone who had taken American correspondence school courses in picture taking, and along with his mining gear he had brought along both a windup movie camera and a Leica for stills.

The extraordinary result was several hours of 16 millimeter film (stored in hundred-foot reels in half a dozen cardboard boxes) and five thousand still photos that for the first time in history, and likely the last as well, photographically documented the way indigenous peoples reacted to the appearance of pale-skinned interlopers.

What we see are looks ranging from the purest astonishment and naked incomprehensibility to thunderstruck terror, looks that Europeans themselves might mimic if confronted by beings from another galaxy far, far away. Making what we see all the more potent is the knowledge that we are witnessing one of history's paradigmatic moments, that Leahy's cameras give us a privileged glimpse of precisely what Columbus and all who came after him must have seen on their arrival in an unprepared world.

It's more than this footage, however, that makes *First Contact* so absorbing. It's also that we get to see and hear the participants in those long-ago events look back from the perspective of the present day and reminisce about what was on their minds when this unimaginable tumult was going on.

Though leader Michael Leahy died in 1979, well before this film was made, we get to hear from two of his brothers, James and Daniel, and their tone is largely defensive. Perhaps unsettled by finding themselves on the wrong side of history in their old age, they talk of the danger they were in, the need to defend themselves and their trade goods from undeniably warlike natives, and insist that they only killed people who otherwise would have killed them.

The New Guinea tribal people, many of whom come from the Mount Hagen area of the Wahgi Valley in the western highlands, have a reputation for oratory and verbal performance. Even in translation it's a pleasure to hear them describe their long-ago thoughts and actions in rich, expressive language, often punctuated by the laughter of amused remembrance.

"I was so terrified I couldn't even look; I cried in fear," one man remembers of his childhood sighting, while another adds, "We'd never seen such a thing. Did they come from the sky?"

Speculation as to where these strange people had come from was on everyone's tongue. The consensus, says one man, was supernatural: "We believed our dead went over there, turned white, and came back as spirits. That's how we explained the white man: our own dead had returned." When the white men panned for gold, it was thought that the ancestors had come back to look for their bones.

Though the highlanders often wore elaborate headdresses and necklaces, their only clothing was the traditional loincloth known as the lap-lap. They had never even imagined the kinds of garments the Leahys wore and, assuming that trousers were part of their bodies, reached an imaginative conclusion. "We thought they must not have body wastes in them," one man remembers, "because they were wrapped up so neatly."

Soon enough, the highlanders noticed that the strangers' did have bodily waste, and that it smelled as bad as their own. And the women found out sooner than the warriors how human the newcomers were. "We had sex together," one woman says pithily, "and then we knew they were only men."

Still, there was no lack of new and strange things these outsiders had at their command. When small transport planes flew in, the local people "fell down and hid our faces, we clung to each other." The introduction of the gramophone, a highlight of Robert Flaherty's *Nanook of the North*, caused a similar sensation: "Our own dead," was the thought, "were crying out from inside that box."

After *First Contact* was finished, Connolly and Anderson committed to staying in the Papua New Guinea highlands to tell a wider story, a story involving Michael Leahy's unacknowledged mixed race son Joe that unfolded in the trilogy's final two parts, *Joe Leahy's Neighbors* and *Black Harvest*, These films are excellent, but it is *First Contact* that you can't get out of your mind. It's not every day that you get to see centuries of world history encapsulated in a single look.

What to Watch Next:

Joe Leahy's Neighbors (1989), directed by Bob Connolly and Robin Anderson.

Black Harvest (1992), directed by Bob Connolly and Robin Anderson.

Further Reading:

First Contact: New Guinea's Highlanders Encounter the Outside World, by Bob Connolly and Robin Anderson.

DISTANT VOICES, STILL LIVES

1988

Directed by Terence Davies. Starring Peter Postlethwaite, Freda Dowie.

You can dissect *Distant Voices, Still Lives*, you can describe and analyze how its elements come together, but that doesn't prepare you for the intensity of the emotional experience. Written and directed by Britain's Terence Davies, this is a landmark in the expressive use of music to enhance images and give them a power that is almost beyond the ability of words to convey.

This power comes from *Distant Voices* being a memory piece, the distilled essence of Davies's unblinking recollections of the pain and pleasures of growing up in a terraced house in working-class Liverpool during the 1940s and 1950s.

Every corner of every frame has deep and specific meaning for the filmmaker, who went to great lengths to use or recreate locations that were as close as possible to how he remembered them. Davies is also especially gifted at conveying the precise emotional tonality of what he experienced.

Davies's key creative decision was visualizing *Distant Voices*, as he himself wrote, as "a pattern of timeless moments." This film is not told chronologically but as a sequence of out-of-sequence vignettes. There is no story per se but rather a progression of incidents, shards of memory that blend together like an emotional dream state. "Film is not 'what happens next,' Davies told a journalist when the film came out. "It's what happens next *emotionally* that's important."

The center of *Distant Voices, Still Lives* (made in linked halves using the same cast and shot with a two-year gap to emphasize the passage of time) is a family based on Davies's memories of his own life as the youngest of ten children. It consists of son Tony (Dean Williams), daughters Eileen (Angela Walsh) and Maisie (Lorraine Ashbourne), and a mother (Freda Dowie) and a father (Pete Postlethwaite) so iconic that the film does not give them specific names.

With the exception of Dowie and Postlethwaite (who went on to an Oscar nomination for *In the Name of the Father*), the fact that most of the performers have unfamiliar faces enhances a sense of verisimilitude so strong that it can be difficult to remember that these are actors working off a script and not real figures conjured up by Davies's intense powers of remembrance.

Towering over everything is Postlethwaite's father, a man of terrible rages and moods as dark as the jet black shirts he favors. Glowering and sadistic, possessed by ungovernable furies that regularly resulted in savage beatings for his wife and children, this man, Davies insisted in interviews, was easier to take than the real thing. "Everything in the screenplay happened," he has said. "I had to tone down my father's level of violence because if I'd put the real levels in, nobody would have believed it."

Yet, unexpectedly, there are warmer aspects to this film's world, a focus on the healing nature of friendship and community, for instance, that temper the darkness. Both aspects of the film, the light and the dark, are enhanced by the two different ways *Distant Voices* works with the singing voices that dominate its soundtrack.

Most noticeable at first is Davies's impeccable taste in what to play when, the way his soundtrack marries classic recordings of songs to specific scenes, inevitably to devastating effect. *Distant Voices'* first major sequence, a series of images revolving around the father's funeral, is set to Jessye Norman's knockout version of the classic Lead Belly spiritual, "There's a Man Going Round Taking Names."

Even more powerful, perhaps because it is unexpected, is a version of Ella Fitzgerald singing "Taking a Chance on Love." The song begins before the visuals, and when we realize that lyrics like "Here I slide again/ About to take that ride again/ Starry eyed again" are being played against a particular brutal beating the father inflicts on the mother, the effect is extraordinary.

Helping keep family members sane in such a hope-free world is the camaraderie of friendship and neighborliness that marked Liverpool in that time and place. This fellow feeling was most visible in the frequent communal singing that occurred most often in pubs after weddings, christenings, and funerals but also in troop railway cars, bomb shelters, anyplace people gathered together.

Davies, who was a small child when the first part of his film took place, often remembered only fragments but not complete songs or their titles. Research led to lyrics for tunes ranging from "My Yiddishe Mama" and "Brownskin Girl" to "Buttons and Bows," "If You Knew Susie," and "Roll Out the Barrel." Everyone heard doesn't have a great voice but the point of the tradition was not high quality but that everyone sang. Song was a way these people related to each other, a way they made sense of the world.

Enhancing these vocal effects is the focused and specific visual plan Davies and cinematographers William Diver and Patrick Duval conceived for the film. The color is desaturated and everything we see, whether slow panning shots across faces in a pub or austere, stark framing shots of houses and situations, seems stately and deliberate, emphasizing that constructing formal tableaux rather than traditional dramatic scenes was the goal.

Though the first part of the film's diptych, *Distant Voices*, focuses on the wartime years when the three siblings were children, it starts with them all as adults on Eileen's wedding day. The father is dead by this point, but the powerful hold he exerts on them despite his outbursts continues, with Eileen saying she wishes her father was there and Maisie saying in voice-over response, "He was a bastard and I bleeding hated him."

Davies, determined to be fair to his reality, includes scenes of the father's infrequent warm moments, showing the three siblings watching in awe as their dad demonstrates uncharacteristic caring while he grooms his cart horse and sings "When Irish Eyes Are Smiling." (The photo of the father and his horse seen on the wall is actually a photo of Davies's father and his animal.)

More often than not, however, kind moments are merely preludes to the worst. The father is all thoughtful smiles as he lovingly decorates a tiny tree on Christmas Eve, but at teatime the next day he hurls all the dishes to the floor and demands that mother clean everything up.

Still Lives, the second part of the story, takes place a decade later (a radio broadcast mentions 1959), a time when postwar prosperity was taking hold but the marriages that the children and their friends made contain difficulties of their own.

Eileen's husband Dave, for instance, insists she give up her close friendships, the relationships that sustained her before marriage, and concentrate completely on him. "Give us a song, Ei," someone in the pub says after she's had yet another run-in with Dave, and her rendition of the Johnny Mercer/Sadie Vimmerstedt lyric "I'll be around to pick up the pieces after somebody breaks your heart like you broke mine" underlines how songs allow otherwise repressed feelings to be expressed in the fullest possible way.

Filmmaker Davies grew up loving movies, musicals in particular, and one of *Distant Voices*' most affecting sequences starts with a sea of drenched umbrellas outside a theater showing *Love Is a Many Splendored Thing* followed by a shot of the sisters weeping inside the theater as that sad love story unfolds. Soon enough, tears shed for a movie blend into real-life tears. Melancholy always overshadows joy in this film, just as joy is always available to push the melancholy away.

Unexpectedly for a film with so much harshness, *Distant Voices, Still Lives* ends on a note of affection and acceptance. Members of the family are shown emerging laughing from a party and fading into the darkness as they head towards home while tenor Peter Pears movingly sings Benjamin Britten's arrangement of "O Waly Waly" (The Water Is Wide) on the soundtrack. The good will endure and survive, we're being told, and song will have played the largest possible part in that.

What to Watch Next:

Hope and Glory (1987), directed by John Boorman.

THE NINETIES

Perhaps because the century was drawing to a close, each of these films felt like an ultimate expression of genre to me, felt like the filmmakers involved had the nerve and skill to take their subject matter as far as it could go.

Leolo is a coming-of-age film, but one with the kind of magical and tragic qualities the genre rarely manages.

Unforgiven has many of the tropes of classic Westerns, but things are turned on their head and the price of violence is emphasized, not ignored.

Even *Howards End* seems particularly uncompromising in presenting the kind of thoughtful, character-driven extravaganza that is becoming increasingly rare. The Merchant-Ivory team made dozens of films, but they never did it better than this.

HOWARDS END

1992

Directed by James Ivory. Starring Anthony Hopkins,
Emma Thompson, Vanessa Redgrave.

Who speaks of *Howards End* these days, who expounds on the virtues of this magnificent drama whose traditional style seems almost as distant as its Edwardian setting. Seen now, decades past its release, it seems not only the Merchant-Ivory team's most polished accomplishment but the high-water mark of a certain kind of filmmaking as well, a landmark example of movies of passion, taste, and sensitivity that touch every emotion.

Certainly *Howards End* was appreciated in its day. Made for only $8 million, it received nine Oscar nominations, including best picture, director, cinematographer, and acting nominations for Vanessa Redgrave and Emma Thompson, who won along with Ruth Prawer Jhabvala's script and Luciana Arrighi and Ian Whittaker's art direction and set decoration.

Paradoxically, perhaps the old-fashioned nature of its strengths is the reason it's been half forgotten. It is based on E.M. Forster's 1910 novel of families in love and in conflict, and its filmmaking techniques owe nothing to modern flash and dash. With a fine script and impeccable acting from people like

Anthony Hopkins, Redgrave, and most especially Thompson, extravagant directorial flourishes would have just gotten in the way.

Experience is essential in sustaining this kind of restraint, and producer Ismail Merchant, director James Ivory, and screenwriter Ruth Prawer Jhabvala had collaborated with each other for thirty years when they undertook this project. Nothing they did, not the splendidly comic *A Room with a View* that came before or the somber *Remains of the Day* that came after, matched this achievement.

What sets *Howards End* apart is the complex emotional life of its characters. This is a film capable of setting off lasting reverberations beneath an exquisite surface: it moves you in different ways every time you see it.

With any number of films in Edwardian dress behind them, the Merchant-Ivory team knew more than how to be literally faithful to the look of those times; they knew how to make that world seem genuinely inhabited. From production designer Arrighi, who was after "how people lived, not a set" to costume designer Jenny Beavan, who wanted "real clothes made in an authentic way," the level of authenticity created is the more convincing because it seems to be so casually done.

Having a novelist as psychologically acute as E.M. Forster to work off of certainly gave a leg up to all concerned. In addition to his facility with character and relationships, Forster in *Howards End* was dealing with a powerful theme, the pangs of a society in terrible flux. There was a serpent loose in the genteel garden that was Edwardian England, the serpent of the modern world, fated to bite everyone and change everything.

Like the novel it follows, *Howards End* begins not head-on but from an angle, with a peripheral but telling relationship. Helen Schlegel (Helena Bonham Carter) is visiting with the Wilcoxes, a family that she and her sister Margaret (Emma Thompson) met the previous spring at Howards End, the Wilcoxes' romantic old pile of an English country home.

Helen and one of the Wilcox sons become briefly infatuated with each other, which leads to the comic intervention of
the Schlegel girls' busybody Aunt Juley (Prunella Scales). The
young people are soon separated, but though everyone assumes
all ties have been severed, the two families are fated to intercon-
nect much more than anyone suspects.

Certainly, the Schlegels and the Wilcoxes would seem to
have very little in common. The three Schlegel siblings (Helen
and Margaret have a rather ineffectual younger brother named
Tibby) are genteel, cultured people with a lively interest in London's intellectual scene. The Wilcoxes, by contrast, are typified
by father Henry (Anthony Hopkins), the essence of triumphant
capitalism, the wealthy head of The Imperial and West Africa
Rubber Company who is abrupt, distant, and often unfeeling.

But when the Wilcoxes come to London for a stay and take
a flat practically next door to the Schlegels, Henry's wife Ruth
(Vanessa Redgrave) and Margaret renew their acquaintanceship.
Very different from her children and her in-laws, who tend to be
venal and small-minded, Ruth is passionate about the old ways,
in love with English tradition in general and with the property at
Howards End, which belongs to her not her husband, in particular. Though she would not seem to have much in common with
the chatty, terribly up-to-date Margaret—she doesn't even believe in giving women the vote—the two find an unspoken emotional kinship growing between them.

At the same time, the impulsive and high-strung Helen takes
an umbrella by mistake (a habit of hers) and inadvertently makes
the acquaintance of one Leonard Bast (Sam West, in real life the
son of actress Scales). The beautifully constructed scene where he
takes off after her, umbrella-less in a downpour, showcases almost
without words their contrasting personalities: she impulsive and
heedless, he dogged and aggrieved.

A low-paid clerk at an insurance company, Bast faces an eco-
nomically precarious situation, and that has made him touchy and

easily offended. Possessed of a terribly earnest, poetic soul, he is dazzled by the Schlegels' easy, spirited ways and by the cultured, idealistic world they so easily inhabit.

Though the Schlegels, Wilcoxes, and Leonard Bast represent different social classes, it is the grace of *Howards End* to make us care desperately about them as people. And though the film's story line intertwines these three groups and involves them in a series of shattering events, it is the depth and breadth of its characters that make it memorable.

Because it is confident of its story and its powers, *Howards End* takes the time to establish itself, to allow its characters the space to demonstrate subtlety and complexity. Far from being presented to us fully formed, these protagonists gradually develop and change, revealing who they are not only to the audience but often simultaneously to themselves and each other as well.

None of this would be possible, of course, without subtle, delicate acting, and *Howards End* so matches performer to part that it's fair to say that these roles must be considered career high points for all concerned.

With her abundant pre-Raphaelite hair, Bonham Carter is perfectly cast as a woman who, in the actress's words, "is all action and impulse and passion." At the opposite end of the emotional scale is Anthony Hopkins's vivid, thoughtful work as a paragon of male energy and achievement, a man who is more indifferent to good than actually bad. Hopkins's previous role was as Hannibal Lecter in *The Silence of the Lambs*—producer Merchant used that film's sound editor to get the actor the script—but this performance is the more resonant.

Though her part is not enormous, Vanessa Redgrave (who agreed to the role when Merchant impulsively doubled her salary) makes a singular impression as Ruth Wilcox, a wan and vulnerable wraith from a dying world. The film's opening, with Ruth wandering around the moody twilight of the Howards End garden and looking in at a bright and lively dinner party inside the house, is a fine way to begin a drama that emphasizes both the need and the difficulty of establishing emotional connections across barriers.

If one performance can be said to lie at the heart of *Howards End*, it would have to be Emma Thompson's. Though she has since gone on to win a screenwriting Oscar for her adaptation of Jane Austen's *Sense and Sensibility*, at the time *Howards End* came out she was best known in this country for being married to actor/director Kenneth Branagh.

This singular role changed Thompson's American reputation overnight. Because, though you don't immediately suspect it, Margaret Schlegel is the force that powers *Howards End*, the only character possessed of the moral strength to cope with a society in extremis.

With her bright smile and chatterbox qualities, given to bustling into restaurants and saying things like "I want to eat heaps," she seems at first glance to be little more than a cheery blithe spirit. But the joy of Thompson's performance is the way she projects emotional intelligence, gradually allows us to see past that surface and realize how wise and substantial Margaret is.

An actress who can break your heart just by widening her eyes, Thompson takes over this part totally, and, as Forster's surrogate in the story, manages the extremely difficult feat of making decency and caring into heroic qualities. The triumph of these virtues, like the triumph of *Howards End*, happens gradually, but to see this exceptional film is to know that the wait has been worthwhile.

What to Watch Next:
Room with a View (1985), directed by James Ivory.

Further Reading:
James Ivory in Conversation: How Merchant Ivory Makes Its Movies, by Robert Emmet Long.

LEOLO

1992

Directed by Jean-Claude Lauzon. Starring Maxime Collin, Ginette Reno, Pierre Bourgault.

Some films haunt you while you watch them; others linger in the mind for days or even weeks afterward. Some films, and some filmmakers, haunt you from beyond the grave.

It happened late one night in 1998. I was leaving Raleigh Studios in Hollywood after a screening, alone and nearly the last one off the lot. I turned left onto Bronson Avenue, the way I always do, when, all in a rush, I felt myself overwhelmed and near tears. And I knew, even before the feeling became a thought, that this was about Jean-Claude Lauzon.

It had been a few months since French Canadian director Lauzon, age forty-three, and his actress girlfriend Marie-Soleil Tougas, had died in the crash of a Cessna 180 he was piloting in a remote and frozen area some 2,400 miles north of Montreal. That corner outside the studio gate was the last place I had seen Lauzon alive, and, against all reason, I could not shake the feeling that his spirit had called out to me from that spot, had forcefully insisted on being remembered.

If anyone had the strength of personality and will necessary to deliver a message from the afterlife to someone who only knew him slightly, it would be Lauzon. As intense as he was sensitive, he was a dazzlingly talented filmmaker who found creativity agonizing. "I cannot make a movie," he had told me, "if I don't suffer for it."

Lauzon also had the unnerving directness that can accompany people who've come up from poverty. "I'm so used to being involved with very, very rough people that even when I'm not so angry people think I'm going to stab them with a knife," he admitted when I interviewed him in 1992 in a Toronto hotel. "It's a habit I took when I was young."

Lauzon directed only two films, but they were among the most honored and successful in Canadian history, so much so that Serge Losique, director of the Montreal World Film Festival, didn't hesitate to call him "a genius . . . the most authentic filmmaker that Canada produced."

His first film, *Un Zoo, La Nuit* (Night Zoo), won an unprecedented thirteen Genies, Canada's Oscars. Reluctant to make features because of the interior pain involved, Lauzon waited five years before turning out *Leolo*, which in 1992 debuted in competition at Cannes and must be considered, despite its uncompromising style and scenes almost too scabrous to describe, as great a film on childhood as has ever been made.

Leolo was a touchstone for me. I saw it exhausted and irritable near the end of the festival. But within minutes I was astonished and involved, and by the time the screening ended I felt that I'd seen something very special.

Leolo is a memoir of the kind of brutal, destructive coming of age that usually leaves survivors without the ability or the desire to remember. Yet Lauzon managed to infuse his story of the squalid desperation of a boy growing up in his old Montreal neighborhood with the all-accepting warmth and humor of remembered experience. It was a cry from the heart of a brutalized poet, of a boy who escaped by merest chance, and you couldn't watch it without knowing that even the worst episodes—especially the worst episodes—had really happened.

Leolo was initially subtitled *Because I Dream*, and that phrase defines its theme. Its twelve-year-old protagonist (Maxime Collin), growing up in the hopeless decay of Montreal's tough Mile End neighborhood, says early on that "people who trust only their own truth call me Leo Lozeau. Because I dream, I am not."

Instead, Leo imagines he is really Leolo Lozone, not French Canadian but Italian, who ends up born in Montreal after his mother, in an especially boggling sequence, makes accidental contact with a sperm-laden Sicilian tomato. Later, sandwiched between two sisters who move in and out of mental hospitals, an obsessive bodybuilder of an older brother and a brutish, packhorse father who cares only about the regular bowel movements of his offspring, it is no wonder that Leolo dreams. And his dreams focus on the power of writing, on passionately believing "there was a secret in words strung together."

Getting hold of the sole book in the house, Leolo ritualistically dons hat and mittens to read it late at night by the chilly light of the refrigerator. And he writes. Continually, compulsively, for no practical reason, not even bothering to save the pages, he commits to paper his heightened, poetic reflections, overflowing with emotion and insight. Only the mysterious Word Tamer, an almost mythological literary scavenger created by Lauzon as a tribute to the real-life teacher who rescued him, appreciates what the boy is writing but is powerless to help him change his life.

As read by a cultivated adult voice, Leolo's writings set an assured, polished verbal tone that counterpoints the rawness of the sometime savagery in which he lives. For this film is definitely not decorous, well-behaved, and suitable for children. It circles again and again, sometimes elegiacally, sometimes with taunting brutality, sometimes with unexpected humor, around the same key events and people in a small boy's life.

There is Leolo's bulked-up older brother, Ferdinand, who "fear had given a reason for living," turning him into a bodybuilder after a humiliating encounter with a cocky local bully.

His sister, Queen Rita, curator of an impressive insect collection, is lulled into tranquillity by the sound of dozens of wings. His mother, enormous in a series of gargantuan housedresses, is the only sane person in the family with "the strength of a frigate plowing through troubled waters." And finally, there is the boy's muddled grandfather (veteran French actor Julien Guiomar), the source of the family's insanity as well as Leolo's rival for the smiles and favors of their lovely Sicilian neighbor Bianca (Giuditta Del Vecchio), Leolo's Italian fantasy.

Because Lauzon remembers this story so exactly, because the emotions are as vivid for him as if it all just happened, he has been able to use nonprofessional actors effectively in several key roles. Surprisingly strong for their lack of experience are Yves Montmarquette, one of Montreal's top bodybuilders, as Ferdinand, and Pierre Bourgault, a political journalist and force for Quebec independence, as the Word Tamer. And Ginette Reno, a woman known as the queen of Quebec's pop singers, embraces the role of Leolo's mother with impressive results.

Leolo also has a splendid, eclectic soundtrack, which Lauzon says he had set in his mind before he began to write the script. Songs by Tom Waits and the Rolling Stones, as well as music from Arabia, Argentina, and Tibet, pull you deeper and deeper into Lauzon's very particular and yet uncannily universal story. For the wonder of *Leolo* is that in his passion to tell his own personal truth, Lauzon has ended up telling everyone else's as well.

A major prize at Cannes seemed inevitable for a film like this, but it didn't happen. Rumors (which the director later confirmed) claimed that Lauzon had destroyed his chances with a provocative sexual remark to an American actress who was on the jury. "My producer was next to me and he turned gray when I said it," Lauzon remembered, but he himself was indifferent. Not a model citizen, simply a survivor of a childhood that should have left him for dead, emotionally if not literally, Lauzon did what he did without concern for consequences.

A director with both an artist's sensitivity and an outlaw's behavior patterns, Lauzon knew he discomfited people who "like you to be either a clean, white hero or a very hard, dark rebel." Yet this dichotomy is what makes his films moving and exceptional.

Lauzon was unapologetic about making films so wrenching "when you come out of the theater, you don't want to talk to anybody, you're on your knees for the next twenty minutes." But what work like this took out of him personally was always a concern.

"After my movies," he said impishly, "people are not coming out and eating from the buffet. I want them to eat from the buffet. I'm always wanting to write nice stuff, so beautiful women will approach me afterwards. I prefer to write easier stuff, I don't want to go through this crap anymore, but these images obsess me. I didn't want to make a movie about kids, I didn't want to be talking about poor people. But when I was sitting down to write, there is something, images recurring, a wave coming back."

"Maybe you'll see me in LA one day, making this kind of easy film," Lauzon said as he saw me to the hotel room door, but, no surprise, that never happened. With dramatic films causing him agony and commercial work remunerative, Lauzon, who was as passionate about flying and the outdoors as he was about directing, never took on another feature.

He occasionally came to LA for meetings, and it was on one of those trips not long after *Leolo*'s American release that I saw him for the last time. I was making that same late-night turn out of Raleigh when Lauzon, who was on foot, saw me and rushed the car, smiling and waving and materializing out of nowhere. But with typical impetuosity he tore off before I could get out and say hello.

It was a casual moment of the kind that is usually forgotten, but I've thought about it a lot since that plane crash, regretting that I didn't hop out of the car faster and give Lauzon a proper greeting. What finally lasts, however, what finally matters, is the quality of his work, and the strength of the emotional connection it continues to make.

Sometime after Lauzon's death, I was at a film festival when the Brazilian director Walter Salles said he had a story to tell me. Visiting Los Angeles, he had bought the *Los Angeles Times* on a Sunday morning and, when he got back to his hotel room, simply tossed it on the bed. The paper had immediately opened to a story I had written about my late-night encounter with the spirit of Jean-Claude Lauzon. Which was how Salles had first found out that his friend had died months before.

The haunting continues.

What to Watch Next:

The 400 Blows (1959), directed by François Truffaut.

Un Zoo, La Nuit (1987), directed by Jean-Claude Lauzon.

UNFORGIVEN

1992

Directed by Clint Eastwood. Starring Clint Eastwood,
Gene Hackman, Morgan Freeman.

Westerns and I go way back, and Clint Eastwood was there from
the beginning.

Eastwood wasn't the first cowboy actor in my life. That
would be William Boyd, whose dozens of Hopalong Cassidy B
pictures were reedited for television just in time for me to embrace their expansive Western images on my family's small TV in
our cramped Brooklyn apartment.

The man has remained a personal favorite for many, myself
included: the Western-themed gift shop at Los Angeles' Autry
National Center reports that nothing moves like Hoppy mer-
chandise, and I recently bought a shiny DVD-filled lunchbox to
prove it. Back in the day, however, along with my immigrant father, who loved Westerns as much as I did despite growing up in
the shtetls of Eastern Europe, I moved on.

Sitting in our living room on side-by-side folding plastic
beach chairs (don't ask), my father and I took in Dale Robertson in
Tales of Wells Fargo, Ward Bond in *Wagon Train*, James Garner in
Maverick, and, of course, Clint Eastwood as lean and lanky cattle

drive ramrod Rowdy Yates in *Rawhide*. At this point in time, I can't remember exactly what it was a ramrod did on those endless drives, but Eastwood's presence was remarkable even then.

Soon after that series ended, Eastwood went on to the Man with No Name trilogy of so-called spaghetti Westerns for Italian director Sergio Leone (*A Fistful of Dollars; For a Few Dollars More; The Good, the Bad, and the Ugly*), and he always remained close to the genre, even after his success gave him a wider choice of roles. It's not only that no other active actor/director has made as many Westerns, Eastwood has also delighted in bending boundaries, in pushing the Western to areas outside the accepted canon.

In addition to the apocalyptic trio of films he directed himself (*High Plains Drifter, The Outlaw Josey Wales, Pale Rider*), Eastwood has done quasi-musical Westerns (*Paint Your Wagon*), modern-day comic Westerns (the surprisingly charming *Bronco Billy*), and even New York City police dramas that were really Westerns in disguise (*Coogan's Bluff*). Which brings us to *Unforgiven*.

Simultaneously heroic and nihilistic, reeking of myth and morality but modern as they come, this is a Western for those who know and cherish the form. Produced by, directed by, and starring Eastwood, this is a film that resonates wonderfully with the spirit of films past while using idiosyncratic characters to stake out a territory quite its own. Even before it won four Oscars, including best picture and best director for Eastwood and best supporting actor for Gene Hackman, it was obvious that this was not cowboy business as usual.

One of the paradoxes of *Unforgiven* is that even though as a finished film it's all but inconceivable in anyone else's hands, David Webb Peoples's exceptional script was originally the property of Francis Ford Coppola. "It was brought to my attention in the early 1980s, when I was looking for a writer to do some stuff for me," Eastwood said when I interviewed him just prior to the film's release. "I thought, 'Gee, I really like this, it's too bad it's all tied up.' But when I called the writer's agent he said,

'Francis gave up the option two days ago; the script is available.'
So I bought it."

Eastwood was shrewd enough to hold onto the script for
more than a decade, until, just past his sixtieth birthday, he felt
he had weathered enough to do the role proper justice. "I always
thought it was a little gem," he told me. "But I figured I had to age
into it."

For *Unforgiven*, the story of a reformed gunslinger who confronts his past, is in its own bleak way an elegiac Western, as melancholy in its fashion as such classics as *The Wild Bunch* and *Ride
the High Country*. As *True Grit* was for John Wayne, this is also
something of a last hurrah for Eastwood's Man with No Name
persona, but because Eastwood is who he is, it is a dark and omi-
nous good-bye, brooding and stormy.

Unforgiven is also, and this is perhaps its most unexpected
aspect, a neat piece of revisionism. It's a film so violent that costar
Hackman considered not accepting the part, but it's also bound
and determined to demythologize killing. Considerable emphasis
is placed on how hard it is to take the life of even one man, on the
destructive interior price that must be paid for each and every act
of mayhem. If there are thrills to be had here, none of them are to
be paid for cheaply.

"I've done as much as the next person as far as creating mayhem in Westerns," Eastwood said, "but what I like about *Unforgiven* is that every killing in it has a repercussion. It really tears
people up when they are violent, and I felt it was time for that
kind of thing in the world." When Eastwood's stone cold desper-
ado says, point-blank, "It's a hell of a thing killing a man, taking
away all he's got and he's ever gonna have," the actor's presence,
command, and cinematic history give the words extra power.

Both the time and setting of *Unforgiven*—1880 in Big Whiskey, Wyoming—emphasize this sense of mortality. The frontier
West is coming to an end, both physically and spiritually, leaving frustration in its wake. In the forbidding high country, a flat,

empty locale under cold blue skies—the fictional Big Whiskey was built from scratch in thirty-two days in a remote part of Alberta, Canada—the West is an angry, hostile place, rife with fury and lawlessness.

In this particular town, however, the law has a definite presence. He is the town sheriff, Little Bill (Hackman) by name, and he is called on in the film's opening moments to adjudicate a dispute at the local whorehouse on a dark and stormy night. A cowboy from the nearby Bar T ranch has viciously slashed one of the prostitutes in the face. When the house's owner complains "no one is going to pay good money for a cut-up whore," Little Bill, ever the friend of capital investment, decrees that the cowboy and a friend who accompanied him must pay the owner six horses as compensation.

This does not sit well with Strawberry Alice (Frances Fisher), the most outspoken of the prostitutes, who has a harsher less mercantile punishment in mind. "Just because we let the smelly fools ride us like horses," she says angrily, giving the film a neofeminist subtext, "doesn't mean we let them brand us like horses." When Little Bill doesn't agree, Alice masterminds a sub rosa scheme to offer $1,000 cash for the death of the two cowboys, no questions asked.

In the normal course of events, none of these events would come to the attention of William Munny (Eastwood), a destitute Kansas farmer whom we saw burying his wife in the film's opening scene. Munny now divides his time between raising their two small children and nonheroically rooting around in the mud with his recalcitrant hogs, a comic situation that Eastwood explained is critical to how he sees his character.

"I've never pictured myself as the guy on the white horse or wearing the white hat on the mighty steed, though I've ridden some good horses periodically," the actor said. "I've always liked heroes that've had some sort of weakness or problems to overcome besides the problem of the immediate script. That always keeps it much more interesting than doing it the conventional way."

This awkwardness notwithstanding, Munny is not just any farmer. Before he met his wife and reformed eleven years earlier, he was an alcoholic killer, "a man of notoriously vicious and intemperate disposition" who was legendary for the heedless death he left in his path. Or so says the self-styled Schofield Kid (Canadian actor Jaimz Woolvett), a callow young blowhard with more bluster than sense who has heard of Munny's reputation ("the meanest goddamn son of a bitch alive, as cold as snow") and rides into his yard offering him half the reward if he'll join up with him.

With an anguished face looking worn, lined, and lived in like no one else's, Munny is clearly not eager for his old life. "I ain't like that anymore," he tells the Kid with conviction. "I'm just a fella now. I ain't no different than anyone else."

But his poverty is a goad, and Munny ends up enlisting his ex-partner, Ned Logan (Morgan Freeman), to join in the quest. As the group heads off for Big Whiskey, the question is several-fold. Are they the same men, can they kill in the same way, and, more crucially, if they can take that one step back down the road to perdition, will they then be able to turn around and return to their quiet lives?

It is one of the pleasures of David Webb Peoples's script, along with period dialogue that mixes menace with a sly and pithy sense of humor, that these kinds of questions come up at all. Peoples, whose résumé includes a shared credit on Ridley Scott's version of Philip K. Dick's *Blade Runner* and Jon Else's documentary *The Day After Trinity*, is intent on de-romanticizing the West. He portrays shootouts and gunplay as drunken, thuggish violence and the world of habitual despair they occur in as a place where randomness, anarchy, and disorganization hold sway.

Not interested in creating conventional heroes and villains, Peoples has come up with a series of vivid, eccentric characters, from small cameos like a one-armed, three-gun deputy to major roles like dime novel scribe and professional mythologizer W.W. Beauchamp (Saul Rubinek) and English Bob, a.k.a. the Duke of

Death, a fancy-pants killer given a nice twist by Richard Harris, all of whom never behave exactly as you'd expect them to.

Most indelible of all, however, is Little Bill, Big Whiskey's sheriff. Ruthless to the point of sadism, he's also possessed of both a sense of justice and a wicked sense of humor, calling English Bob "the duck of death." A house-proud homebody with a weakness but not an aptitude for carpentry, Little Bill has the easy confidence of someone who makes up the rules as he goes along. And in playing him, Gene Hackman gives one of his most powerful and least mannered performances, displaying an implacable resolve and controlled passion that form the essential counterbalance to Eastwood's own considerable force.

For *Unforgiven* is finally very much an Eastwood film. As an actor he is exactly right in a role that is as comfortable as a worn hat, as a producer he has the sense and nerve to cast this film for ability, not box office, and, perhaps most important, as a director he has infused it all with his sure, laconic, and unexpectedly emotional style.

Eastwood dedicated this film to the two directors who were most influential in his career, Sergio Leone and Don Siegel, and perhaps the most telling thing that can be said about *Unforgiven* is that these two masters would doubtless be flattered and approve.

"If I was ever to do a last Western," Eastwood told me, "this would be it because it kind of sums up what I feel. Maybe that's why I didn't do it right away. I was kind of savoring it as the last of that genre, maybe the last film of that type for me."

What to Watch Next:
Mystic River (2003), directed by Clint Eastwood.

Further Reading:
Clint Eastwood: A Biography, by Richard Schickel.

THE NEW CENTURY

Nothing emphasized to me how much I've come to depend on the sustenance of films from overseas to keep my hopes high and spirits alive as the realization that all eight of the films I'd selected as favorites from the new century came from countries other than my own.

It was not a shock to find films from France (*A Prophet* and *Of Gods and Men*), a country whose movies are perennial favorites of mine, but these choices went beyond those familiar confines.

On my list are productions from Japan (*Spirited Away*), Italy (*The Best of Youth*), Denmark (*The Five Obstructions*), Israel (*Footnote*), and other spots as well. These foreign films did not land with the cultural explosion that accompanied the French New Wave, but they sustained me every bit as much.

SPIRITED AWAY

2001

Directed by Hayao Miyazaki. Starring Rumi Hiiragi, Miyu Irino.

Prepare to be astounded by *Spirited Away*. The members of the Berlin Film Festival jury certainly were. I ought to know: I was one of them.

The year was 2002 and though I knew about the work of the master Japanese animator Hayao Miyazaki and had even experienced his previous *Princess Mononoke*, I wasn't prepared for the visual floodgates his fierce and fearless imagination was capable of opening.

And though I was entranced by *Spirited Away*, it's a mark of how uncompromisingly idiosyncratic the film is that I was determined to speak up about it even if, as I feared likely, the other jury members would think I'd lost my mind.

As it turned out, the rest of the panel felt exactly the same way: simultaneously passionate in their approval and unsure whether even one other person would share their zeal. In fact, this darkly joyous feature so held the jury in its power that out of nowhere *Spirited Away* became the first animated feature in the Berlin festival's fifty-year history to win the Golden Bear (sharing the top prize with Paul Greengrass's very different *Bloody Sunday*) and went on to take home the Oscar for best animated feature as well. "My jaw was open from beginning to end," said Pixar's John Lassiter, a longtime admirer, and the rest of the Academy felt the same way.

Written and directed by Miyazaki, this visually intoxicating example of Japanese anime will be a revelation to anyone familiar only with Hollywood animation. The style is more painterly, the feeling unmistakably Japanese, and the mood, even when it's light, is almost never jokey or cartoonish.

Even for Miyazaki, there is something special about *Spirited Away*. Though it shares the otherworldly ambiance that characterizes his most beloved work, the charming and joyful *My Neighbor Totoro*, this is a heroic adventure story worthy of *The Arabian Nights* with an ordinary ten-year-old girl named Chihiro as the heroine.

Added to this magical air of once upon a time is the unnerving atmosphere of the unexpurgated Brothers Grimm, an intimidating world where boys can turn into terrible dragons, evil spirits can't go back on their word, and horrific sludge monsters take the weekend off to grab a hot tub and chill out at the local bathhouse.

Although possibly too scary for the smallest children, *Spirited Away* also manages, in a casual, offhand way, to teach lessons about the power of love and friendship, the importance of self-reliance and knowing who you are, the corrupting nature of greed, and how much is possible for those who believe.

It's a testament to the importance Miyazaki places on the wonder and enchantment of his visuals that, unlike the way things work at other places, he always animates first and then makes the dialogue fit the performance. Miyazaki's inventiveness never flags despite this film's two-hour–plus running time, and it expresses itself across a gamut that is remarkably wide.

For though it comes to the sweetest possible ending, *Spirited Away* is as at home with disturbing scenes of the ghastly, terrifying Kaonashi or "No-Face" throwing up as it is with images of piercing tranquillity and purity: the unforgettable vision of a train gliding to nowhere on tracks submerged in water could have come from a painting by Magritte.

Miyazaki no doubt intended the effect the opposition of these images has on us. Dream and nightmare, the grotesque and the beautiful, the terrifying and the enchanting, all come together to underline the oneness of things, to point out how little distance (much less than we might imagine) there is between these seemingly disparate states.

For a film that does so much, *Spirited Away* starts quietly, with a skittish, reluctant Chihiro sulking in the backseat of a car taking her and her parents to their new suburban home. She's unhappy at leaving familiar surroundings behind and not at all mollified when her mother says her new life will be an adventure.

Though using girls as intrepid heroines is nothing new for Miyazaki, Chihiro has a very particular starting point. "He met this young girl, the daughter of a friend, and he was surprised at how apathetic she was about everything," Lassiter has explained. "He noticed that this was a problem in Japan with young girls. They just didn't care; they were bored. So, he said, I want to make a movie for them."

That adventure starts sooner than anyone anticipates. In classic fable fashion, Chihiro's father takes a wrong turn and thinks he sees a shortcut through the woods that will solve his problems. The family ends up in front of a mysteriously beckoning tunnel that leads to what looks like an abandoned theme park (based on the real-life Edo-Toko Open Air Architecture Museum).

Wise beyond her years, Chihiro doesn't want to enter, but her mother and father, lured by delicious smells, insist the family plunge ahead. Although no one's around, they discover tables piled high with food so irresistible that the parents, suddenly losing all restraint, dig in with savage gusto.

"Don't worry," Chihiro's father says between heaping mouthfuls, "you've got Daddy here." (Yasuko Swaguchi, the actress who played Chihiro's mother, gnawed on Kentucky Fried Chicken during the recording session to make her line readings sound authentic.) Suddenly everything goes terribly wrong, and Chihiro finds herself on her own in this decidedly spectral environment.

In a panic, she comes upon an enormous building and watches in an astonishment we share as a ferry pulls up and unloads one of the strangest cargoes ever. The structure turns out to be a bathhouse for the gods, a place where all kinds of nonhuman spirits come to refresh, relax, and recharge. Miyazaki shows them all with a dazzling variety (especially hard to miss is the enormous walrus-like Radish Spirit) that words can't hope to equal.

"In my grandparents' time," Miyazaki has written, "it was believed that gods and spirits existed everywhere . . . in trees, rivers, insects, anything. . . . In fact, in Japanese, there is an expression—'*yaoyorozu no kami*'—which means 'eight million gods.' However, as far as I know, nobody has actually seen any of these gods and spirits. So I had to make up their faces and shapes. Some of them are based on beliefs, traditions, legends, and other materials."

Coming to Chihiro's aid is Haku, a severe-looking boy with a Prince Valiant haircut. "Don't be afraid, I just want to help you," he says, calm and collected, and Chihiro begins to feel a connection with him she cannot place.

Haku sends Chihiro to one of the bathhouse's oddest corners, the boiler room, where tiny, skittish soot gremlins (familiar to Miyazaki regulars from their appearance in *Totoro*) deliver coal to the furnace one lump at a time and the wily six-armed Kamaji, looking like a hipster-anarchist with his round dark glasses and bushy mustache, is the creature in charge.

Kamaji sends Chihiro to see Yubaba, a strange and powerful witch who runs the bathhouse despite looking like a petticoat-wearing, hair-in-a-bun nineteenth-century Victorian lady. She lives with her gargantuan infant son, Boh, literally the world's biggest baby, and three disembodied green heads that roll around her apartment for no apparent reason like a trio of mumbling, grumbling beach balls.

Chihiro is given a job assisting bathhouse attendant Lin, and here her adventures truly begin. Starting as a spoiled girl who never worked a day in her life, Chihiro gains confidence and ability as she copes with the singular challenges Miyazaki has prepared for her.

"This story is not a showdown between right and wrong," the director has written. "It is a story in which the heroine will be thrown into a place where the good and bad dwell together, and there she will experience the world. . . . She manages not because she has destroyed the 'evil,'" but because she has acquired the ability to survive."

Miyazaki's name, as it turns out, is the last image to appear on the screen after the final credits roll. It's hard to think of a filmmaker who deserves that prominence more.

What to Watch Next:
My Neighbor Totoro (1988), directed by Hayao Miyazaki.

Further Reading:
Starting Point: 1979–1996, by Hayao Miyazaki.

THE BEST OF YOUTH

2003

Directed by Marco Tullio Giordana. Starring Luigi Lo Cascio,
Alessio Boni, Jasmine Trinca.

Intimate, epochal, memorable, *The Best of Youth* defies logic and
expectation. Made for Italian television with no thought of ex-
port, a quirk of fate led it to turn out better than it might have.
Rank snobbery should have kept it from captivating the rarefied
international film festival world, and its unplayable six-hour
length should have kept it from an American theatrical release.
To see it at all is not to believe your luck. It is that satisfying, that
engrossing, that good.

Directed by Marco Tullio Giordana from a complex six-
hundred-page script by Sandro Petraglia and Stefano Rulli, *Youth*'s
story compellingly intertwines one family's personal narrative
with nearly forty years of the defining events of recent Italian history, constructing a story line whose various threads play out from
the mid-1960s to the early days of the twenty-first century.

Rather than pushing the envelope to terra incognita, *Youth*'s
creative team concentrated on pushing a different kind of envelope, on making mainstream, traditional cinema as good as they
could make it. This is a kind of filmmaking we sometimes forget

exists—serious, adult storytelling on a grand scale that deals with dramatic events whose unfolding patterns are a source of continual delight. The only way not to be captivated is not to see it in the first place.

Despite its strengths, if not for a series of fortunate events *Youth* would likely never have made it out of Italy. Even a year later, when I was introduced to him in Cannes, director Giordana was still surprised by what had happened. He told me that a managerial crisis at RAI, Italy's national broadcasting company and the film's production entity, had freed him from the at times stifling oversight of cultural bureaucrats and left him alone to make his film his way. An Italian scout for Cannes tipped the festival off to *Youth*'s qualities, and it appeared out of nowhere in the Un Certain Regard section in 2003.

Just as surprising was the emotional impact the film had on proverbially hard-bitten Cannes audiences: people seated near me at its first screening were reduced to tears at times. Adding surprise to surprise, *Youth* took home Un Certain Regard's top prize. The New York and Telluride film festivals took notice, as did theatrical distributors in Italy, where the film did remarkably well on the big screen before finally appearing on television (in four 90-minute installments) considerably later than had been anticipated.

The qualities that led to this success start with the scope of *Youth*'s story, which is basically the story of the generation that came of age in the cataclysmic 1960s. Though the film's events are as specifically Italian as its locations (Rome, Turin, Palermo, Tuscany, the Appenines), the overarching turmoil and upheaval, the sense of living in tumultuous times rife with social and political crisis, have parallels everywhere.

Given that American culture is convinced it all but invented the 1960s, it's more than a little ironic that the great film about that period should come from somewhere else. Yet if *Youth* has a subtext, it is the power and influence of American music and poetry, with references in the script to Sherwood Anderson and Allen Ginsberg's "Howl" and everything from the Four Tops "Reach Out I'll Be There" to both "Time After Time" and "I'm Through with Love" from Dinah Washington on the soundtrack.

Sensitively personalizing this story, using internal parallels between characters and situations to elaborate on its themes of the strength of family and the necessity of embracing life, was the veteran Italian writing team of Petraglia and Rulli, whose credits include Gianni Amilio's memorable *Stolen Children*.

Their *Youth* screenplay focuses on the Carati family, giving time to both parents and all four offspring but concentrating on the two middle children, brothers only one year apart in age, and the variety of emotional bonds they form. This film does not pretend human connection is easy, but it does insist that it is all we have, the only thing that can save us from the abyss.

The film begins in the summer of 1966, when the warm and lively Nicola (Luigi Lo Cascio) and the more reserved, broodingly handsome Matteo (Alessio Boni) are about to take a seasonal break from their university studies. Matteo is a prodigy in literature, while Nicola is just getting by in medicine. But, in a telling moment, a professor rates him highly because of his innate empathy, telling him "unsympathetic is the worst thing a doctor could be."

The brothers plan to hook up with friends and go to Norway, but a chance encounter Matteo has with Giorgia (Jasmine Trinca), an enigmatic, ethereally beautiful obsessive-compulsive patient in a psychiatric hospital, the Villa Quieta, ends up having a profound effect on both brothers' lives.

Their attempt to help Giorgia is an early manifestation of 1960s idealism that leads to the inevitable recognition that the world is more difficult and complicated than they realized. Their experience with this young woman underlines reality's unyielding, unsympathetic nature and compels the brothers to take different paths in response to the tides of history, to engage with and even confront an often unjust society in ways that couldn't be more different.

One of the great virtues of *Youth*'s length is its refusal to be rushed into establishing character. We reconnect to its protagonists at a series of pivotal crossroads, as they define themselves against the backdrop of changing times. While they make decisions about love, careers, the very stuff of life, we see how difficult it is to know which choice to make, how simple actions have unexpected consequences. Everyone we meet grows not only older but more complex than the person we initially encountered, at once different from but completely consistent with that first impression.

All-in performances by superior actors are essential in making all that happen, and *Youth* is filled with uniformly strong acting which ensures that we are dealing with individuals, not types. First among equals are Lo Cascio, the film's emotional center, and Boni, who plays a character so convincingly hot-tempered and unfathomable ("brave and sad like Achilles," says his brother) we never feel we completely understand him no matter how much we desperately want to.

Those who've seen Nani Moretti's *The Son's Room* will remember actress Trinca, whose haunting, hunted look is one of the film's touchstones. Also excellent are the two actresses, Sonia Bergamasco and Maya Sansa, whose characters play important roles in the brothers' lives. In some ways towering over everyone as the family matriarch is the veteran Adriana Asti, whose career extends back to another family epic, Luchino Visconti's *Rocco and His Brothers*, and whose work for directors like De Sica, Pasolini, and Bertolucci gives her both unquestioned authority and formidable skill.

Directing a film this ambitious, which could easily have turned into a standard miniseries, was a feat both logistically and emotionally, and Marco Tullio Giordana met both challenges.

Working with cinematographer Roberto Franzo, who makes good use of TV's inevitable close-ups, and shot in super 16 millimeter later blown up to 35 millimeter, Giordana oversaw a no-frills, twenty-four-week shoot that utilized some 240 sets and had actors noticeably age several times.

On an emotive level, Giordana's direction is a case study in the effectiveness of unobtrusive work. He allows all characters, no matter what their actions, the same dignity and respect. The decency and careful intelligence that run through this film give everything the feeling of reality. This restraint with the story's sensational material lets coincidences feel organic and allows the heart-stopping, melodramatic things that tend to happen in multipart family sagas to convince us rather than turn us off.

Youth also deftly works the events of the day into its personal story. There are small moments that only Italians will likely remember, like losing a World Cup match to North Korea in 1966, as well as situations with worldwide repercussions like cataclysmic floods in Florence, industrial unrest in Turin, and the government's fight with the Mafia in Palermo. Also represented are country-wide movements like the struggle for legal rights for mental patients (the screenwriters made a documentary on the subject called *Fit to Be Untied* in 1975) and the depredations of the murderous Red Brigades.

And despite its length, *The Best of Youth* (the title comes from a Pasolini poetry collection as well as an old Italian song) is characterized by its determination to pay attention to detail. The smallest roles are memorably cast (director Giordana says he chose even the extras personally) and the film's sense of the music of the period—including excerpts from Georges Delerue's *Jules and Jim* score, the Animals' version of "House of the Rising Sun," and Italian jukebox hits like "Amado Mio" and Fausto Leali's "A Chi" in addition to that American music—is immaculate.

Like other great popular melodramas, *The Best of Youth* has a pull that is strong enough to register as gravitational. Its length enables us to be involved in its characters' lives to a thrilling extent, and its warmth and intimacy, its belief that, as someone says, "What is the purpose of life but to live," make that involvement worthwhile, no matter how much time is needed to make it happen. Commit to watching *The Best of Youth* over two nights, remember it for a lifetime.

What to Watch Next:
Amarcord (1973), directed by Federico Fellini.

Further Reading:
A History of Italian Cinema, by Peter Bondanella.

THE FIVE OBSTRUCTIONS

2003

Directed by Jørgen Leth, Lars von Trier.

The Five Obstructions is a hypnotic original. This ingenious film won't remind you of anything else because there's nothing else quite like it. In only ninety minutes it encourages you to reexamine the nature of cinema, the sources of creativity, and the unexpected joys of the unanticipated moment. More than that, it takes the concept of the remake, ordinarily a bane of the cinematic universe, and creates a documentary blend that's enormously fun to watch.

Obstructions results from the fusion of energies of a pair of Danish codirectors who would seem to have little in common. Lars von Trier, the Palme d'Or winner for *Dancer in the Dark* who was unprecedentedly declared persona non grata at Cannes in 2011 for press conference remarks he made about Nazism and Adolf Hitler, is abrasive, provocative, difficult. Jørgen Leth, a maker of shorts and experimental works who's nearly twenty years von Trier's senior, is elegant, composed, unflappable, and little known in this country.

What both men do share is a keen intelligence, a passion for cinema in general and for one film in particular, a twelve-minute 1967 short called *The Perfect Human* that Leth directed. Von

Trier, who met Leth when both worked at the Danish Film Institute in the 1970s, says he's seen it at least twenty times and claims it as one of his all-time favorites. He loves it so much, it turns out, that he wants to destroy it.

For despite his avowed passion, von Trier, the born troublemaker, has a decidedly ambivalent attitude toward *The Perfect Human*, a whimsical, precisely composed mock anthropological examination of the male and female of the species. "It's a little gem," he says to its creator with unconcealed enthusiasm, "we are now going to ruin."

So the two directors make a pact. Leth agrees to remake his film five separate times, with each new version conforming to a series of conditions, the obstructions of the title, decreed by the increasingly diabolical von Trier.

This results in a feature put together from a range of parts. To begin with, *The Five Obstructions* shows major sections of Leth's original opus as well as each of the five films he makes to the exacting specifications of von Trier, who goes so far as to take an *Obstructor* credit in the final film.

On view, too, is vérité footage of Leth going out and making those five films. Also shot on the fly, and perhaps most involving of all, are the conversations between the two men, often held over elaborate vodka and caviar repasts, that occur both when von Trier presents Leth with the obstructions to be overcome and when, over a two-year period, Leth comes back to present his interlocutor with the finished responses.

The key thing about this interchange is that it is not just anyone formulating the obstructions; it is another filmmaker of formidable intelligence, as well as someone who truthfully says, "There are few areas in which I am expert, and one of them is Jørgen. I know more about him than he does."

These conversations follow the same irresistible pattern, the exhilaration of intellectual combat of a high order that Leth compares to a tense aesthetic tennis match. "It's very much a dialogue playing back and forth across the net," the director explains. "He serves hard and we return as hard as nails. He serves again, a deadly serve, and we have to pull our best shot out of the bag to return."

First serve always goes to von Trier, determined to make Leth as miserable as possible, to "banalize" his fellow Dane by forcing him to mar the flawless surface of his classic film.

Leth invariably responds by moaning and groaning, talking about Valium and claiming to be completely flummoxed by his adversary. "It's completely insane," he is wont to say of a von Trier obstruction, "it's impossible, totally destructive. What the hell does he expect me to do?"

Then, always the gifted counterpuncher, Leth coolly goes out, fulfills the conditions, and makes fine short films in the process. When von Trier complains, "You're so clever that whatever I do inspires you" and Leth riposts, "I can't help that," you have this process in a nutshell.

In his first set of obstructions, among other things, von Trier insists the remake be shot in Cuba, a country Leth has never visited, and doesn't allow the filmmaker any shots that last longer than twelve frames, or half a second of screen time. "Twelve frames, that was vicious of me," von Trier says, pleased with himself, when the film is delivered. "Satanic," Leth enthusiastically agrees, but soon enough von Trier realizes "twelve frames were a gift."

In his second group of conditions, von Trier makes Leth go to the most miserable place on earth (it turns out to be the heart of Bombay's red light district) and play the lead in the film himself, a ploy meant to get Leth to empathize with his surroundings and abandon the pose of the uninvolved observer. But, as increasingly becomes the norm, situations have a tendency not to work out the way von Trier anticipates.

One of the pleasures of *The Five Obstructions* is that the more exasperated von Trier gets, the more fascinating the film becomes. At one point the Obstructor, admittedly "furious when it turns out there are solutions" to his conditions, ups the ante on his obstacles, becoming, if possible, even more devious.

"The trouble is you're so clever everything I say inspires you; not a mark has been left on you," von Trier grumbles as he tightens the screws still further, studiously ignoring Leth's complaints that the new conditions are "really diabolical" and "below the belt."

It wouldn't be fair to reveal what von Trier insists on and how Leth responds, but each new set of challenges takes both Leth's filmmaking and the philosophical underpinnings of the exercise, the question of whether obstacles enhance or limit creativity, to a new, even more involving level.

What is perhaps most satisfying about this crossroads of amiable sadism and film art is the way it makes you believe again in the power of cinema to create mood and magic. "The Five Obstructions" is a billboard for the infinite possibilities inherent in the filmmaking process. And something more.

For it turns out there is an unanticipated aspect to von Trier's pervasive scheming, and to the man himself. See this impish film for its intellectual provocations, for its thrilling examinations of the creative process and receive, as an unexpected bonus, glimpses of humanity where you least expect them. That's how remarkable, how truly original *The Five Obstructions* is.

What to Watch Next:
Adaptation (2002), directed by Spike Jonze.

Further Reading:
Trivial Everyday Things, by Jørgen Leth.

STRANDED
I'VE COME FROM A PLANE THAT CRASHED ON THE MOUNTAINS

2007

Directed by Gonzalo Arijon.

SENNA

2010

Directed by Asif Kapadia.

Though the uninitiated may not know or care, we are living in a golden age of documentary filmmaking. Never before in cinematic history have so many people made so many high-quality nonfiction films.

Key among the reasons for this is the increasing sophistication and decreasing cost of digital equipment. Not to get too Marxist about it, putting the means of production into the hands of the workers has had marvelous results.

Equally important has been the existence of outlets that give these films exposure and help bang the drum for them, broadcast entities like HBO Documentary Films under the leadership of Sheila Nevins and festivals like IDFA in Amsterdam and Full Frame in Durham, North Carolina.

The top of that list, at least for me personally, is the Sundance Film Festival, the annual Park City, Utah, event that gave docs equal footing with independent dramatic features long before it was fashionable to do so.

Sundance has hosted the world premiers of innumerable excellent docs, films strong enough to make my annual ten best film selection. Just in the past few years, the list includes *20 Feet from Stardom*, *The Square*, *The Summit*, *Blackfish*, *The Invisible War*, *Marina Abramovic: The Artist Is Present*, *Ai Weiwei: Never Sorry*, and *Buck*. And that doesn't include docs like the pair of Israeli standouts, *The Gatekeepers* and *The Law in These Parts*, that played Sundance without premiering there.

As opposed to the two compelling documentaries from the 1980s described earlier—*The Day After Trinity* and *First Contact*—*Senna* and *Stranded* are both part of this newer Sundance-supported generation.

And though their subject matter—glamorous Brazilian Formula One driver Aryton Senna and the skeletal Uruguayan survivors of a disastrous airplane crash—could not sound more disparate, these films end up having a great deal in common beyond their Sundance origins, South American story component, and titles that begin with the same letter of the alphabet.

Both films deal with experiences we can barely imagine, even after hearing about them in exceptional detail. Though their documentary styles convey information in quite different ways, both are also intent on detailing as best they can the truth behind the myths that surround their subjects.

More critically, both *Senna* and *Stranded* surprise us with a very particular and unexpected emphasis. These films share a

deeper, more profound theme, a major spiritual component dealing with the presence of life in the midst of death that is more
potent in both cases for being completely unanticipated.

More than most documentaries, *Senna* helps itself by having
the pace of a thriller, a tale of motors and machines that doesn't
fail to tell a gripping human story.

Brazil's Aryton Senna was the boy genius of Formula One
racing, winner of three world championships and forty-one races
before dying in a 1994 Grand Prix crash at age thirty-four, a racer
BBC Sport recently voted the greatest Formula One driver who
ever lived.

But if all Senna could do was race, this wouldn't be much of a
story. Though he could drive like the devil, Senna was a spiritual
person who believed deeply and profoundly in a higher power. A
philosophical mystic with a jewel thief's nerves and a poet's sensitivity, not to mention killer good looks, Senna was an altogether
remarkable individual. And a deeply contradictory one.

"You are doing something that nobody else is able to do,"
he says. "But at the same moment that you are seen as the best,
the fastest, and somebody that cannot be touched, you are enormously fragile. Because in a split second, it's gone. These two ex-
tremes are feelings that you don't get every day. These are all
things which contribute to—how can I say—knowing yourself
deeper and deeper. These are the things that keep me going."

As that quote indicates, Senna was a thoughtful, articulate
man who wore his heart on his racing sleeve, someone your own
heart can't help but go out to as he tries to maintain a sense of
decency and dignity in cutthroat surroundings.

But Senna was also the fiercest competitor imaginable, someone who lived to win and never hesitated to push cars beyond
their design capabilities. Triumphing at Formula One, he tells
one interviewer, is "something so strong, like a drug. Once you
experience it, you search for it all the time."

More than anything, Senna was a driver who wouldn't play the game, an upright individual who loathed the politics and the injustices he felt he saw all around him and refused to compromise when he was sure he was right. It's not for nothing that *Senna* begins with the driver talking about his teenage years as a go-kart racer in Europe. "It was pure driving, pure racing," he says, looking back with undisguised longing. "There was no money, no politics, it was real racing."

Senna's story is so compelling that at various times directors like Michael Mann, Oliver Stone, Ridley Scott, and Antonio Banderas were reportedly contemplating features. Yet *Senna*'s director, Asif Kapadia, turned out to be someone who'd never been to a race and was not particularly a Formula One fan.

But Kapadia (whose debut feature, *The Warrior,* was a British academy award winner) brings essential gifts to the table. He has a keen sense of drama, a talent for narrative drive, and the kind of unerring eye necessary to cull 104 minutes of film from 15,000 hours of archival footage from ten countries, so much footage that the project took four years to edit and complete.

Not just any footage, either. Aided by screenwriter Manish Pandey, a Formula One enthusiast who was essential in getting the cooperation of both Senna's family and the equally protective Formula One hierarchy, Kapadia and his editors Gregers Sall and Chris King had access to material no one else had been able to use before.

This includes intimate home movie footage, onboard camera shots taken from inside Senna's car, and riveting footage of frequently tempestuous drivers-only meetings held before each race. Looking at endless interviews with the benefit of translators, the filmmakers realized that Senna had been more candid and forthcoming when talking to Brazilian TV than previously recognized.

Director Kapadia also conducted numerous contemporary interviews for *Senna,* recording both the driver's family and experienced journalists like ESPN's John Bisignano and Brazil's Reginaldo Leme. He also made the bold decision not to show the people interviewed as conventional talking heads, instead using their comments as voice-over accompanying vintage footage. It turns out to be a wise choice, keeping viewers inside the driver's reality and ensuring that nothing pulls us out of the intense moments of this world, this story.

The games Senna detested started with his first significant race, the 1984 Monaco Grand Prix, where the Brazilian, described as a genius in the rain, came from thirteenth place to almost win the event before a controversial decision gave it to France's Alain Prost. "Formula One is political," Senna said afterward. "It is money and when you are still small you have to go through this."

Prost, a four-time world champion, turned out to be Senna's bête noir, a driver whose calculating, legalistic personality led to his being nicknamed "The Professor." The savage rivalry between these two (aided and abetted by Jean-Marie Balestre, the president of Formula One's governing body) is something to behold, leading to on-track encounters at both the 1989 and 1990 Japanese Grand Prix that have such potent symmetry it's difficult to believe they actually happened.

Aryton Senna was such an innately dramatic personality that every race he took part in felt like the most intense possible. Until you see the next one. Perhaps his most emotional race was the 1991 Brazilian Grand Prix, an event which Senna, idolized in his home country, was desperate to win. The emotional and physical strain this exceptionally arduous event put him through—you can literally hear him screaming in pain on the car's camera—beggars belief no matter how many times you watch it unfold.

Speaking at Sundance, where the film won the world documentary audience award, screenwriter Pandey talked about showing the film to Ron Dennis, the head of the McLaren Group that Senna raced for in his prime, a man known for being unemotional and for being so conscious of not wasting a minute of his time he has a car and driver waiting for him with the engine running everywhere he goes.

"After the film ended, Ron Dennis cried for ten minutes," Pandey remembers. "Then he sat and talked about Senna for two hours." Such is the power of this man, and this film.

While the drama of Aryton Senna may be unfamiliar unless you are a Formula One fan, the narrative of *Stranded: I've Come from a Plane That Crashed on the Mountains* tells a story, one of the twentieth century's most astonishing tales of resilience and survival that we all think we know, and demonstrates that we haven't really known it at all.

Stranded's narrative is well-known because, under the title *Alive*, it was both an international best-selling book (5 million copies sold in English alone) and a Hollywood movie starring Ethan Hawke. Who doesn't have at least a vague knowledge of the story of the Uruguayan airliner that slammed into the Andes in 1972, and of the sixteen young men who survived for seventy-two days stranded in the mountains in part because they did the unthinkable and ate the flesh of those who died.

But it is only now, some thirty-five years after the fact, that all those who made it out alive agreed to tell their story from the inside, to talk on camera with candor and startling detail about the nature of their experience and what their thoughts about it are today. The result is a deliberate and powerful narrative that ends up as elevating as it is disturbing.

These stories do not shortchange the horror of the situation but, under the direction of Gonzalo Arijon, *Stranded* understands that out of disaster can come the purity of transcendence. The survivors' experience turns out to have been a surprisingly spiritual one, a story of intimate religious communion.

As *Alive* author Piers Paul Read noted in the book's acknowledgments, some survivors have always felt that "the faith and friendship which inspired them . . . do not emerge in these pages. . . . Perhaps it would be beyond the skill of any writer to express their own appreciation of what they lived through." Now, with this film, that appreciation has taken tangible form.

One reason these men felt comfortable finally talking was that veteran documentarian Arijon, born in Montevideo but a resident of Paris for nearly thirty years, was a boyhood friend of many of the young men who boarded that plane on Friday October 13, 1972.

The *Stranded* survivors turn out to be persuasive, articulate talkers, astonished at the arbitrariness of fate. "How does destiny work?" one of them asks. "Why you and not me? What is the formula, what is the equation that underlies this kind of logic?" We hang on these words as voices combine to remember every moment with an awful vividness and an immediacy that can overwhelm.

Aside from getting the interviews, director Arijon did other things to make his narrative especially effective, starting with utilizing the film's delicate, otherworldly score by composer Florencia Di Concillo-Perrin to add a disturbing air to the proceedings.

Unlike *Senna*, which had thousands of hours of footage to work with, *Stranded* had to make its peace with the fact that no film exists of the crash experience (with the exception of newsreel footage of the rescue). So Arijon centers the film around contemporary talking heads and made the risky decision to use re-creations to help tell the story.

Though this technique can be heavy-handed, here, as shot in super 16 millimeter by cinematographer Cesare Charlone, Oscar nominated for *City of God*, the opposite is true. Someone with his own connection to the tragedy—he was nearly a passenger on that doomed flight—Charlone has crafted quiet, effective scenes that grow on us, taking on a reality of their own. Because no one in the re-creations speaks, the sequences come off as dreamlike and haunting, which is as it should be.

The re-creations are also an effective companion piece to *Stranded*'s other contemporary footage, which follows the adult survivors as they take a summertime trip back to the Valley of Tears in the Andes, the crash site, and try to convey to their children the nature of what they went through.

In 1972 these men were just nineteen years old, players on a rugby team whose members had graduated from a Catholic high school, headed for a game in Santiago, Chile, and what they thought would be a weekend "full of adventure and excitement."

The crash instantly killed more than a dozen of the forty-five passengers, and numerous others died from a combination of injuries and hunger. When survivors heard on their radio that the search for them had been abandoned, they came around with tremendous reluctance to the notion of what they had to do to survive.

Stranded emphasizes that what kept this Catholic group together was its "strong sense of unity and solidarity" and that the decision to eat human flesh was done in the respectful spirit of the most serious religious ritual. Instead of feeling exploitative, the scenes where the decision and its consequences are discussed are the most deeply moving of the film. "It was a very intimate communion for all of us," one of the group explained at their first post-rescue press conference. "That's what helped us survive."

Also stirring are the descriptions of how the group was finally rescued, how two of their number walked for ten days before reaching help, going so far (44 miles over peaks that reached 13,000 feet) that the rescue helicopter pilots they guided back to their friends thought they couldn't possibly have covered so great a distance.

Roberto Cannessa, one of the two who walked out, appeared at *Stranded*'s Sundance premier, and it's no exaggeration to say that his experience on the mountain turned him into a figure of enormous charisma and grace, with the kind of magnetism even the greatest film stars would be hard-pressed to match. Asked to reflect on it all, he replied quietly, "Make plans for one hundred years, but you must be ready to die at any moment." Words to live by, and, like *Senna*, a film impossible to forget.

What to Watch Next:
Downhill Racer (1969), directed by Michael Ritchie.
Into the Wild (2007), directed by Sean Penn.

Further Reading:
Alive, by Piers Paul Read.

A PROPHET

2009

Directed by Jacques Audiard. Starring Tahar Rahim, Niels Arestrup.

Genre is powerful, especially in the hands of as masterful a film-maker as France's Jacques Audiard. *A Prophet* is an answered prayer for those who believe that revitalizing classic forms with contemporary attitudes makes for the most compelling kind of cinema.

Part prison film, part crime story, part intense personal drama, this all-consuming narrative became something of a phenomenon after it received the Grand Jury Prize at Cannes. A *Sight & Sound* magazine poll of critics worldwide named it the best film of 2009; it took Britain's prestigious Bafta foreign language award and was one of the five Oscar nominees in that category (inevitably losing to Argentina's more sentimental *The Secret in Her Eyes*). *A Prophet* also won nine Césars, France's Oscar, including best picture, director, screenplay, cinematography, editing, and two acting awards. Yes, it is that good.

None of this was a surprise to followers of cowriter (with Thomas Bidegain) and director Jacques Audiard, a meticulous craftsman whose four previous films, including US art house successes *Read My Lips, A Self-Made Hero,* and *The Beat That My*

Heart Skipped, displayed a passion for well-constructed, emotionally connected narratives and gripping, visceral storytelling that *A Prophet* takes to even higher levels.

So while those familiar with *The Big House* prison movies or tales of criminal enterprise featuring gang rivalries, intricate drug deals, and double and triple crosses will feel at home here, that's not the end of the story. What's particularly satisfying about *A Prophet* is seeing how the ruthless arsenal of modern filmmaking—uncompromisingly gritty characterization, explicit violence (doled out in graphic bursts that are brief but terrible), unlooked-for surreal elements like ghosts catching fire, and eclectic music from the likes of Jimmy Dale Gilmore and Sigur Ros—has reinvented and reinvigorated the gangster film for the modern age.

As a filmmaker Audiard not only believes in this style of storytelling in and of itself, he values it for what it can clandestinely say about larger issues. "What interests me about genre," the director said when I interviewed him at Cannes, "is that the public connects immediately with it; it has certain rules, certain codes the audience recognizes. I like that it's a popular form of cinema with mass appeal. Art cinema aspects and elements can be inserted and reach the widest audience."

What Audiard especially wanted to insert in *A Prophet* is the unexpectedly empathetic character of its protagonist, a rootless young Arab named Malik El Djebena. Raised in a juvenile center and in and out of institutions his whole life, Malik arrives at a French prison at age nineteen to begin doing a six-year stretch. "You're in with the big guys," his lawyer laconically tells him, and so it frighteningly proves to be.

Friendless, barely literate, and highly vulnerable in the savage, balkanized prison environment, Malik is initially fresh meat, someone who soon enough gets his shoes stolen and his body beaten. Though the young man's fiery core resists backing down, he gains our sympathy because Tahar Rahim's César-winning performance is able to project vulnerability and openness in addition to nerve and fury.

Audiard met the young actor when they shared an automobile ride from a film set, and "I looked at him and that was that, though I didn't trust my instincts and auditioned forty other actors before I chose him. When I looked into his eyes there was no melancholy, no tragedy, just someone very open, very full of life."

Unfortunately, Malik catches a terrible break early on. Not only does an older Arab prisoner named Reyeb (Hichem Yacoubi) proposition him for sexual favors, but César Luciani, the frankly terrifying crime boss who runs things on the inside, notices this and decides to use it to his advantage.

If Malik is at the bottom of the prison pyramid, César is at the very top, a Mr. Big who isn't exaggerating when he says of himself and the wolf pack cadre of Corsican mobsters who follow him everywhere, "we run this place." As played by Niels Arestrup (who won a César as the cold father in *The Beat That My Heart Skipped* and added another one here), this is a brutally violent man with the icy dead eyes and quick-strike instincts of a cobra who intimidates hard cases just by looking at them.

A Prophet is the tale of what happens to Malik during his six years inside. It's a story complex enough to need two and a half hours to play out as Malik navigates a postgraduate course in criminal behavior and receives the most unsentimental of educations, one that allows him to gain an authentic sense of his potential, both as the person he never knew he could be and as part of an Islamic culture he barely knew existed.

Because, as it turns out, the title *A Prophet* and the spiritual mythologizing that goes along with it is very much intentional on filmmaker Audiard's part. As a series of chilling scenes demonstrate, Malik can see dead people, and having prophetic visions is not outside his capacities. Even the memorable criminals created by James Cagney never went down this particular route.

Malik's trajectory inside the walls is intricately intertwined with his relationship with the deadly overlord César. A career criminal who can go from seeming lassitude to rage in a moment, César functions as both mentor and slave master to the young man, taking him under his wing but holding him contemptuously at arm's length because he is an Arab.

Gradually, almost imperceptibly, *A Prophet* reveals stirrings of ambition on Malik's part, bits and pieces of an entrepreneurial spirit, a clandestine yearning to make something of his life. While the film deftly echoes *The Godfather* saga, it's played out in an alternate universe where Don Vito Corleone matches wits with his son Michael.

Though *A Prophet* was shot in a set constructed in an abandoned factory, it goes to great lengths to feel authentic, including hiring former convicts, "the only people," the director says, "who know about prisons. For scenes in corridors, I'd just ask them to act naturally. When we had to stage fights, they would say, 'That's not very realistic; that's not how it's done.'"

Essential to creating *A Prophet*'s completely enveloping ambiance is Stephane Fontaine's intense and jittery camerawork. So bleak and claustrophobic is this world that a glimpse of a passing airplane from the exercise yard looks like an image from another cosmos. Fontaine's camerawork also nicely captures this story's small yet telling moments, for instance, the way a convict on leave reflexively mimics prison procedure by opening his mouth while going through an airport security screening.

Since it feels so realistic, Audiard's film, much to his surprise, sparked debate in France about conditions in prison and penal reform. His goals, he said in Cannes, were more cinematic, his intention to create mythic figures, icons for those, like the Arabs in France, who don't have them.

But because his characters are so individual and alive, Audiard's film transcends those goals, catching us up completely in Malik's individual quest to come into his own. We not only worry about this young man's survival, we worry about what ensuring that survival will do to him. For this is a world where nothing is predictable, nothing is safe, and no one leaves you alone.

What to Watch Next:
Read My Lips (2001), directed by Jacques Audiard.

OF GODS AND MEN

2010

Directed by Xavier Beauvois. Starring Lambert Wilson, Michael Lonsdale.

Dramatic tension isn't found only in obvious places. Complex moral dilemmas can compel viewers just as easily as heroines in jeopardy or runaway trains. The austere yet provocative *Of Gods and Men* is an adventure of the spirit that's as thrilling as anything James Bond ever appeared in.

Directed by Xavier Beauvois and based on the true story of a profound life-and-death crisis faced by a group of French monks in a monastery in Algeria's Atlas Mountains in the mid-1990s, *Of Gods and Men* takes its name from somber lines from Psalm 81. They begin the film and leave no doubt as to the seriousness of purpose of what we're about to see: "ye are gods and all of you are children of the most high. Yet ye shall die like men, and fall like one of the princes."

European cinema especially has a history of films dealing with the power of spirituality and belief. You can almost trace a dramatic line that goes back to the magisterial work of Denmark's Carl Theodor Dryer (*The Passion of Joan of Arc, Day of Wrath, Ordet*) and includes the more recent films of Belgium's Dardenne brothers, especially *La Promesse*, in which a thoughtlessly amoral young boy discovers the existence of a difference between right and wrong. Few of these films, however, have caused as much of a sensation as *Of Gods and Men* did in its native France.

The film won the Cannes Grand Jury Prize and was nominated for eleven Césars, including best picture, director, screenplay, cinematography, and a trio of acting nods. It not only won three (picture, cinematography, and supporting actor for the veteran Michael Lonsdale), but also, even more impressive for a film with monks and more monks as protagonists, *Of Gods and Men* exploded commercially in France, getting more than 2 million admissions in only its first five weeks in theaters.

Director Beauvois, whose previous film was the excellent crime drama *Le Petit Lieutenant*, accomplished this not by making it easy for the audience or sensationalizing Etienne Comar's thoughtful script. Rather, he's taken the opposite approach and selected rigor and restraint to be his most effective tools.

Though it works up considerable dramatic heft, *Of Gods and Men* is careful to start quietly, choosing to emphasize, in Caroline Champetier's luminous cinematography (the film was actually shot in Morocco, not Algeria), the tranquil setting of the Cistercian monastery in the remote community of Tibhirine.

In a way that echoes *Into Great Silence*, Philip Groning's immersive documentary about monastic life, *Of Gods and Men* could not be in less of a hurry. It opts to slowly absorb viewers in the monks' daily lives as they move through sacred prayer rituals and secular tasks like gardening, cleaning, building, and making honey. The objective is to make the monks' tranquil rhythms our rhythms, to make us feel we live here, too, so that the disruption that shocks these men shocks us just as much.

Not surprisingly, given its title, there is a special focus in all of this on the community's elaborate, melodic, white-robed prayer rituals. The repetition of prayer services emphasizes that what we're seeing shouldn't be confused with cinematic local color: it is the essence of who these men are and what they do.

The film also emphasizes from the start how well the monks, who are unmistakably there to do service, not to proselytize, fit into the fabric of the town's Muslim community. Benevolent but never paternalistic, insistent that relationships not be based on power, they are invited to family celebrations, they sell their Miel de l'Atlas honey in the market, enjoy easy relations with the local religious leaders and, in the form of brother Luc (Lonsdale), provide minimal but essential medical care to more than a hundred people a day.

We meet all the monks eventually, from the ancient Amedee to the worrier Christophe, but the one who makes the biggest impression, aside from Luc, is Christian, who has been elected by the others to be their prior, or leader. As played by Lambert Wilson, best known to American audiences for his role as the Merovingian in the *Matrix* films, Christian is forceful and articulate, someone whose clear sense of what the monks should be doing drives the action and makes him seem both sure of himself and, at times, intransigent and unwilling to compromise.

This scene setting is delicately done, and along with it comes the sense that these monks and villagers are living in a paradise on earth, small problems notwithstanding. As is the case with almost all paradises, however, it is inevitable that there will be a shattering fall.

The first intimations of this are reports that an eighteen-year-old girl in a nearby town was stabbed on a bus for not wearing the hijab, or traditional Muslim head covering. The local imam is as horrified as the monks at these first stirrings of Islamic fundamentalism. "This is new, no one understands," he says, adding "the world's gone mad."

Then things come closer to home, and we watch as a gang of terrorists led by the implacable Ali Fayattia (Farid Larbi) slaughters a group of nearby Croatian construction workers, cutting the throats of men whose only crime is that they are not Muslims. A visit to the monastery by Ali and his men—"where is the Pope?"

they scream—underlines that despite all that has gone before, the deadly threat to the monks could not be more real.

Of Gods and Men compellingly examines the ways the monks, at one and the same time men and men of God, deal with this stark change in their reality. Though their dilemma can be framed in the simplest terms—should they stay or should they go—the factors they have to consider make the decision extraordinarily complex.

For one thing, staying would mean accepting military protection from a corrupt government the monks are not in sympathy with, a government that tells them their stubbornness is putting them in unnecessary danger.

But leaving would mean abandoning the village that depends on the community. When one of the monks tries to explain the touch-and-go nature of their decision by saying "we are birds on a branch," he is contradicted. No, a villager says, "we are the birds, you are the branch. If you go, we will lose our footing."

In addition to these factors, issues of personal responsibility, of religious vocation, of how you lead your life, loom large, leading to crises of faith that are different for each of the monks. "I didn't come here to commit collective suicide," one man insists, while another asks, "Would dying here and now serve a purpose?" There are no easy answers to questions like these, and the film has the grace not to pretend otherwise.

What *Of Gods and Men* does do is emphasize the role of prayer in how the final decision is made. When Cristophe has severe doubts, it is God he cries out to, sobbing, "Help me, help me, don't abandon me." Prayer is these men's habit and sustenance. They trust with unwavering absoluteness that guidance will come through worship. Once a decision is reached, a simple supper served to the rapturous concluding music from *Swan Lake*, a ballet that also emphasizes the triumph of love over death, raises the monks, and the audience, to the highest possible plane.

As noted, *Of Gods and Men* was a surprising success in France, so much so that the country's major newspapers speculated editorially on the possible reasons. *Le Monde* was perhaps most eloquent and acute, observing that the monks "incarnate everything that the public, from the left to the right, no longer finds in society—nobility of spirit, a sense of sacrifice, freedom, sincerity, daily ecology, meditation, reflection on death." Gone from society, and gone from movie screens as well, which is why this contemplative but emotional film makes the kind of impact it does.

What to Watch Next:

Into Great Silence (2005), directed by Philip Groning.

FOOTNOTE

2011

Directed by Joseph Cedar. Starring Shlomo Bar-Aba,
Lior Ashkenazi.

Footnote speaks volumes. Intensely specific in story yet universal
in themes, with a tone that turns on a dime from comic absurdity
to near tragedy, this is brainy, bravura filmmaking, a motion picture that is as difficult to characterize as it is a pleasure to enjoy.

The fourth work by writer/director Joseph Cedar, Israel's
most accomplished filmmaker, *Footnote* did not lack for recognition. It took the best screenplay award at Cannes, won nine Israeli Oscars (including picture, script, and direction for Cedar,
plus a pair of acting awards) and, like Cedar's last film, the very
different *Beaufort*), was one of five nominees for the best foreign
language Oscar. All despite subject matter that could not sound
more parochial or even obscure.

Set in the spirited precincts of Jerusalem's Hebrew University, *Footnote* deals with the implacable rivalry between two schol-
ars of the Talmud, the complex and sacred primary text of the
Jewish religious tradition: the misanthropic, unsmiling Eliezer
(Shlomo Bar-Aba) and the gregarious Uriel (Lior Ashkenazi),
who happen to be father and son.

"The Talmud is our primary text, our tradition; it's something I want to deal with if I am making movies in Israel," filmmaker Cedar, whose own father is a celebrated Hebrew University scientist, said when I interviewed him after the film's Cannes debut.

"Talmud is known for being the smallest and toughest department at the university. There are stories of epic rivalries, of people being stubborn in a way that is concrete solid, where you don't compromise on anything, ever. These are people who have dedicated their lives to something esoteric, and they've done it with the drive of Julius Caesar."

Emphasizing that point, the director talked about conversations he had while the film's poster art was being planned. "One idea I had was to create an image from a boxing movie; *Raging Bull* would have fit. In boxing, everyone is comfortable saying, 'I want to knock you out,' but the further you get from sports, the harder that is for people to admit. What I'd really like is to get those intellectuals into a boxing ring."

It is Cedar's particular talent to find a way to endow the infighting and the rivalries of this recondite world with broader interest and make it speak to larger concerns. *Footnote*'s nominally miniature canvas turns out to encompass with casual grace themes as large and involving as the price of ambition, the perhaps inevitable tension between fathers and sons, and the human requirement for recognition.

"Recognition is something you need to live, but to get it you may have to compromise your integrity," the director said at Cannes. "That's something that I dread, and something that's a big part of the relationship between individual Israelis and the Israeli establishment. You need it but you feel shameful about it. To be embraced by a country is not a little thing. And there is a price tag that comes with it."

More than just the nature of these conflicts, however, makes *Footnote* stimulating. The inventive, playfully cinematic ways Cedar presents the drama and the information—like using the form of unspooling microfilm as a recurring visual theme—also factors in.

The film's opening segments, daringly set to music reminiscent of Bernard Herrmann's compositions for Alfred Hitchcock thrillers (Amit Poznansky did the score), skillfully present many of the plot elements that will play out unexpectedly as the story progresses.

After the words "The most difficult day in the life of Professor Shkolnick" appear on the screen, we immediately see an older academic-looking man, presumably the individual in question, and hear a voice-over extolling extensive and impressive professorial credentials: international recognition, nine books, dozens of papers, the respect of his peers, and so on.

Only gradually does it register that while it is the father Eliezer Shkolnik we are looking at, the voice is proclaiming the virtues of his son Uriel, and it is the father's difficult day because seeing his son be inducted into the Israeli National Academy of Science—an honor he himself has not received—is eating him alive. It's simply the first of many delicious reversals *Footnote* specializes in presenting.

At this point, quickly and with considerable visual flair, *Footnote* fills us in on the background of both Shkolniks, starting with father Eliezer, a scholar, it will come as no surprise to anyone, of fierce and almost terrifying integrity.

The elder Shkolnik is a philologist, a close textual researcher into language, who spent more than thirty years painstakingly analyzing different versions of the Jerusalem Talmud only to have rival scholar Yehuda Grossman (Micah Lewesohn, with a forehead furrowed like the sands of the Negev) beat him to publication because of a fluke discovery.

The pride of Eliezer's life is a footnote dedicated to him in a monumental analysis of the Talmud by the legendary P. Feinstein, making him the only living person mentioned by name among thousands of notes. (In one of the film's many real-life correlations, there is apparently just such a footnote in a book by Y.N. Epstein, the father of modern Talmudic scholarship.)

If Eliezer is a fussy minimalist, son Uriel very much sees the big picture. Beautifully played by Israeli star Ashkenazi (*Late Marriage, Walk on Water*), who grew an impressive beard for the part, Uriel is a born schmoozer who writes expansively and conceptually on what the Talmud might mean without worrying overly much about the specific words, an approach that is anathema to his father.

Uriel is a difficult man in his own way—he likes telling students that their work has things in it that are new and correct, "only the new things are not correct and the correct things are not new"— but, in conversations with both his wife Dikla (Alma Zak) and his long-suffering mother Yehudit (Alisa Rosen), it's clear that he cares more about the father-son relationship than the older man does.

Though both actors won Israeli Academy Awards for their work, *Footnote* is impossible to imagine without Ben-Aba's fearless performance as the cantankerous born contrarian Eliezer. Primarily a stage and television performer known for antic comedy, Bar-Aba is marvelous as a man who holds it all inside, conveying considerable subtleties of emotion through an expression that on some level appears never to change.

With all this information as back story, *Footnote* kicks into gear when a bombshell hits and Eliezer, of all people, is notified that he has won the highly coveted Israel Prize, the country's top academic honor.

Uriel is just beginning to get used to what that means when, in a brilliant scene that initially echoes the claustrophobic stateroom commotion in the Marx Brothers' *A Night at the Opera* and then goes somewhere else entirely, comedy and tragedy fatally intertwine in a way that feels classically Jewish and completely new. Amusing and disturbing in equal measure, *Footnote* does more than ask the provocative question, What is more important than truth? It attempts to answer it as well.

What to Watch Next:
The Gatekeepers (2012), directed by Dror Moreh.

Further Reading:
The Israelis: Founders and Sons, by Amos Elon.

ORSON WELLES DOUBLE FEATURE

It's happenstance as much as anything else that gives Orson Welles a position of prominence all his own at the end of this book—as opposed to my other double bills, the two films I've chosen for him are from different decades—but I can't say I mind.

I've often named Welles as my favorite director, a man whose passions ignited the screen but made the practicalities of his day to day filmmaking existence precarious. His glories have not faded in my eyes and showcasing them is always the greatest of pleasures.

TOUCH OF EVIL

1958

Directed by Orson Welles. Starring Charlton Heston,
Janet Leigh, Orson Welles.

CHIMES AT MIDNIGHT

1965

Directed by Orson Welles. Starring Orson Welles, Keith Baxter, John Gielgud.

I met Orson Welles only once. The meeting was brief and a few of the details are vague, but the memory has endured.

It happened in the early 1980s at a Los Angeles hotel where Welles was scheduled to receive some kind of minor award. A room had been set aside for the preliminary cocktail reception, and right in the middle of it, at his ease in an enormous armchair like some unlooked-for combination of benign potentate and Hasidic bridegroom, the immense director held court.

When I was brought over and introduced, I told Welles what I felt, that he was the greatest of American film directors. Then I added, in a sense apologizing for wasting his time with so commonplace and pedestrian a sentiment, "But you probably hear that all the time."

Welles hadn't responded to my first sentence, but he put his head back and literally roared with laughter at the second. "You can't," he said with conviction born of experience, "hear that too often."

When I think about it now, there's a poignance to Welles's response that I didn't completely understand at first. If the praise and opportunity that goes with extraordinary ability is a given for most master directors, Welles's career had followed a very different, more uncertain arc.

While access to all the technical resources 1940s Hollywood had to offer ("the biggest electric train set any boy ever had," he famously said) had allowed Welles to debut as a feature director with the exceptional *Citizen Kane*, for half a century the number one film in *Sight & Sound* magazine's once-a-decade greatest movies poll, the karmic balance the cinema gods decreed meant nothing would ever be so easy for him again.

Although Welles directed another dozen features, each of them had its difficult, thorny aspects, either in terms of financing, distribution, or control of final cut. Critics argue ceaselessly over why someone so gifted faced so many hardships—was the problem Hollywood's intransigence, Welles's personality, or some combination of the two?—but talking about him as a director is curiously equivalent to talking to baseball fans about the plight of the often injured New York Yankee Mickey Mantle: how great could these men have been if they'd been able to operate at the peak of their powers?

Yet as far as the films Welles was able to complete are concerned, this is not as unremittingly bleak a story as it sounds. Even working under the variety of constraints and the daunting odds that became business as usual for him, Welles, congenitally incapable of ordinary work, was able to do some truly exceptional things. Don't even think about giving him points for degree of difficulty; he doesn't need them.

Though their tone and sensibility are quite different, both *Touch of Evil* and *Chimes at Midnight*, sometimes known as *Falstaff*, share several qualities. Both are adaptations, though of wildly different material (Whit Masterson's pulp novel *Badge of Evil* in the first case, the historical plays of Shakespeare in the second), and both star Welles in metaphysically—and literally—larger-than-life roles it's difficult to imagine anyone else inhabiting. And both demonstrate as well the kind of filmmaking gifts, the ability to do bravura work without having it come off as show-offy, which is Welles's directing trademark.

Perhaps the most surprising thing about *Touch of Evil* is the way it continues to surprise. Repeated viewing can't dull the edge of its sinister ambience or soften the visual excitement Welles brought to this quintessentially cinematic film noir.

This has been especially true since 1998, when producer Rick Schmidlin and editor Walter Murch, following the detailed instructions Welles offered in a celebrated fifty-eight-page memo he wrote after seeing what Universal had done to his cut, came up with a version that was closer to the director's conception of the film than anything that had been available before.

The most conspicuous of those changes is hard to miss: the credits that were once superimposed on the superb three-minute Chapman crane tracking shot, one of the most celebrated openings in American film, have now been moved to the film's ending, so much the better to appreciate the mastery of what Welles and cinematographer Russell Metty achieved.

That complex shot tracks a bomb from the moment when it's planted in the trunk of a massive Cadillac in Mexico (doubled by Venice, California) to the resulting explosion in America that kills a stripper named Zita and Rudy Linnekar, one of the most prominent men in the mythical American border town of Los Robles. "Welcome Stranger to Picturesque Los Robles," reads a criminally deceptive billboard, "the Paris of the Border."

The showstopping visuals begin unassumingly with a close-up of a few sticks of dynamite and a timer and then breathlessly pulls you smoothly up and out without losing focus on the Cadillac. When a pair of lovers walk into the frame, the camera leaves the car momentarily to travel with them, then returns to the vehicle just in time for Zita (Joi Lansing) to say she can't get a curious ticking sound out of her head as the car crosses the border and explodes.

When the bomb goes off the two lovers, who just happen to be crusading Mexican police official Miguel "Mike" Vargas (Charlton Heston), chairman of the Pan American Narcotics Commission, and his brand-new American wife, Susan (Janet Leigh), are nearby. Since the bomb originated in his country and Vargas is nothing if not conscientious, he immediately involves himself in the investigation.

That doesn't sit too well with Los Robles law enforcement legend, "our local police celebrity" as someone calls him, Capt. Hank Quinlan. Touchy about his prerogatives, alternately bullying, whining, dismissive, and aggrieved, Quinlan is as memorable a piece of acting as Welles (who reportedly weighed close to 300 pounds but added 60 more via padding) ever did. It's a brilliant and grotesque characterization that commands attention from the first moment to the last.

Quinlan is described in *Touch of Evil*'s shooting script as "a grossly corpulent figure in an overcoat, a huge cigar in the middle of his puffy face," but even that image doesn't do justice to the huge, malignant toad Welles creates on camera. That flapping overcoat hangs off him like a Bedouin tent, the cigar juts from his mouth in an act of perpetual hostility, and the man himself drips sarcasm, corruption, and disdain.

Introduced in a wide close-up as he maneuvers his way out of a car, a vanity-free choice by Welles that emphasizes the character's unnerving bulk, Quinlan projects a lived-in life. Venality and inner demons have marked the man, and they're especially visible in his face, where frequent tight close-ups reveal tiny, gleaming slits of eyes fighting for life amid expanses of corrupt, bloated flesh. Yet Welles doesn't let us forget that this is also a man of shrewd intelligence ("Just because he speaks a little guilty," he says of one suspect, "that don't make him innocent") who can convey a sense of remembered romantic pleasure he doesn't seem capable of.

The presence of Vargas and his wife soon draws the interest of crime boss Joe Grandi (a wheedling Akim Tamiroff), whose drug-dealing brother is one of those Vargas has imprisoned. Grandi is soon laying complex plans to embarrass and compromise the Mexico City cop, and he has no qualms about involving Vargas's naive young wife in his schemes.

Though their presence is the catalyst for much of the plot, Vargas and his wife are the least compelling people in *Touch of Evil*. It's rather the film's gallery of unsettling characters we remember, like the unnerving blind woman who sits prominently in the frame as Vargas tries to have a romantic telephone conversation with his young bride. "If you are mean enough to steal from the blind," the sign behind her says, "help yourself."

Other performances, even if they are small, have become close to legendary, like Mercedes McCambridge as the sinister leader of a drug-using gang, or Dennis Weaver, who improvised much of his role as a twitchy, unbalanced motel night man, the prototype for *Psycho*'s Norman Bates, who totally loses control at just the mention of the word "bed."

Best of all is Marlene Dietrich, one of several of Welles's friends and collaborators, including Joseph Cotten as the American coroner and Zsa Zsa Gabor as the owner of a Mexican strip club, to appear in a series of cameos.

Dietrich, however, is in a class of her own, putting on a black wig to play Tanya, the owner of a local dive who delivers nothing but drop-dead lines. "You're a mess, honey," she laconically tells the whale-like Quinlan early on after advising him to "lay off those candy bars." Later, when he asks her to read his future in the Tarot cards, she comes back with a blood-freezing, "You haven't got any. Your future is all used up."

Photographed by Metty, *Touch of Evil* exemplifies the kind of eye-catching camera work Welles favored. Expressionistic in the extreme, filled with darker-than-night shadows, unexpected angles, and cinematic flourishes, the film raises the standard brooding nightmare ambience of film noir to a poetic level few other pictures have achieved. As Janet Leigh said in a 2008 interview, with Welles "nothing was ever mundane, nothing was ever boring, nothing was ever ordinary." But striking though they are, the visuals are not there for their own sake but to advance the story.

Welles's original December 5, 1957, memo about *Touch of Evil* was first published in its entirety in 2008, and in its own way it's one of the more heartbreaking documents to come out of Hollywood. Visible on every page is how much Welles cared about his work, his deep knowledge of the craft of filmmaking, his passion for detail, and, ever sensitive to his lack of influence, how polite, well-spoken, even deferential he could be in making his case. This is no arrogant auteur laying down the law but a man pleading for his creative life.

Resigned as he is "to the fact that a great majority of my previous notes and suggestions have been disregarded," Welles is completely aware that he's "the very last person whose opinion will likely carry any weight." Still, he can't help but appeal to the powers that be not just for his version of the film but also for the kind of simple fairness that would allow him to be part of the team in what he knew to be a collaborative art.

"Do please—please give it a fair try," he says at one point, "do please give the question some thought," he adds at another.

The closest Welles got to exasperation was when he wrote, "I must ask that you open your mind for a moment to this opinion from the man who, after all, made the picture." They didn't, and Welles never made a film in Hollywood again.

If a number of Welles's post-*Kane* films have a make-do quality about them, the sense of being called into being against daunting odds by a virtuoso on a budget, *Chimes at Midnight* has it more than most. The director's resources had become inescapably fewer—the film was made, Welles memorably commented, by "cutting corners, and then cutting the cuts"—and the uneven results of budget-driven decisions like shooting in Spain instead of England and employing extensive postproduction sound recording are hard to avoid.

Yet as Welles's difficulties intensified over time, his gifts also deepened. While the strains limited spending put on the production were unfortunate—the director claimed that in one particular scene, all seven key actors had to be played by stand-ins—Welles's work simultaneously became more effortless and more profound. So much so that the director came to claim *Chimes* as the favorite among his films: "If I wanted to get into heaven on the basis of one movie," he told the BBC in 1982, "that's the one I'd offer up."

A meditation on aging, friendship, betrayal, and coming to terms with life's profound contradictions interspersed with antic humor and some of the greatest battle scenes ever filmed, *Chimes at Midnight* can't escape the air of majestic melancholy that begins with the opening scene, a wintry conversation between Welles's Sir John Falstaff and his old friend Master Shallow (Alan Webb) that gives the film its name: "We have heard the chimes at midnight, Master Robert Shallow," Falstaff says, to which the venerable man replies, "That we have, that we have, that we have."

That exchange, though it is said in a different physical context, comes from *Henry IV, Part II*, one of several Shakespeare plays (the others include *Henry IV, Part I, Henry V, Richard II,* and *The Merry Wives of Windsor*) that Welles mined for situations and lines of dialogue involving the inescapably roguish Sir John, a character so intoxicating that the director considered him to be "Shakespeare's greatest creation."

Though it could be supposed that Welles took on the film because few roles were available for a man of his size, in truth he had been fascinated by Falstaff for most of his life. He played the character while a student at the Todd School as well as in a 1938 Mercury Theater multiplay pastiche called *Five Kings* that was revamped into a 1960 stage version also called *Chimes at Midnight*.

But though Sir John in a sense stands alone due to his comic energy and his girth ("how long is it, Jack," someone asks in all seriousness, "since thou has seen thy knees?"), it is Welles's inspiration to play him off against a strong opponent as *Chimes'* plot goes back and forth between, if you will, the rascals and the royals.

The key royal, and Falstaff's spiritual adversary, is not the ultimately treacherous Prince Hal (Keith Baxter), but his father, the usurping monarch Henry IV, brilliantly played by John Gielgud. Though his time on set was apparently limited to ten days (some reports say that all the actor's over the shoulder shots were done with a double), Gielgud defines magisterial as the icy monarch all too aware of the precariousness of his situation.

One of the virtues of *Chimes* is that Welles's lifelong familiarity with Shakespeare meant that he treated the language as something alive and vital, spoken by real people. The spectacular Gielgud is his best ally here, and hearing him speak celebrated lines like "can no man tell me of my unthrifty son" and "uneasy lies a head that wears a crown" is to have them come alive and sing as if no one had ever spoken them before.

It's a good thing that Gielgud's work is so vivid, because Welles's Falstaff is overpowering. A born rogue and lover of drink, Sir John in Welles's view is less a liar than a Baron

Munchausen–type fabulist, someone who considers life to be a performance and reality a mere construct he can alter according to his whim. His life force is so irresistible that by the time Falstaff pleads to the prince, play-acting as his own father, "banish not him thy Harry's company, banish plump Jack and banish all the world," we have no choice but to agree.

It is Prince Hal who provides the link between these two exemplars, and he initially prefers Sir John to his father because the large man is an alluring source of merriment. The prince and his friend Poins concoct a plan to personally make Falstaff flee a robbery for the simple pleasure of hearing how he will lie his way out of his cowardice. Sure enough, Falstaff describes being attacked by ever-multiplying numbers of "misbegotten knaves in Kendal green." But when Hal confronts him with the damning truth, Falstaff, in Welles's perfectly pitched performance, casually shrugs it off: "Was it for me to kill the heir apparent?" he insists. "I was now a coward on instinct."

But when rebels against the king's rule force Prince Hal to take arms along with his father at Shrewsbury, his loyalty starts to look homeward. Those battle scenes, again shot with restrictions—Welles only once had as many as 180 extras, otherwise considerably fewer—are marvels of imagery and rhythmic editing. A frenzy of smoke, horses, and murderous men all but immobilized by ever present mud, these beautifully photographed sequences give an almost unparalleled sense of war's savage brutality.

After the battle was won, it was only a matter of time until Prince Hal abandoned Falstaff once he became king. Welles believed that Hal's betrayal of his old comrade is this story's core; he told an interviewer it was "one of the greatest scenes ever written, so the movie is really a preparation for it."

But even though we can sense it coming, the former prince's withering "old man, I know thee not" and Falstaff's shocked response are devastating. Falstaff had come to believe his own fantasies, had convinced himself that he had a relationship with those in power. So, in his own way, did Orson Welles, and that belief was perhaps a factor in his undoing the same way Falstaff's was in his.

What to Watch Next:

Double Indemnity (1944), directed by Billy Wilder.

Henry V (1944), directed by Laurence Olivier.

Further Reading:

Orson Welles: The Road to Xanadu and *Hello Americans*, by Simon Callow.

Touch of Evil, edited by Terry Comito.

Put Money in Thy Purse: Filming of Orson Welles' Othello, by Michael MacLiammoir.

THE FIFTY-FIFTH FILM

Deciding that fifty-four was the number of films to be included in this collection was relatively simple. Deciding exactly which films would be chosen was harder than I anticipated, especially as I got closer to the end. Much harder.

I started with an initial list of more than one hundred films compiled more or less off the top of my head, a list I added to after using reference books and other compilations to prod my sometimes stubborn memory. To be fair to those who've read my previous collections of reviews, the only stricture I put on myself was not to include too many films (I ended up with some half a dozen) from my books *Never Coming to a Theater Near You* and *Now in Theaters Everywhere*.

Rather than come up with an ironclad list of fifty-four before I started to write, I also decided to choose the films as I wrote about them, one at a time. I selected these in no particular order. When I was ready to begin an essay, I'd look at my list, decide which title spoke to me most strongly, what film I felt like seeing at that moment in time, watch it again, and begin writing.

What this system did, though I didn't realize it when I began, was give my inventory of choices a fluid, quicksilver quality, making it in my eyes into an ever-changing, almost living thing. While some films were always going to be there, others gained or lost status and momentum as my mood changed and the list grew in size and shape.

The closer I got to finishing, the more difficult, even excruciating, choosing the final films became, because at this late stage picking one film inevitably meant another title would be left by the wayside.

By the end, I felt each of the contending films calling out to me, pleading with metaphorical tears in its eyes, "Pick me, choose me, take me with you. Remember how much I've meant to you, don't leave me behind in the darkness." Right up to the last minute, I was remembering and agonizing over new titles—where was *Downhill Racer, Mystic River, The Man Who Would Be King*—that I had not found room for. When Peter O'Toole died, I kicked myself for leaving *Lawrence of Arabia* out of the top fifty-four. It was, as I say, a difficult decision.

Finally I broke the logjam by holding auditions for the fifty-fourth film, watching half a dozen contenders before I made my choice. It was, appropriately enough for a list compiled in Los Angeles, Roman Polanski and Robert Towne's *Chinatown*, as good a film about this city as has been made, that was my final selection.

But what if I hadn't been so draconian, what if I'd allowed myself a fifty-fifth film, what would that have been? True to the spirit of how arduous it was getting to fifty-four, I decided to split my fifty-fifth choice between two very different films, Jean Cocteau's *Beauty and the Beast* and Sam Fuller's *Pickup on South Street*.

Cocteau's retelling of the Jeanne-Marie Leprince de Beaumont fairy tale starring Josette Day and Jean Marais is a spectacular romance. It benefits from the director's transporting, fantastical visual sense (cinematographer Henri Alekan's images are legendary) and the magisterial dignity Cocteau and star Marais bring to the character of the Beast.

Richly dressed and having a realistic leonine face, the Beast is the image of self-command and ironic self-knowledge. "Don't call me 'sir,'" he says on meeting Beauty's stunned merchant father. "I am called the Beast. I do not like compliments."

Pickup on South Street (1953) is set in another universe, with the opposite kind of star, the self-aware Richard Widmark, as amoral Manhattan pickpocket Skip McCoy, Jean Peters (later Mrs. Howard Hughes) as Candy, the former good time girl who loves him, and a cell of scheming communists who both bring them together and threaten to tear them apart. It has the energy of a coiled spring and characters who are bursting with the vigor and purpose that, in typical Sam Fuller fashion, allows them to live life with more intensity than seems possible.

But *Pickup* also has a lasting emotional resonance that is rare with Fuller, a quality that earned it a level of mainstream acceptance his work only infrequently managed. The film won the Bronze Lion at Venice, and it is also the only work of Fuller's to earn any kind of Oscar recognition, a best supporting actress nomination for Thelma Ritter as the enigmatic stool pigeon Moe.

Different, yes, but perhaps there are similarities between these two films as well. Both are created by strong directorial personalities whose admittedly divergent styles are, once seen, equally indelible. And both, in their dissimilar ways, turn out to be romances that spend a lot of time at the dark end of the street. What could be better than that?

A SECOND FIFTY-FOUR

IN THE BEGINNING

7th Heaven, director Frank
  Borzage, 1927
Show People, director King
  Vidor, 1928

THE THIRTIES

Baby Face, director Alfred E.
  Green, 1933
Footlight Parade, director Lloyd
  Bacon, 1933
The Sin of Nora Moran, director
  Phil Goldstone, 1933
Top Hat, director Mark
  Sandrich, 1935
Camille, director George
  Cukor, 1936
Crimes of Monsieur Lange,
  director Jean Renoir, 1936
The Adventures of Robin Hood,
  directors Michael Curtiz,
William Keighley, 1938
Pygmalion, directors Anthony
  Asquith, Leslie Howard,
  1938

THE FORTIES

City for Conquest, director
  Anatole Litvak, 1940
Citizen Kane, director Orson
  Welles, 1941
How Green Was My Valley,
  director John Ford, 1941
The Maltese Falcon, director
  John Huston, 1941
Yankee Doodle Dandy, director
  Michael Curtiz, 1942
Double Indemnity, director Billy
  Wilder, 1944
I Know Where I'm Going, direc-
  tors Michael Powell, Emeric
  Pressburger, 1945

White Heat, director Raoul
Walsh, 1949

THE FIFTIES

Outcast of the Islands, director
Carol Reed, 1951
From Here to Eternity, director
Fred Zinnemann, 1953
On the Waterfront, director Elia
Kazan, 1954
East of Eden, director Elia Ka-
zan, 1955
Paths of Glory, director Stanley
Kubrick, 1957
North by Northwest, director
Alfred Hitchcock, 1959

THE SIXTIES

Eyes Without a Face, director
Georges Franju, 1960
The Misfits, director John Hus-
ton, 1961
Lawrence of Arabia, director
David Lean, 1962
To Kill a Mockingbird, director
Robert Mulligan, 1962
A Hard Day's Night, director
Richard Lester, 1964
Dr. Strangelove, director Stan-
ley Kubrick, 1964
Up series, director Michael
Apted, 1964–2012

Coogan's Bluff, director Don
Siegel, 1968

THE SEVENTIES

Amarcord, director Federico
Fellini, 1973
The Godfather II, director
Francis Ford Coppola, 1974
The Man Who Would Be King,
director John Huston, 1975

THE EIGHTIES

Broadcast News, director James
L. Brooks, 1981
Blade Runner, director Ridley
Scott, 1982
E.T. the Extra-Terrestrial,
director Steven Spielberg,
1982
Fanny and Alexander, director
Ingmar Bergman, 1982
Witness, director Peter Weir,
1985
Hannah and Her Sisters,
director Woody Allen,
1986
Hope and Glory, director John
Boorman, 1987
Decalogue, director Krzysztof
Kieslowski, 1988
My Neighbor Totoro, director
Hayao Miyazaki, 1988

THE NINETIES

The Fugitive, director Andrew
Davis, 1993

Hoop Dreams, director Steve
James, 1994

Toy Story, director John
Lasseter, 1995

La Promesse, directors
Jean-Pierre and Luc
Dardenne, 1996

L.A. Confidential, director
Curtis Hanson, 1997

After Life, director Hirokazu
Koreeda, 1999

THE NEW CENTURY

Crouching Tiger, Hidden Dragon,
director Ang Lee, 2000

Kitchen Stories, director Bent
Hamer, 2003

Sideways, director Alexander
Payne, 2004

Animal Kingdom, director
David Michod, 2010

ACKNOWLEDGMENTS

With a book that encompasses an entire lifetime of film-going, it would take a volume all its own to properly thank all the people who've made my viewing life possible. Rather than write that book, I've decided to focus on a small number of essential people who I could not imagine this endeavor without.

I have to start with the late Judith Crist, whose class on film reviewing I took at Columbia University's Graduate School of Journalism. She was the first person who told me I could do this for a living, and as anyone who met her can testify, when Judith Crist talked, you listened.

Also, in the spirit of the Yiddish tradition of *di goldene keit*, the golden chain that links the generations, I'd like to thank the students who've taken my film reviewing course at both USC and UC Berkeley, some of whom have gone on to become excellent critics in their own right. Sharing their journey has been a privilege.

I have to thank as well my steadfast and insightful agent Kathy Robbins, as well as Peter Osnos, founder and editor at large of PublicAffairs, who has published three of my books and displayed a loyalty and perspicacity that is becoming increasingly rare.

I also want to thank Clive Priddle, PublicAffairs' editor in chief, whose insights and ideas have helped enormously in shaping this particular book.

It's a pleasure to thank the staff of the Academy of Motion Picture Arts and Sciences' Margaret Herrick Library, a beautiful building that is one of my favorite places in the world, and one of the most useful as well.

Finally, I want to thank my wife, Patty Williams, still the source of all that's good in my life, and the friends and family—you know who you are—who accompany me to my endless screenings and put up with my viewing habits and eccentricities. Gratitude goes as well to my editors and colleagues at the *Los Angeles Times*, fellow critics I've shared opinions with, as well as the often unappreciated publicists and projectionists who do the heavy lifting. You've all made this long journey easier, and for that I will always be grateful.

INDEX

Academy Awards
  All About Eve, 130
  Bicycle Thieves, 100
  Casablanca, 79
  Garson, 85
  McCarey, 12–13, 40–41, 48
  Sanders, 116
  Signoret, 133
  Sturges, 69
  Towne, 219
Achard, Marcel, 148
Adaptation, 281
Adrian, 53, 57
The Adventures of Robin Hood, 325
An Affair to Remember, 21, 40–41, 48
After Life, 327
Agee, James, 14
Aldrich, Robert, 156–157
Alekan, Henri, 322
Alexander Nevsky, 33, 189
Alison, Joan, 81
Alive (Read) and *Alive*, 287, 290
All About Eve, 113, 115–119, 130
Allain, Marcel, 5, 7
Allen, Woody, 79–80, 326
Alonzo, John, 219
Amarcord, 277, 326
An American in Paris, 142, 143

American Prometheus (Bird; Sherwin), 231
Anderson, Lindsay, 183
Anderson, Maxwell, 174
Anderson, Robin, 232–235
Animal Kingdom, 327
Anna Christie, 21
The Annotated Godfather (Jones), 216
Ansky, S., 34–35, 172
Applause, 118
Apted, Michael, 326
Arcand, Denys, 191
Arestrup, Niels, 292, 293
Arijon, Gonzalo, 282, 287–288
Arletty, 90, 92
Armes, Roy, 6–7
Arrighi, Luciana, 245, 246
Arrival of a Train at a Station, 225
The Art of Buster Keaton, 10
Art of Noir (Muller), 159
Ashbery, John, 6
Ashkenazi, Lior, 301, 304
The Asphalt Jungle, 113, 120–124
Asquith, Anthony, 137–140, 325
Audiard, Jacques, 291–295
Aulier, Dan, 177
Austen, Jane, 53–54, 56, 58, 74, 249
Auteurs/auteur theory, 152, 171, 316
The Awful Truth, 40, 48

Baby Face, 72, 325
Bacon, Lloyd, 325
Bad Day at Black Rock, 197
Badge of Evil (Masterson), 313
Bafta awards, 285, 291
Band Wagon, 145
Bann, Richard W., 13
The Barefoot Contessa, 28, 131
Barefoot Gen, 231
Barrault, Jean-Louis, 90, 91, 93
Bart, Peter, 214
Baxter, Anne, 115–116
Baxter, Keith, 311, 318
The Beat That My Heart Skipped,
   291–292, 293
Beauty and the Beast, 322–323
Beauvois, Xavier, 296–297
Beavan, Jenny, 246
Beavers, Louise, 30, 45
Becker, Jacques, 132–134, 136
Beckett, Samuel, 14
Bell, Book, and Candle, 174
Bellah, James Warner, 184–185
Benny, Jack, 59, 64
Bergamasco, Sonia, 272, 275
Bergman, Ingmar, 326
Bergman, Ingrid, 79–81, 83, 176
Berlin, Irving, 143
Berman, Henry, 195
The Best of Youth, 265, 272–277
Bethe, Hans, 227–229
Between Two Worlds (Ansky), 35
Bezzerides, A.I. "Buzz," 157
Bicycle Thieves, 51, 100–104, 149, 203
Bird, Kai, 231
Bishop, Christopher, 17
Black Harvest, 235
Blade Runner, 169, 260, 326
Boetticher, Budd, 160–164
Bogart, Humphrey, 79–83
Boileau, Pierre, 172
Bombshell, 21, 28–31, 125
Bondi, Beulah, 39, 44, 47
Bonham Carter, Helena, 246, 248

Boni, Alessio, 272, 274, 275
Boone, Richard, 162
Boorman, John, 192–196, 240, 326
Borzage, Frank, 40, 325
Bourgault, Pierre, 250, 253
Bow, Clara, 29, 128
Boyer, Charles, 39, 41–42, 147–148,
   176
Brackett, Charles, 126
Bradley, David, 202, 203
Brando, Marlon, 211, 213–215
Brasseur, Pierre, 90, 93
Breathless, 198
Breon, Edmund, 5, 7
Bressart, Felix, 62, 68
Bridge of Light (Hoberman), 34–35, 38
British Academy of Film and Televi-
   sion Awards. *See* Bafta awards
Broadcast News, 326
The Broadway Melody musical, 142,
   144
Brooks, James L., 326
Brown, Harry Joe, 160
Brown, Nacio Herb, 142–143, 144
Browning, Tod, 40
Brownlow, Kevin, 3, 96, 97, 99
Budapest, 61
Bunuel, Luis, 14
Burnett, Murray, 81
Burnett, W.R., 120–121
Burns, Robert E., 24–25, 27
Buster Keaton: Interviews (Sweeney),
   18

Caan, James, 211, 213–214
Cagney (McCabe), 78
Cagney, James, 75–78, 293
Callow, Simon, 320
Camille, 325
Canadian Oscars (Genies), 24, 251
Cannes Film Festival
   Best of Youth, 273
   Footnote, 301–302
   Of Gods and Men, 296–297

Lauzon, Jean-Claude, 251, 253
  Palme d'Or prize, 105, 203, 278
  A Prophet, 291–294
  Un Certain Regard prize, 273
  von Trier, 278
Cannessa, Roberto, 289–290
Carey, Harry, 183
Carey, Harry, Jr., 187
Carné, Marcel, 90–92, 94
Casablanca, 51, 76, 79–84, 86
Casque d'Or, 113, 132–136
The Catcher in the Rye (Salinger), 85
Cecchi d'Amico, Suso, 101, 102
Cedar, Joseph, 301–303
César Awards, 291, 292–293, 297
Champetier, Caroline, 297
Chandler, Raymond, 128, 217–218,
  220
Chaney, Lon, Jr., 42
Chaney, Lon, Sr., 40, 232
Charlone, Cesare, 288
Child of Paradise: Marcel Carné . . .
  (Turk), 94
Children of Paradise, 51, 90–94
Chimes at Midnight, 313–320
Chinatown, 209, 217–221, 322
Cicognini, Alessandro, 103
Cinema Europe: The Other Hollywood
  documentary series (Brown-
  low), 3
Cinematography
  Asphalt Jungle, 121
  black and white, 96, 106, 121
  Distant Voices, Still Lives, 238
  Earrings of Madame . . . , 148, 150
  Godfather, 212
  Of Gods and Men, 297
  Great Expectations, 97
  Kes, 204
  neo-noir, 26
  A Prophet, 291
  Sweet Smell of Success, 167
  Third Man, 106
  Touch of Evil, 313–314, 316

Vertigo, 175
Citizen Kane, 69–70, 79, 116, 142,
  169–171, 312, 325
City for Conquest, 325
Classics of the Foreign Film (Tyler),
  33–34
Clint Eastwood: A Biography (Schickel),
  261
Clothier, William, 163
Coburn, Charles, 69, 72–73
Cocteau, Jean, 6, 69, 71, 322
Coli, Tonino Della, 189
Collin, Maxime, 250, 252
Colman, Juliet Benita, 89
Colman, Ronald, 85–89
Comden, Betty, 142–143, 145
Comito, Terry, 320
Company of Heroes (Carey Jr.), 187
Connolly, Bob, 232–235
Consent Decree of 1948, 51
Conversations with Wilder (Crowe),
  131
Coogan's Bluff, 257, 326
Cooper, Maxine, 156, 158
Coppel, Alec, 174–175
Coppola, Francis Ford, 211–216, 257,
  326
Costumes
  To Be or Not to Be, 66
  Casablanca, 83
  Earrings of Madame de . . . , 148
  of Edith Head, 173
  Howards End, 246
  Importance of Being Earnest, 138
  Pride and Prejudice, 56–57
  Vertigo, 174
Cotten, Joseph, 105, 107–108, 315
Creelman, Eileen, 67
Crime films, 120–124, 198–201,
  291–295, 297
Crimes of Monsieur Lange, 325
Criss Cross, 221
Crouching Tiger, Hidden Dragon, 327
Crowe, Cameron, 131

Crowther, Bosley, 67, 85, 151, 192
Cukor, George, 325
Curtis, James, 72
Curtis, Tony, 165, 168–169
Curtiz, Michael, 78, 79, 81, 325

Dabholkar, Pratibha A., 143, 146
Dancer in the Dark, 278
Dardenne brothers, 203, 296–297, 327
Darrieux, Danielle, 147, 148–149
Dassin, Jules, 120, 124
David Lean: A Life in Film (Brownlow), 96, 99
Davidson, Max, 3, 9–13, 15, 17, 18
Davies, Terence, 236–239
Davis, Andrew, 327
Davis, Bette, 115–117
Davis, Tim, 188
Dawson, Beatrice, 138
The Day After Trinity documentary, 225, 227–230, 260, 283
De Beaumont, Jeanne-Marie Leprince, 322
De Havilland, Olivia, 75, 77–78
De Niro, Robert, 215
De Sica, Vittorio
   as actor, 147, 149
   as director, 100, 102–104, 203, 275
Deburau, Jean-Gaspard, 91
Decalogue, 326
Deliverance, 195
Delmar, Vina, 44
Delon, Alain, 198, 199–200
Demarest, William, 72, 128
DeMille, Cecil B., 128, 130
D'entre les Morts (Boileau; Narcejac), 171–172
Desti, Mary, 70–71
Devine, Andy, 184, 185
Di Concillo-Perrin, Florencia, 288
Diaghilev, Serge, 69, 71
Dickens, Charles, 95–96, 98–99, 129
Dickinson, Angie, 192, 194

Dietrich, Marlene, 315, 316
Distant Voices, Still Lives, 225, 236–240
Divine Images: A History of Jesus . . . (Kinnard; Davis), 188
Documentaries, 8, 225–235, 278, 282–290, 297
Dog Day Afternoon, 141, 209
Dogs, 29, 53–54, 108
Doherty, Thomas, 24, 32
Donen, Stanley, 141–144
Double Indemnity, 320, 325
Dowie, Freda, 236, 237
Downhill Racer, 290, 322
Dr. Mabuse The Gambler, 3, 8
Dr. Strangelove, 326
Drazin, Charles, 106, 109
Dryer, Carl Theodor, 296–297
Dunaway, Faye, 217, 220
Duncan, Isadora, 70–71
Dunne, Irene, 39, 40, 41–42, 48
Duvall, Robert, 211, 213, 214
Duvivier, Julien, 84
The Dybbuk, 21, 33–38, 172
Dyson, Freeman, 229, 230

The Earrings of Madame de . . . , 113, 147–150
East of Eden, 326
Easter Parade, 143
Eastwood, Clint, 228, 256–261
Eisenstein, Sergei, 33, 189
Elon, Amos, 305
Else, Jon, 227–228, 260
The Emperor and the Wolf (Galbraith), 155
Epstein, Julius and Philip, 76, 78, 81
Ernst Lubitsch: Laughter in Paradise (Eyman), 68
E.T. the Extra-Terrestrial, 326
Ethnic comedy, 11, 12, 13
Evans, Edith, 137, 139
"Everybody Comes to Rick's" unproduced play (Burnett; Alison), 81

Eyes Without a Face, 326
Eyman, Scott, 68

The False Magistrate, 6
Fanny and Alexander, 326
*Fantômas in the Shadow of the
    Guillotine*, 6
Fantômas serial/Fantômas character,
    3, 5–8
Fantômas vs. Fantômas, 6
Farber, Manny, 165–166
Farewell, My Lovely (Chandler), 128,
    220
Farr, Robert, 13
Farrell, Glenda, 25
Fellini, Federico, 103, 277, 326
Feuillade, Louis, 5–8
The Film Noir Encyclopedia (Silver;
    Ward; Ursini), 159
Film noir genre
    Asphalt Jungle, 121
    Chinatown, 218
    Kiss Me Deadly, 156–159
    Sunset Boulevard, 126
    Touch of Evil, 313, 316
The Films in My Life (Truffaut), 67
The Films of Akira Kurosawa (Richie),
    155
Fiordin, Hugh, 146
First Contact documentary, 225,
    232–235, 283
*First Contact: New Guinea's Highland-
    ers . . .* (Connolly; Anderson),
    235
The Five Obstructions, 265, 278–281
Five Screenplays by Preston Sturges (ed.
    Henderson), 74
Fleming, Victor, 28, 29
Fonda, Henry, 69, 71–74, 104, 173
Fontaine, Stephane, 294
Footlight Parade, 325
Footnote, 265, 301–304
Ford, John, 183–187, 325
Forster, E.M., 245, 246

The 400 Blows, 255
Franju, Georges, 326
Franzo, Roberto, 276
Freed, Arthur, 142–143, 144
Freeman, Morgan, 256, 260
French cinema, 3–8, 113, 133, 198,
    202, 265, 291–295. *See also* César
    Awards
French New Wave, 133, 171, 198, 202,
    265
From Here to Eternity, 326
The Fugitive, 327
Fuller, Sam, 159, 322, 323

Galbraith, Stuart, IV, 155
The Gang That Couldn't Shoot Straight,
    215
Garbo, Greta, 21, 62
Garson, Greer, 53, 55, 56, 85–89
The Gatekeepers documentary, 283,
    305
Gaumont, León, 6
Gehring, Wes D., 48
Geist, Kenneth L., 119
General Della Rovere, 150
Gershwin, George, 143
Gibbons, Cedric, 53, 88
Gibson, Mel, 188
Gielgud, John, 311, 318
Giordana, Marco Tullio, 272–273,
    275–276
Godard, Jean-Luc, 63–64, 133, 198
The Godfather, 79, 209, 211–216, 294
The Godfather II, 215, 216, 219, 326
The Godfather Legacy (Lebo), 215
*The Godfather Papers and Other
    Confessions* (Puzo), 216
Going My Way, 12–13
Goldbeck, Willis, 184–185
Goldsmith, Jerry, 219
Goldstone, Phil, 325
Gone with the Wind, 104, 152
Goodbye, Mr. Chips (Hilton), 86
Gordon, Robert S.C., 103, 104

The Gospel According to St. Matthew, 181, 188–191
Grant, Cary, 40–41, 48, 104
The Grapes of Wrath, 71–72
Great Expectations, 51, 95–99
Green, Adolph, 142–143, 145
Green, Alfred E., 325
Green, Guy, 97
Green, Howard J., 24–25
Greenberg, James, 217, 218–219, 221
Greene, Graham, 105–109
Greenstreet, Sydney, 80–81, 83
Greenwood, Joan, 137, 138
Griffith, D.W., 10, 13
Griffithiana journal, 13
Groning, Philip, 297, 300
Groves, Leslie, 228–229
Guilol, Fred, 13
Guinness, Alec, 95, 98, 166

Hackman, Gene, 256–259, 261
Hagen, Jean, 120, 123, 145
Hal Roach Studios, 10–11, 13, 40
Hamer, Bent, 327
Hamlet play (Shakespeare), 64, 65
Hammett, Dashiell, 217
The Hanging Tree, 184
Hannah and Her Sisters, 326
Hanson, Curtis, 327
A Hard Day's Night, 326
Hardy, Oliver, 10, 40
Harlow, Jean, 28–30, 148
Harmetz, Aljean, 80, 84
Hayden, Sterling, 120, 122, 212
Hayworth, Rita, 75, 76–78, 101
Hello Americans (Callow), 320
Henreid, Paul, 80, 83
Henry IV, Part I play (Shakespeare), 212, 317
Henry IV, Part II play (Shakespeare), 317–318
Henry V, 320
Heroes for Sale, 24, 26, 27
Herrmann, Bernard, 173, 176, 303

Hess, Earl J., 143, 146
Heston, Charlton, 311, 314
High Plains Drifter, 257
Hiiragi, Rumi, 267
Hilton, James, 86–87
Hines, Barry, 202, 203, 205
Hiroshima, 230
Hiroshima, Mon Amour, 34, 196
Hitchcock (Truffaut), 177
Hitchcock, Alfred, 170–177, 303, 326
Hitchcock's Notebooks (Aulier), 177
Hitler, Adolf, 64, 68, 278
Hoberman, J., 34–35, 38, 100
Hobson, Valerie, 95
Hogue, Peter, 14
Holden, William, 125–127
Holm, Celeste, 115–118
Holmes, Brown, 24–25
Hoop Dreams, 327
Hope and Glory, 240, 326
Hopkins, Anthony, 245–248
Horizons West (Kitses), 164
House television program, 130
How Green Was My Valley, 325
Howard, Betty, 57–58
Howard, Leslie, 140, 325
Howards End, 243, 245–249
Howards End (Forster), 245, 246
Howe, James Wong, 76, 167
The Hunter (Westlake), 192–193
Huston, John, 120–121, 124, 217, 220, 325, 326
Huxley, Aldous, 51, 53–54, 55–56

I Am a Fugitive from a Chain Gang, 21, 23–27, 88
I Am a Fugitive from the Georgia Chain Gang (Burns), 24, 27
I Know Where I'm Going, 325
The Importance of Being Earnest, 137–140
The Importance of Being Earnest play (Wilde), 137, 140

In Search of the Third Man (Drazin), 106, 109
In the Name of the Father, 237
Into Great Silence documentary, 297, 300
Into the Wild documentary, 290
Irazoqui, Enrique, 188, 190
Israel, 265, 283, 301–305
Israeli Academy Awards, 301, 304
The Israelis: Founders and Sons (Elon), 305
Italy, 11, 102, 189–190, 265, 272–277
Ivory, James, 243, 245–246, 249

Jackson, Michael, 128
Jaffe, Sam, 120, 122, 123
James, Steve, 327
James Ivory in Conversation (Long), 249
Japan, 46, 63, 113, 151–154, 265, 267–270
Jerome, Helen, 54
Jesus, 181, 188, 190–191
Jesus of Montreal, 191
Jewish Prudence short film, 11, 18
Jhabvala, Ruth Prawer, 245, 246
Joe Leahy's Neighbors documentary, 235
Johnson, Dorothy M., 184–185
Jones, Jenny M., 216
Jonze, Spike, 281
Joyce, James, 6
Juve vs. Fantômas, 6

Kael, Pauline, 13–14
Kapadia, Asif, 282, 285–286
Karas, Anton, 106
Kazan, Elia, 215, 326
Keaton, Buster, 3, 9–18, 128, 232
Keaton, Diane, 213
Keaton, Eleanor, 13, 14–15, 17–18
Keighley, William, 325
Kelly, Gene, 141–145
Kemp, Phillip, 133

Kennedy, Burt, 160–163
Kennedy, Joseph P., 127
Kes, 181, 202–205
A Kestrel for a Knave (Hines), 202, 205
Kieslowski, Krzysztof, 203, 326
Kinnard, Roy, 188
Kiss Me Deadly, 113, 156–159
Kitchen Stories, 327
Kitses, Jim, 164
Koch, Howard, 81
Kore-eda, Hirokazu, 327
Kosma, Joseph, 92
Krasker, Robert, 106
Kubrick, Stanley, 120, 326
Kurosawa, Akira, 151 155

La Cava, Gregory, 119
L.A. Confidential, 327
La Promesse, 296–297, 327
Ladd, Alan, 128
The Lady Eve, 41, 51, 69–74
The Ladykillers, 166
Lambert, Gavin, 133
Lancaster, Burt, 165–168
Lang, Fritz, 8
Lasseter, John, 327
Lassiter, John, 268, 269
The Last Tycoon (Fitzgerald), 54
Laszlo, Ernest, 157
Laszlo, Nikolaus, 62
Lathrop, Philip, 195
Laughton, Charles, 40, 326
Laurel, Stan, 10, 40
Laurel and Hardy, 10, 40
Lauzon, Jean-Claude, 250–255
Lawrence, Jennifer, 44
Lawrence of Arabia, 95, 99, 322, 326
Le Cercle Rouge (Melville), 201
Le Giornate de Cinema Muto, Pordenone, Italy, 11
Le Monde newspaper, 300
Le Petit Lieutenant, 297
Le Samouraï, 181, 198–201

Leahy, Joe, 235
Leahy, Michael, 233–235
Lean, David, 95–99, 326
Lebo, Harlan, 215
Lee, Ang, 327
Lehman, Ernst, 165, 166
Leigh, Janet, 311, 314, 316
Leigh, Vivien, 55, 56
Leisen, Mitchell, 68
Lengyel, Melchior, 64
Leo McCarey: From Marx to McCarthy (Gehring), 48
Leolo, 243, 250–255
Leonard, Robert Z., 53, 55, 57
Leone, Sergio, 257, 261
LeRoy, Mervyn, 23–26, 85, 88
Les Enfants du Paradis. See Children of Paradise
Lester, Richard, 326
Leth, Jorgen, 278–281
A Letter to Three Wives, 116
Levant, Oscar, 143
Liebgold, Leon, 34, 37, 38
The Light Ahead, 38
Liliana, Lili, 33, 37, 38
Little Caesar, 26, 88
Litvak, Anatole, 325
Lo Cascio, Luigi, 272, 274, 275
Loach, Ken, 202–204, 205
Lombard, Carol, 59, 64–65
The Lonely Life (Davis), 117
Long, Robert Emmet, 249
Lonsdale, Michael, 296, 297, 298
Loos, Anita, 55–56
Lopate, Phillip, 148
Lorca, Federico Garcia, 14
Lorre, Peter, 80–81, 82
Los Angeles, 125–130, 156–159, 217–220
Los Angeles Times newspaper, 170, 218, 255
Losique, Serge, 251
Love Affair, 12–13, 21, 40–43, 148
Lubitsch, Ernst, 59–68

Lucky Star, 3, 40
Lumiere brothers, 225

Mackendrick, Alexander, 165–168
MacLiammoir, Michael, 320
Maddow, Ben, 120, 121
Maggiorani, Lamberto, 100, 101, 103
Magritte, René, 6, 269
Mahin, John Lee, 29
Make Way for Tomorrow, 12–13, 21, 40, 43–47
Malle, Louis, 7
The Maltese Falcon, 325
A Man Called Horse, 184
The Man in the White Suit, 138, 166
The Man Who Shot Liberty Valance, 181, 183–187
The Man Who Would Be King, 322, 326
Manhattan Project, 228–229
Mankiewicz, Herman, 116
Mankiewicz, Joseph L., 115–119
Marais, Jean, 322
Marshman, D.M., Jr, 126
Martin, Mildred, 67
Marvin, Lee, 160, 162, 183–184, 186, 192–196
Marx, Harpo, 40
Marx Brothers, 40, 304
Masaki, Mori, 231
Masterson, Whit, 313
The Matrix, 8
Mayer, Louis B., 13, 54, 55, 125, 142
McBride, Joseph, 187
McCabe, John, 78
McCarey, Leo, 12–13, 18, 21, 39–48
McGuire, Kathryn, 9, 15–16
McIntire, John, 124
McWilliams, Carey, 218, 221
Meeker, Ralph, 156, 157
Melchior, Georges, 7
Melville, Jean-Pierre, 198–201
Melville on Melville (Nogueira), 200, 201

Menges, Chris, 204
Merchant, Ismail, 243, 245–246, 248, 249
Metty, Russell, 313, 316
Meyer, Edwin Justus, 64
MGM studios, 53–56, 85–88, 125, 142–145, 193
Michell, Roger, 58
Michod, David, 327
Mifune, Toshiro, 151, 153–154, 155
Miles, Vera, 173–174, 176, 184–185
Mills, John, 95, 98
Milne, Tom, 199
Milner, Marty, 169
Minnelli, Vincente, 145
The Misfits, 326
Missa Luba, 189
Miyazaki, Hayao, 267–271, 326
Miyu Irina, 267
Monroe, Marilyn, 116, 118–119, 122, 123
Montana, Lennie, 215
Montand, Yves, 132
Montreal, 250–253
Monturi, Carlo, 103
Moore, Victor, 39, 44, 47
Moreh, Dror, 305
Moretti, Nani, 275
Morgan, Frank, 60, 62
Mosher, John, 61
Motion Picture News, 10
Mrs. Miniver, 85, 86, 89
Muller, Eddie, 159
Mulligan, Robert, 326
Muni, Paul, 23, 25
Murch, Walter, 313
The Murderous Corpse, 6, 8
Murfin, Jane, 53–54
Musical scores and soundtracks
  Asphalt Jungle, 121
  Best of Youth, 273–274, 276
  Bicycle Thieves, 103
  Casablanca, 81

Distant Voices, Still Lives, 237–238, 239, 240
Footnote, 303
Of Gods and Men, 299
Gospel According to St. Matthew, 189
Leolo, 251
Stranded, 288
Third Man, 106–107
Vertigo, 173
Musicals, 118, 141–145, 239, 257
My Darling Clementine, 184
My Fair Lady, 138
My Man Godfrey, 63, 64
My Neighbor Totoro, 268, 270, 271, 326
My Wonderful World of Slapstick (Keaton; Samuels), 18
Mystic River, 261, 322

Napoleon, 3, 34
Narcejac, Thomas, 171–172
Navarre, Rene, 5, 7
Nazis, 63, 65–68, 81–82, 83, 278
Neorealism, 100, 102–103, 149, 190
Never Coming to a Theater Near You (Turan), 321
New York City, 165–169, 257, 273
New York Sun newspaper, 67
New York Times newspaper, 61, 66, 166
New Yorker magazine, 170
Nicholson, Jack, 217, 220
A Night at the Opera, 304
Night of the Hunter, 326
Nilsson, Anna Q., 128
Ninotchka, 62, 68
Noda, Kogo, 46
Nogueira, Rui, 200, 201
Norman, Jessye, 237–238
North by Northwest, 177, 326
Novak, Kim, 170, 173–175
Now in Theaters Everywhere (Turan), 321

O'Brien, Edmond, 184, 185
O'Connor, Carroll, 194–195
O'Connor, Donald, 141, 143–145
O'Connor, Una, 77, 87
Odets, Clifford, 165–168
Odetta, 189
O'Donnell, Spec, 9, 12
Of Gods and Men, 265, 296–300
The Old Curiosity Shop (Dickens), 95–96
Oliver, Edna May, 56
Olivier, Laurence, 53, 320
Olsen, Nancy, 125, 129
On Film-making (Mackendrick), 169
On Sunset Boulevard (Sikov), 127, 131
On the Town, 142–143
On the Waterfront, 326
One Sunday Afternoon play, 76
An Open Book (Huston), 124
Ophuls, Max, 147–150
Oppenheimer, Frank, 228, 230
Oppenheimer, J. Robert, 228–231
Orr, Mary, 115
Orry-Kelly, 83
Orson Welles: The Road to Xanadu (Callow), 320
Oscars. *See* Academy Awards
O'Steen, Sam, 219
O'Toole, Peter, 322
Our Gang series, 10, 40
Ouspenskaya, Maria, 39, 41, 42
Outcast of the Islands, 108, 109, 326
The Outlaw Josey Wales, 257
Outside the Law, 40
Ozu, Yasujiro, 21, 46, 48

Pacino, Al, 211, 213, 214–215
Paint Your Wagon, 257
Pale Rider, 257
Pandey, Manish, 285
Papua New Guinea, 232–235
Paramount Studio, 47, 60, 61, 70, 71, 128–129, 214–215
Paris, 90–94, 132–135

Partie de Campagne, 134
Pasolini, Pier Paolo, 188–191, 275, 276
Pass the Gravy, 9, 11–13, 40, 232
The Passion of the Christ, 188
Paths of Glory, 326
Payne, Alexander, 327
Peabody Award, 227
Peckinpah, Sam, 196
Penn, Sean, 290
Peoples, David Webb, 228, 257, 260–261
Peoples, Janet Webb, 228
Pepe Le Moko, 84
The Perfect Human, 278–279
Persuasion, 58
Petraglia, Sandro, 272, 274
Phantom of the Opera, 232
Pickford, Mary, 3
Pickup on South Street, 159, 322, 323
Picture Play magazine, 13
Pictures Will Talk (Geist), 115, 119
Pierson, Frank, 141–146
Poetic realism, 90–91
Point Blank, 181, 192–197
Poland, 35, 63–67
Polanski, Roman, 217–219, 221, 322
Polito, Sol, 26
Postlethwaite, Peter, 236, 237
Powell, Michael, 325
Power, Tyrone, 128
Pre-Code films, 24, 26, 30, 32, 72, 75. *See also* Production Code
Pre-Code Hollywood (Doherty), 24, 32
Pressburger, Emeric, 325
Preston Sturges by Preston Sturges (Sturges), 74
Prévert, Jacques, 90–92
Pride and Prejudice (Austen), 53, 54, 56, 58
Pride and Prejudice, 51, 53–58, 86
Princess Mononoke, 267
Production Code, 21, 24, 42, 74, 124, 157. *See also* Pre-Code films

Prokofiev, Sergei, 189
A Prophet, 265, 291–295
Prost, Alain, 285
*Pulp Surrealism: Insolent Popular
    Culture . . .* (Walz), 8
Put Money in Thy Purse (MacLiam-
    moir), 320
Puzo, Mario, 212, 213–214, 216
Pygmalion, 138, 140, 325

Queen Kelly, 127
The Quiet American (Greene), 107

Rabe, I. I., 228, 230
Radio City Music Hall, New York,
    57, 86
Rahim, Tahar, 291, 292–293
The Rain People, 214
Raines, Claude, 79, 80–81, 82
Random Harvest, 51, 85–89
Ranown cycle, 160, 162, 163–164
Raphaelson, Samson, 62
Rapoport, Shloyme Zanvyl, 34. *See
    also* Ansky, S.
Rattigan, Terence, 138
Rawhide television program, 256–257
Read, Piers Paul, 287–288
Read My Lips, 291–292, 295
Reap the Wild Wind, 10
Red Dust, 29
Redgrave, Michael, 137, 138
Redgrave, Vanessa, 245–246, 248–249
Reed, Carol, 105–109, 326
Reed, Walter, 161
Reggiani, Serge, 132, 133, 135
Remains of the Day, 246
Remember the Night, 68, 72
Reno, Ginette, 250, 253
Renoir, Jean, 39, 92, 94, 134, 325
Renoir, Marguerite, 133–134
Renoir, Pierre, 92
Resnais, Alain, 7
Reynolds, Debbie, 141, 142, 144, 145
Richie, Donald, 155

Rififi, 120, 124
Ritchie, Michael, 290
Ritter, Thelma, 116, 118, 323
Robinson, Casey, 81
Rodgers, Gaby, 156
Roman Polanski: A Retrospective
    (Greenberg), 221
Rome, 101–102, 103, 273
Ronald Colman: A Very Private Person
    (J. B. Colman), 89
Room at the Top, 133, 202
A Room with a View, 246, 249
Rossellini, Roberto, 150
Rosson, Harold, 121
Round Up the Usual Suspects
    (Harmetz), 80, 84
Rozsa, Miklos, 121
Ruddy, Al, 214, 215
The Rules of the Game, 94, 142
Rulli, Stefano, 272, 274
Russell, Gail, 160, 161
Russo, Gianni, 214
Rutherford, Ann, 57
Rutherford, Margaret, 139
Ruttenberg, Joseph, 88

Salerno, Enrico Maria, 190
Salinger, J.D., 85
Salles, Walter, 255
Salo, 188
Samuels, Charles, 18
San Francisco, 172, 175–176, 193, 196,
    214
Sanders, George, 116–117
Sandrich, Mark, 325
Saturday Evening Post magazine, 89
Schenck, Nicholas, 13
Schickel, Richard, 261
Schmidlin, Rick, 313
Scoop (Waugh), 209
Scorsese, Martin, 157, 165
Scott, Randolph, 160–164
Scott, Ridley, 260, 285, 326
The Searchers, 183

Searching for John Ford (McBride), 187

Seberg, Jean, 198

Selznick, David O., 55, 104, 106–107

Senna, Aryton, 283–287

Senna documentary, 282–287, 290

Sense and Sensibility, 249

Seven Chances, 18

Seven Men from Now, 113, 160–164

Seven Samurai, 113, 142, 151–155

Seventh Heaven, 3, 325

7th Heaven, 40

Shakespeare, William, 64–66, 92, 151, 211–212, 313, 317–318

Shearer, Norma, 29, 54

Sherlock Jr., 13–17

Sherwin, Martin J., 231

Shimura, Takashi, 151, 153

Shoeshine, 102, 103, 104, 149

The Shop Around the Corner, 51, 60–63

Short films, 10–11, 40, 116, 134, 278, 280

Should Second Husbands Come First, 11

Show People, 3, 28, 32, 325

Sideways, 327

Siegel, Don, 81, 261, 326

Sight & Sound magazine, 100, 109, 142, 170–171, 291, 312

Signoret, Simone, 132–135

Sikov, Ed, 127, 131

The Silence of the Lambs, 248

Silent films, 1, 3–17, 28, 40, 115, 126–129, 142–143, 190

Silver, Alain, 159

Sin in Soft Focus (Viera), 32

The Sin of Nora Moran, 325

Sinatra, Frank, 216

Singin' in the Rain, 123, 141–146

Singin' in the Rain: The Making . . . (Hess; Dabholkar), 143, 146

Sinyard, Neil, 105

Siodmak, Robert, 221

Sleepless in Seattle, 40–41

Social consciousness and Clifford Odets, 167

of Ken Loach, 202–203

neorealist films, 102

pre-Code movies, 24–25

The Son's Room, 275

Southern California Country (McWilliams), 218, 221

Souvestre, Pierre, 5, 7

Spielberg, Steven, 106, 151, 326

Spirited Away, 265, 267–271

Spirituality

Dybbuk, 37

Of Gods and Men, 296–300

Gospel According to St. Matthew, 188–191

A Prophet, 293–294

Senna and *Stranded*, 283–284, 287–288

Spoto, Donald, 170, 174

Stack, Robert, 59, 65

Stage Door, 119

Stagecoach, 184, 187

Stagg, Sam, 119

Staiola, Enzo, 100, 101, 103

Stanwyck, Barbara, 69, 71–74

A Star Is Born, 28

Starace, Gino, 6

Stark, Richard, 192, 197

Steamboat Bill Jr., 232

Steiner, Max, 81

Stevens, George, 13

Stewart, James, 59–63, 170–176, 183–185, 326

Stranded documentary, 282–284, 287–290

Strauss, Richard, 151

Strawberry Blonde, 75–78

Sturges, Preston, 31, 41, 67–74, 197

Sturges, Solomon, 70, 71

Sullavan, Margaret, 59, 61–63

Sullivan's Travels, 31, 67–68, 74

Sundance Film Festival, 102, 171, 283, 286, 289

Sunset Boulevard, 28, 113, 115, 125–130

Surrealism, 7, 13–14
Swanson, Gloria, 115, 125–127, 130
Sweeney, Kevin W., 18
Sweet Sixteen, 205
Sweet Smell of Success, 113, 165–169
Sylbert, Anthea and Richard, 219

The Tall T, 162, 164
Taxi, 75
Taylor, Samuel, 174–175, 176
Thalberg, Irving, 54–55, 142
The Third Man, 51, 105–109, 232
Thompson, Emma, 245–246, 249
Throne of Blood, 155
Time magazine, 170
To Be or Not to Be, 51, 59, 60–61,
    63–68
To Kill a Mockingbird, 326
Tokyo Story, 21, 46, 48
Top Hat, 323
Touch of Evil (Comito), 320
Touch of Evil, 311, 313–316
Touchez Pas au Grisbi, 136
Towne, Robert, 215, 217–220, 322
Toy Story, 327
Tracy, Lee, 28, 31
Trauner, Alexandre, 92
Trinca, Jasmine, 274, 275
True Detective Mysteries magazine, 24
True Grit, 258
Truffaut, François, 67, 133, 172, 173,
    175, 177, 255
Turk, Edward, 94
Tyler, Parker, 33–34

Ulmer, Edgar G., 38
The Ultimate Buster Keaton Collection
    compilation, 10
Un Zoo, La Nuit, 251
Unforgiven, 228, 243, 256–261
United Artists, 65
Universal Studios, 313
Up series, 326
Ursini, James, 159

Uruguay, 283, 287

Valli, Alida, 105, 107
Variety magazine, 13, 57, 138, 192, 214
Veidt, Conrad, 80–81, 83
Vertigo, 113, 170–177
Vidor, King, 32, 325
Vienna, 105–108
Viera, Mark A., 32
Vilmorin, Louise de, 147–148
Vilna Troupe, 35, 36
Violence on screen
    Distant Voices, Still Lives, 237
    Godfather, 215–216
    Kiss Me Deadly, 156–157
    Point Blank, 192
    pre-Code films, 24
    A Prophet, 292–293
    Unforgiven, 243, 258–260
Von Stroheim, Erich, 125, 127
Von Trier, Lars, 278–281

Wademant, Annette, 148
Wager, Anthony, 97
Waiting for Godot play (Beckett), 14
Walker, Alexander, 190
Walsh, Raoul, 75–78, 326
Walz, Robin, 8
Ward, Elizabeth, 159
Warner, H.B., 128
Warner Bros., 24–25, 80, 117
Wasserman, Lew, 174
Waszynski, Michael, 33, 34
Waugh, Evelyn, 209
Wayne, John, 10, 161, 183, 184, 186,
    258
Weir, Peter, 326
Welles, Orson
    Citizen Kane, 116, 169, 170–171,
        325
    on *Make Way for Tomorrow*, 44, 46
    Third Man, 105, 108, 232
    Touch of Evil, Chimes at Midnight,
        311–320

Wellman, William, 24, 27

West, Mae, 40, 126–127

Westlake, Donald, 192–193. *See also* Stark, Richard

Westmore, Wally, 47

When in Disgrace (Boetticher), 161

White Heat, 75, 78, 326

Whittaker, Ian, 245

Why Girls Say No, 11

Wild Boys of the Road, 24

Wilde, Oscar, 137

Wilder, Billy, 59, 63, 125–128, 320, 325

Willis, Gordon, 212

Wilson, Lambert, 296, 298

Wilson, Robert, 229, 230

Winchell, Walter, 166

The Wind That Shakes the Barley, 203

Witness, 326

Woo, John, 198

Wood, Robin, 170

Workers Leaving the Factory, 225

The World of Entertainment: Holly-wood's . . . (Fiordin), 146

World War I
  and European cinema, 3
  Random Harvest, 51
  veterans as characters, 24, 25

World War II, 225
  Army of Shadows, 199
  Casablanca, 80
  Children of Paradise, 90
  Pride and Prejudice, 51, 55–56, 57
  Shop Around the Corner, To Be or Not to Be, 60–61, 63–67

The Wrong Man, 173

Wyler, William, 59, 89

Yankee Doodle Dandy, 75, 78, 86, 325

The Years Are So Long (Lawrence), 44

Yiddish language films, 21, 33–35, 38

Young Mr. Lincoln, 71–72

Zanuck, Darryl F., 24–25, 118

Zavattini, Cesare, 101

Zeffirelli, Franco, 189

Zinnemann, Fred, 214, 326

Kenneth Turan is film critic for the *Los Angeles Times* and NPR's *Morning Edition*, as well as director of the *Los Angeles Times* Book Prizes. He has been a staff writer for the *Washington Post* and *TV Guide* and served as the *Times'* book review editor. He is the author of *Free for All: Joe Papp, the Public, and the Greatest Theater Story Ever Told* and *Never Coming to a Theater Near You*, and is coauthor of *Call Me Anna: The Autobiography of Patty Duke.*

PublicAffairs is a publishing house founded in 1997. It is a tribute to the standards, values, and flair of three persons who have served as mentors to countless reporters, writers, editors, and book people of all kinds, including me.

I. F. STONE, proprietor of *I. F. Stone's Weekly*, combined a commitment to the First Amendment with entrepreneurial zeal and reporting skill and became one of the great independent journalists in American history. At the age of eighty, Izzy published *The Trial of Socrates*, which was a national bestseller. He wrote the book after he taught himself ancient Greek.

BENJAMIN C. BRADLEE was for nearly thirty years the charismatic editorial leader of *The Washington Post*. It was Ben who gave the *Post* the range and courage to pursue such historic issues as Watergate. He supported his reporters with a tenacity that made them fearless and it is no accident that so many became authors of influential, best-selling books.

ROBERT L. BERNSTEIN, the chief executive of Random House for more than a quarter century, guided one of the nation's premier publishing houses. Bob was personally responsible for many books of political dissent and argument that challenged tyranny around the globe. He is also the founder and longtime chair of Human Rights Watch, one of the most respected human rights organizations in the world.

·   ·   ·

For fifty years, the banner of Public Affairs Press was carried by its owner Morris B. Schnapper, who published Gandhi, Nasser, Toynbee, Truman, and about 1,500 other authors. In 1983, Schnapper was described by *The Washington Post* as "a redoubtable gadfly." His legacy will endure in the books to come.

Peter Osnos, *Founder and Editor-at-Large*